EMOTIONALLY
~ FREE ~

Letting Go
of the Past
to Live in
the Moment

DAVID VISCOTT, M.D.

CONTEMPORARY BOOKS

Library of Congress Cataloging-in-Publication Data

Viscott, David S., 1938-
    Emotionally free : learning to let go of the past and live in
the moment / David Viscott.
        p.   cm.
    ISBN 0-8092-4460-8 (cloth)
        0-8092-3817-9 (paper)
    1. Self-actualization. (Psychology)   2. Self-realization.
3. Self-acceptance.   4. Emotions.   I. Title.
BF637.S4V57   1992
152.4—dc20   92-4987
                                                        CIP

Copyright © 1992 by David Viscott
Published by Contemporary Books
An imprint of NTC/Contemporary Publishing Company
4255 West Touhy Avenue, Lincolnwood (Chicago), Illinois 60646-1975 U.S.A.
All rights reserved. No part of this book may be reproduced, stored in a retrieval
system, or transmitted in any form or by any means, electronic, mechanical,
photocopying, recording, or otherwise, without the prior permission of
NTC/Contemporary Publishing Company.
Manufactured in the United States of America
International Standard Book Number: 0-8092-4460-8 (cloth)
                                                        0-8092-3817-9 (paper)
20   19   18   17   16   15   14   13   12   11   10   9   8

For Matt Small

Contents

Acknowledgments

The author wishes to thank:

Elizabeth Viscott Sullivan for her organizational contribution. She helped focus the work and keep the manuscript coherent.

Christine Benton and Julie Walski for their editing and their assistance in making the manuscript clearer and more direct.

Debra White-Christensen and Craig Underwood for their assistance in preparing countless versions of the manuscript, listening to me read it aloud, over and over again, and seeming to be interested even when they'd heard it a dozen times that day.

Harvey Plotnick for believing in this project and having the courage to view the expansive early stages of the manuscript without losing faith in the final work.

My wife, Katharine Random, for her continual, loving, and supportive rereading of the manuscript without getting tired or bored and for her help in keeping all this at a human level.

And special thanks to my patients and the thousands of callers to my programs who allowed me the special privilege of sharing their lives firsthand.

Author's Note

This book asks you to look at aspects of yourself you may not be proud of.

It asks you to examine feelings that may make you uncomfortable.

It asks you to look at your life's direction and question whether you are living the right life.

The theories and advice contained here are based on twenty-five years of clinical practice and interviews with tens of thousands of people. I have attempted to share a lifetime of experience in these pages to help you find your way and live your best life.

To do this you will take a unique look at yourself and discover where you can still grow and how to take the next step toward achieving emotional freedom. In the process you will discover some new strengths and abilities and develop a greater belief in yourself. I know from experience that what I am going to share with you is true. I know it can make a difference in your life. My goal is to help you become free and motivated to give your gift to the world.

There was never a time when your contribution was needed as much as it is now.

Introduction

Emotional freedom is the natural feeling state of the evolved mature person. It constitutes your ability to react honestly to events in the present without the intrusion of prejudices from the past. It reflects your capacity to act in your own best interest without seeking approval or permission. It is the result of settling life's conflicts as they occur rather than avoiding or displacing them.

Because emotional freedom is born of self-acceptance, when you are emotionally free you have nothing to prove. You are also aware of a sense of commonality with other people so that when you act freely you do not compromise the rights of others, but allow them to be free as well. Ultimately, emotional freedom embraces a dream of world peace and a global community in which living as a free person and making a contribution to a better world are inseparable.

To be emotionally free you need to remove the obstacles that keep you in emotional debt. Emotional debt is any accumulation of unresolved old feelings that causes you to distort your view of the present. These unresolved feelings

1

can be as old as unfair treatment in childhood or as recent as this morning's undeserved parking ticket. When you are in emotional debt, you consume so much energy trying to conceal old feelings that you have insufficient energy left to work effectively or to love with commitment. Unexpressed feelings also have great power to prejudice your judgment and oversensitize you, causing you to take innocent events personally, overreact to them, lose control, and in so doing, lose faith in yourself.

The first source of emotional debt is the emotional restrictions that your particular character type imposes on you. Those constraints include your defenses, blind spots, prejudices, and weaknesses, which interfere with your ability to face and resolve your feelings as they occur and therefore cause you to hold your feelings inside, in emotional debt. This armor represents the legacy of your early life experience. You acquired your particular mixture of defenses to protect you from danger as you grew up. As you matured, you became more secure and could risk being more open and less defensive. If the stresses you encountered in a particular developmental period were severe, the defenses you acquired during that period would naturally be more deeply developed and longer lasting, and your character would likely reflect the defensive style of that particular period.

Over the years I've discovered that each person is a composite of, to varying degrees, three basic personality traits: dependent, controlling, and competitive. Each of these has its origin in a corresponding stage of personality development. The dependent trait of needing another person to be complete emanates from the earliest period of life, when you were an infant totally dependent on your parents. The controlling trait of having to be in charge originates from the stage when you struggled to master control of your body and language skills. Finally, the competitive trait of needing to be better than others developed in your early school years, when you defined yourself by comparing yourself to other children. Some people bear the stamp of one period so strongly we call them either dependent, controlling, or competitive; but under certain circumstances everyone is capable of making all three personality responses because everyone is a unique blend of all three types. It is important to become aware of the constraints of the personality traits that bind you so that you can act spontaneously rather than being limited to one rigid response pattern.

While we all share a common developmental path, the world you experienced during childhood was different from everyone else's. Even siblings in the same household are cared for in different ways and develop unique styles of dealing with life's disappointments and injuries. Your character represents the defensive shield you put together and has become your style of perceiving reality and expressing emotions. Not only was your character formed by stress, but it continues to determine the way you react *to* stress. Your character flaws represent the weaknesses that keep you from dealing with the world in an honest and forthright manner. To achieve emotional freedom—to break the cycle of emotional debt—it is important to understand your character weaknesses and how they continue to distort your perception. Your goal is to grow and become as open as possible.

While the first source of emotional debt is the emotional restrictions that your individual character type imposes, the second is the distorting pressure unexpressed feelings exert on your perceptions and experience. Unexpressed emotional obligations to past events demand expression in the present, often inappropriately. When you're emotionally indebted, you distort the present with your old emotional business. To free yourself from emotional debt you must understand the meaning of your feelings and learn to express them directly. The goal is to resolve feelings in the present by dealing with them as they come and releasing them as they pass. This is an essential key to emotional freedom that not only prevents unexpressed feelings from building up but allows you to release old hurts as well.

The third source of emotional debt is the result of failing to discover your gift. What is more painful than knowing you have not discovered and developed your talent, that you have missed your opportunity to make your mark on the world? Often people justify not taking the right risks by insisting they have no talent, that they cannot afford to risk, that it is too late, or that they have too much invested in their present life to change. What nightmare is worse than living with the realization that you're unhappy because you're living the wrong life?

The right life is one in which you are free to say and feel what you want and make your contribution to the world. Discovering your true gift and following it are essential to being happy. Giving of your gift is necessary if you are to feel your life has meaning. While this may seem a distant and even inaccessible goal at this moment, it is the only one that will allow you to have the life you deserve. The journey to emotional freedom is lifelong, but the rewards begin as soon as you commit to taking it.

This book will help you understand the patterns created by your reaction to your early emotional environment. You will see how you contribute to your own difficulties and regain control over your direction and purpose. It will also explain how your feelings work, what blocks their expression, and how to be emotionally open in the present and preserve your ability to make the right choices. Releasing claims the past has on you will help you be more complete in expressing feelings in each moment and will reduce your emotional indebtedness. As a result you will be free of distractions from the past, able to concentrate on the present, and thus better able to decide what is best for you.

Emotional freedom is being able to do what you want when you want to do it. Being emotionally free also means that you choose to do what is best for you because it pleases you to do so. When you're emotionally free, you believe in your own goodness and act to increase your worth. You understand that whatever interferes with this belief is false, and you seek to exclude it.

Being emotionally free comes down to being free to

believe in yourself and in your specialness and being free to make the most of it. This in turn depends on believing you are good. All of this requires that you be free in expressing your emotions, because if you hold in pain you become a creature filled with unexpressed anger. When you're brimming with resentment, it's hard to feel good about yourself. You think you don't deserve success. It becomes difficult to take positive action on your own behalf.

Be aware, however, that with emotional freedom comes emotional responsibility. You cannot separate the two. You can be emotionally free only if you assume responsibility for yourself not as a duty or burden but as a right and privilege.

You are the sum total of everything that has ever happened to you. It has taken everything good and bad you've experienced to bring you to the point of reading this sentence. An important part of attaining emotional freedom comes from accepting responsibility for everything in your life. If this seems too severe, it is also liberating. It is true that many things that happened to you were not your fault, but in each case you chose to *react* in your own way. Even if you were too young to protect yourself, knew too little, trusted too much, or were terrorized by the threat of retaliation or rejection, you are still responsible for your reactions, and for freeing yourself from these past hurts.

Accepting responsibility for your reactions to events diminishes the blame you can place on others but also empowers you to change and move on. After all, in the words of the Swahili saying, it is not what name others call you that matters but what name you respond to that determines who you are.

The secret of life is that there is no secret of life. It's all hard work. Yet you still have to find the right work and be free to choose the direction that is best for you.

The purpose of life is to discover and develop your gift.

The meaning of life comes from sharing your gift with others.

This book is offered in love and encouragement. You

may be stimulated by what you read or disagree with it. Be patient. This work is intended to have many readings and be a companion to life. You will find that the material in these pages seems to change as you grow.

No set course is prescribed here. Rather I have taken care to leave room so each of you can chart your own way through life, making adjustments as life situations require. But at the center of this book is the common core of the human spirit, seeking to be released, demanding its birth-right to be free.

I invite you to take the first step.

PART I

WHERE YOU CAME FROM

1

Identifying Your Strengths and Weaknesses

You can never be free of the way you are. All you can do is understand yourself, know what kind of person you are, and be aware of your strengths and weaknesses. If you understand your weaknesses, you can acknowledge them and take them into consideration rather than suddenly being stymied when they appear. Your weaknesses become most apparent at the precise moment when they can do you the most damage: when you take risks. Using your strengths effectively depends on knowing where your weaknesses lie.

If anyone is going to get in your way and hurt you, it is probably you yourself. Therefore, your weakness admitted is your greatest strength.

Not being aware of your strengths and weaknesses is like being a prisoner who understands neither the bonds that confine him nor how he can strive to break loose of them. No one really changes. People do get better, healthier, more open, and more honest, and they also get worse, but they always remain fundamentally the same people, with the same defenses and the same inclinations to deceive themselves. When we say someone has changed, we mean that person has grown into more of his best. When you act your best, you have less need to conceal the truth, and thus your defensiveness is lowered. The less you use defenses, the more honest a person you are. Of course, when stress is high, even the healthiest people tend to become defensive. Their saving grace, however, is that they know their weakness and how it affects them, so they can take it into consideration and get back on the right road as quickly as possible.

Understanding a strength is straightforward. For example, if one of your strengths is being open, you easily admit how you feel about your successes and failures. You're open to hearing criticism and advice.

Understanding a weakness is a bit more complicated. Your weakness can manifest itself either as the opposite of your strength or as your strength taken to extremes. For example, if your strength is being open, your weakness is either to close others out from knowing how you feel or to be open to a fault, too revealing about yourself. In other words, your weakness is either understating or overstating your strength. Typically you overstate a character trait because you feel rigid or self-protective and understate it out of compliance or a wish to avoid conflict. Your good and weak points always coexist, stemming from the same basic character trait.

If your strength is honesty, your weakness is to be dishonest as well as to be honest to a fault. If you pride yourself on your honesty, you may take exception to this and take pains to point out how honest you are. But if you consider those times when you were not your best, when you got into trouble and suffered the most, you'll discover that your dishonesty played a significant role in your difficulties. If you are truly honest, you will be aware of your dishonesties and admit them with the ease of recognizing an old friend.

Everyone has several strengths. Think of the strength of which you are proudest, the strength you display when you're being your best. The opposite quality of this strength is your weakness, the way you tend to act when you are defensive or avoiding something painful.

When you are mature, you know your weakness intimately.

The character trait you most value is tarnished by the very quality you most despise and are most loath to admit. The weakness that embarrasses you is part of the very same trait you take pride in. It is no wonder that people often vacillate between a worthy self-image and one that is contemptuous. It is important to realize that your negative trait still exists even when you are operating from your strength. Accepting this paradox of opposite traits allows you to examine your life and grow. Failing to understand the coexistence of your good and weak points, on the other hand, leads to feelings of instability and brittleness. You become especially dismayed by the reappearance of the negative qualities you sought to hide, for there is nothing as discouraging as discovering you haven't changed and are still making the same old mistakes.

When you accept only your strengths, the weaknesses you deny end up limiting those strengths. Accepting your weaknesses allows you to become flexible. You can hear, see, and feel without censoring out data that may threaten your self-image. You want to know. You want to let in information about yourself.

Weaknesses are most likely to reveal themselves to others at the very moment you try to conceal them. Even a small hidden weakness can blemish the reputation of a powerful person. Newspapers focus on such faults, especially *because* they are concealed. The weakness you admit is your protection and grace. The weakness you conceal dishonors you and is your undoing.

The opposite—accepting only your weaknesses—carries its own problems. People who do not want to accept responsibility for themselves often play down their strengths. They fear that if they reveal they can fly they will be thrown out of the nest. Even though many of us deny it, we all doubt our strength. These hidden doubts tend to surface just at the moment of taking a risk. Those who are immature use fear as an excuse for not acting; those who are mature use it to guide them through the risk. Fear is a coward's excuse and a brave man's wisest counsel.

The following list of character traits and their strengths and weaknesses is not intended to be complete but to give you an idea of how weaknesses and strengths relate to each other. These will be discussed more completely in Chapter 2, where they will be related to the three basic character types mentioned in the Introduction.

As you examine the list, try to identify those positive traits that apply to you. If you've chosen accurately, a moment's reflection on your past successes will reveal how these traits played an important role.

Be open as you examine the weakness range next to these positive traits. As you do so, consider the most difficult mistakes and failures you've experienced. You will realize that these corresponding weaknesses played a major role in your difficulty. It is common for everyone to find these weaknesses unfamiliar and unflattering and to wish to deny them. Try to be open and accept the possibility that these corresponding weaknesses exist in you even if it is distasteful to do so. Mastery of your strengths depends on it.

Again, if you're not aware of the way your weakness works, it will eventually entrap you. Fortunately, each mistake you make provides another chance to learn this lesson. Admitting mistakes is the work needed to become free. While you need to know your weakness, it is also important to understand that the way to overcome a weakness is not to oppose it but to act through the strength. You don't become honest by hating dishonesty but by loving honesty.

The love of your strength gives you the special insight and sensitivity needed to develop it. For example, the musical gift lies in hearing, being able to tell when something sounds good. The curse of the gift of hearing is

CHARACTER TRAITS

STRENGTH	WEAKNESS RANGE	
	Understated	Overstated
Believing	Doubtful	Abandons judgment
Fair	Unfair	Everyone is so equal that no one is treated justly
Forgiving	Vindictive	Doormat
Giving	Withholding	Martyr
Loyal	Treacherous	Follows blindly
Open	Closed	Too revealing
Patient	Restless	Apathetic
Trusting	Suspicious	Gullible
Supportive	Critical	Sycophant
Analytical	Guesses	Needs too much information
Clear	Confused, can't see at all	Unfocused, sees too much
Determined	Disillusioned	Can't let go
Frugal	Spendthrift	Self-denying
In control	Out of control	Rigidly controlled
Intelligent	Plays dumb	Pedantic
Wise	Ignorant	Know it all, but no action
Measured	Impulsive	Can't risk
Systematic	Disorganized	Too many rules
Brave	Cowardly	Foolhardy
Charming	Irascible	Con artist
Creative	Mechanical	Too many ideas
Good salesperson	Skeptic	Easily sold
Original	Imitative	Has to reinvent the wheel
Poetic	Prosaic	Style matters more than meaning
Self-confident	Self-doubting	Pushy
Sincere	Phony	Self-righteous
Visionary	Nearsighted	Unrealistic dreamer

knowing when something doesn't sound right. The goal is to become your own judge and set your own standards. When your gift is great, it's difficult to please yourself. As a performer you may be unable to enjoy receiving applause because you did not achieve the effect you wanted—a failure that no one else even noticed. Your sensitivity, the force that drives you forward, also measures you relentlessly against a standard that continues to grow just one step ahead of you.

The object of all this is to encourage you to recognize your gift and use the special sensitivity it provides to reveal your weakness, not obscure it. This is a difficult challenge because the standards that a gift imposes on you are higher than the standards others apply to you. It is easier to please others than yourself. Honest people fret over even the slightest misrepresentations they make, while others dismiss them as unimportant "white lies."

As frustrating as this may seem, without knowledge of the weakness the gift is incomplete and, in a sense, without meaning. The gift that is not in touch with its imperfection is out of touch with its humanness and so cannot relate to others. To become universal and lead you to the potential of greatness, a character strength has to exist in a dynamic balance between its weak extremes. All great characters in literature embody this struggle between strength and flaw, while imitations of great art appear as caricatures because they mimic extremes and do not capture this sense of balance. Life is the struggle between strength and weakness.

Art and understanding your feelings, strengths, and weaknesses fit together because man, at his essence, is a creative artist. Everything touched by human hands is the direct result of someone's creativity. All creativity, all of art, is a celebration of some perceptual sense. Music celebrates hearing. Painting instructs us how to see. Dance shows us how to move and master our position sense, the gift of proprioception. The culinary arts refine our sense of taste. Some arts combine motion and sight, some sight and sound, some understanding and insight, but all require the celebration of a strength, a gift that is revealed through the senses, and mastery of a weakness, the imperfections that the very same talent illuminates.

Your life is your creation. As the artist of your own life your role is to create the happiest set of circumstances in which to flourish as your best. You need to understand and develop your character as if it has the potential for greatness.

The following chapters discuss the three basic personality character types. Though every individual is complex and unique, and to a greater or lesser degree every person has traits typical of all three types, it is possible to identify virtually everyone as *generally* one of three types. The foundation for this classification system is the path of human early development. How we pass through each of three specific stages of early life determines which of three character types we become. Each personality type has inherent strengths and weaknesses. Each strength entails a special capacity to understand and to act, as well as a negative side with the capacity to discourage risk taking. You should always be seeking the proper balance, because the strength that reveals your potential for true happiness also allows you to see your faults and to convince yourself you're not so special at all. Do not despair. Your object is to accept your weaknesses and become free.

Each of the three character types has its own preconceived notion of how the world appears or should be, views distorted according to the strength and weakness of each type. Understanding what kind of character type you are is important because you cannot really see the truth unless you know how you distort it.

The truth is the truth no matter what portion of it you choose to accept. Remember the story of the blind men who touched an elephant for the first time. One touched the tail, one the trunk, and another the tusk. Each described the elephant differently, and each report was correct, but the truth each observer perceived was incomplete.

In the same way, your particular character type leads you to focus on one part of the truth and assume that the whole is like that part. If you are unaware of how you distort, you will be unable to correct for that distortion and act effectively.

The way your particular personality was formed leads you to expect the world to treat you in a certain way. For example, if you were brought up in a critical home, you may be overly sensitive to criticism and see the world as judgmental. Such a view may seem true, but even if you could cite examples proving you were right, your view would still be a distortion.

Your character traits cause you to exaggerate or minimize reality, to see a world that is uniquely your own and, for that matter, uniquely distorted. It is only by understanding what kind of person you are and how you got that way that you can begin to recognize how you distort your view of the world.

2

Getting to Know Yourself: A Workbook

DEFINING YOUR CHARACTER TYPE

The kind of personality you are represents the emotional legacy of your upbringing. Your character type determines your emotional reactions, what you're sensitive to, what subjects you find emotionally provocative, what you see as hurtful or fearful, and how you deal with pain. Your personality determines how you see the world.

The three basic personality types mentioned earlier are the dependent, the controlling, and the competitive. You are a unique composite of traits of each type, but under stress you tend to act in a characteristic style. This workbook will help you define what sort of person you are. Later on we'll look at how you got that way and examine in depth the implications of your particular character traits.

It's important to realize that having a particular character type is not necessarily a bad thing but merely reflects a style of reacting. For example, having a dependent character doesn't mean you are weak or needy but that the most profound influences in shaping your personality occurred during the dependent period of your development and made you especially sensitive to issues of dependency in yourself and in others. While the vogue today is to think of a dependent personality only in terms of weakness and vulnerability, in fact being well loved and cared for in infancy—the dependent period—develops a strong nurturing capacity. Of course someone who always needs another person to feel comfortable is a handicapped dependent type, but strong, loving people owe their positive character traits to the same developmental period. Therefore, to call such people dependent personalities is misleading unless you remember that this label can connote strengths as well as weaknesses.

The two extremes, dependent and independent, represent the dependent personality at its weak and strong positions. The dependent person can continue to grow more independent, and under stress the independent person may feel or act dependent. In similar fashion, controlling and competitive personalities owe their special positive strengths to the same period that instilled their vulnerabilities and also have the potential for growth and regression under stress. Let's define your character type more clearly.

Defining Your Strengths and Weaknesses: An Inventory

Your character is the sum total of your strengths and weaknesses. Let's look at your strengths one at a time. The list of strengths and weaknesses you reviewed in Chapter 1 is reprinted here, but this time it's divided into three sections. For now, don't worry about what those divisions mean. Also don't concern yourself with evaluating your weaknesses. The weaknesses still apply, but because we all find it easier to identify our strengths readily, refer only to the strengths. Rate each strength according to the following scale:

    0—does not apply to you
    1—applies to you very little
    2—sometimes applies to you
    3—usually applies to you
    4—almost always applies to you

Take your time and be as honest as you can. Try to give the inner answer, the answer you would have difficulty admitting to others.

CHARACTER TRAITS

STRENGTH	WEAKNESS RANGE	
	Understated	Overstated

------------------------------ SECTION I ------------------------------

Believing	Doubtful	Abandons judgment
Fair	Unfair	Everyone is so equal that no one is treated justly
Forgiving	Vindictive	Doormat
Giving	Withholding	Martyr
Loyal	Treacherous	Follows blindly
Open	Closed	Too revealing
Patient	Restless	Apathetic
Trusting	Suspicious	Gullible
Supportive	Critical	Sycophant

------------------------------ SECTION II ------------------------------

Analytical	Guesses	Needs too much information
Clear	Confused, can't see at all	Unfocused, sees too much
Determined	Disillusioned	Can't let go
Frugal	Spendthrift	Self-denying
In control	Out of control	Rigidly controlled
Intelligent	Plays dumb	Pedantic
Wise	Ignorant	Know it all, but no action
Measured	Impulsive	Can't risk
Systematic	Disorganized	Too many rules

STRENGTH	WEAKNESS RANGE	
	Understated	Overstated

——————————————— SECTION III ———————————————

Brave	Cowardly	Foolhardy
Charming	Irascible	Con artist
Creative	Mechanical	Too many ideas
Good salesperson	Skeptic	Easily sold
Original	Imitative	Has to reinvent the wheel
Poetic	Prosaic	Style matters more than meaning
Self-confident	Self-doubting	Pushy
Sincere	Phony	Self-righteous
Visionary	Nearsighted	Unrealistic dreamer

Scoring Your Test

Now add up your score for each of the three sections. The maximum score for any section is 36.

Section I: Your Dependent Profile

- 25–36: Your personality is strongly influenced by dependent needs, which greatly influence the way you make decisions and how you feel.
- 13–24: Dependent concerns exist but have less impact on decision making.
- 0–12: You are not driven by dependent concerns and may even be isolated from others.

Dependent personality talents: People who score high in this category are excellent team players, nurturers, teachers, and healing professionals because they have therapeutic personalities.

Dependent personality detriments: People who score high may also exaggerate the value of other people's opinions and the importance of being cared for.

Section II: Your Controlling Profile

- 25–36: Your personality has many controlling features that influence your decisions. Being in control is so important to you, in fact, that you will be more likely to decide to stay in control than to do what may be best for you.
- 13–24: Control is important to you but not your main concern. Your controlling strengths help you organize work efficiently and economically.
- 0–12: You invite other people to take control of your affairs.

Controlling personality talents: People who score high in this range are strong managers, organizers, directors, administrators, lawyers, and planners.

Controlling personality detriments: People who score high may also have an exaggerated need for order over content, obedience over initiative, and routine over true understanding.

If you scored low in Section II and also scored high in the dependent category, you probably suffer feelings of self-doubt and inadequacy.

A high score in the controlling category combined with a high score in the dependent category reveals that your controlling behavior may have developed as a means of protecting you from being abandoned or controlled by others. As such you should consider yourself a dependent person who uses controlling means to protect yourself.

Section III: Your Competitive Profile

- 25–36: You have a competitive personality. A score above 30 in particular is typical of strongly motivated people who desire success and seek activities that promote their self-esteem and win others' appreciation and approval.
- 13–24: You can be competitive if the situation calls for it, but you have no strong need to win just for winning's sake.

- 0–12: You would rather not compete or put yourself on the line. Security appeals to you. Taking a risk stops you cold.

Competitive personality talents: High scores are typical of artists, athletes, salespeople, leaders, and innovators.

Competitive personality detriments: People who score high may also have an exaggerated need to win for the sake of winning, a tendency to get addicted to the highs of life and too discouraged by the lows. They are easily misled by victory for its own sake and may turn outside themselves looking for external approval when they should be asking themselves what would make them happy.

A high score in this category combined with a high score in the controlling range indicates that your competitiveness may have a compulsive quality to it; that is, you may appear driven or obsessed to others. It may also reflect some lack of freedom in your creative expressiveness due to low self-esteem caused by the self-criticism typical of the controlling personality.

A high score in this category accompanied by a high score in the dependent category indicates that you are a high performer, but your need to win others' approval may be a way of feeling better about yourself, and that pleasing others may have too much importance in your life and may inhibit your work. *Great* teachers and healers are in this category.

Balanced Scores

A score of 20–25 in all three categories indicates emotional balance.

A score above 26 in all three categories suggests that you are an emotionally mature person.

A score above 32 in all three categories suggests that you have manipulated the test because you're insecure about revealing yourself. Most likely your highest score is in the controlling category, suggesting you are a controlling person with a capacity for manipulating others.

A score of 11–19 in all three categories suggests some

guarding, a lack of spontaneity, or preoccupation. It would be useful to retake the test, being as open as possible.

A score under 10 in each of the three categories reflects low self-esteem and depression. The validity of your test may be in question, but it's likely that your personality falls into the dependent category.

Defining Your Character Type by Behavioral Weaknesses

At certain times we all have the potential to act immaturely, specifically the way a child at a particular developmental stage might act. See which column you identify with the most in the following chart. Later, we'll examine these negative elements in detail. For now it's important only that you identify which elements of each type make up your personality.

THREE CHARACTER PORTRAITS

By now you should be getting some idea of your basic character type. If you're like most people, you have identified some dependent, controlling, and competitive traits in yourself. The following portraits define the three basic character types in greater detail. Again, you'll see some part of yourself in each of them, but one type will probably feel more like you than others.

The Dependent Person

You are concerned with belonging to another person. You're a people person, concerned with feelings, sharing, and identifying with others' suffering and struggle. You are highly empathetic toward human conditions such as hunger and homelessness. You are a feeling member of the community of humankind, easily brought to tears by the plight of starving children and most likely to send a contribution to help. You put your faith in others and in the

Stress	Dependent Response	Controlling Response	Competitive Response	Mature Response
When you are rejected by a loved one	You become desperate, plead, beg, cling.	You pursue, try to block the other's exit, manipulate and demand, reason and explain, and make your case over and over.	You pretend you really weren't that involved, that the other person never really mattered to you, that you couldn't care less if he or she left.	You're hurt and saddened. You try to figure it all out. You ask to talk about it but accept the inevitable and seek peace and closure.
When your parent is unfair	You barely hold in your resentment; you may sulk or pout or be self-destructive to win the parent's sympathy	You point out your parent's weaknesses, analyze his or her motivations, being cold and distant while doing so.	You may act hurt and hold in your resentment out of pride and then later make a big scene to embarrass or hurt your parent.	You redefine limits. You say you feel unfairly treated and ask why. You don't add fuel to the fire.
When you hurt someone	You apologize copiously and act more fearful of losing the other person's love than sorry for hurting him or her.	You point out how the other person brought it all on himself or herself.	You pretend it was an accident, a mistake, or that you were only kidding or teasing.	You apologize, take responsibility for the hurt you caused, say "I'm sorry," and *mean* it.

Stress	Dependent Response	Controlling Response	Competitive Response	Mature Response
When your efforts start to go wrong	You panic. You're afraid your mistakes make you unlovable. You anticipate rejection and blindly seek support wherever you can.	You cover up and insist your methods work. You fear showing weakness. You blame others for spoiling things.	You pretend that the way events turned out was exactly how you intended they should.	You reexamine your procedures and beliefs. You want to know why and how you failed so you can prevent recurrences.
When you are passed over for a promotion, recognition, or reward	You run to your peers for support and ask them to validate your belief that you were treated unfairly. May stir up unrest in the ranks.	You become obstructive and vindictive. You want to get even. You make a plan to do so and become preoccupied with it. You hold a grudge.	You become deeply hurt. You may get haughty and refuse to listen to explanations or take advice and may quit impulsively, saying you don't need your employer.	You reevaluate your performance. You may ask for a job review, reconsider your goals, efforts, and sincerity. You question and examine your methods.

Stress	Dependent Response	Controlling Response	Competitive Response	Mature Response
When you fail	You look to others to tell you that you are still good in spite of your imperfections. You become convinced you are no good and no one wants you.	You try to prove that it was someone else's fault. Besides, you're not so sure you did fail, especially if one checks *your* figures and notes.	You're secretly shattered but pretend that you weren't really trying, that you never wanted to win in the first place, or that it was all just a game.	You're saddened but not demoralized. You seek to understand your weaknesses and address yourself to correcting them.
When someone beats you	You say you weren't very good.	You blame your equipment/tools or claim your busy schedule has gotten you out of practice or claim to have been cheated.	You demand another chance on the spot or claim you didn't really try.	You thank your opponent for the opportunity to participate.

divine. When in trouble you're inclined to seek to be rescued through the intercession of others.

You represent the mass of humanity, trying to hold family together, finding love where you can, looking for security and protection, struggling to take care of your own. You are the backbone of all work forces, the foot soldier in the army, the person who does the dirty work. While others invent and plan, you are the one who gets it all done.

At your best you are loyal, affectionate, warm, giving, accepting, loving, sweet, sincere, touching, caring, and emotional. You are the long-suffering sports fan who goes to every game even in a losing season. You are a good friend, a devoted spouse, a caring parent, and a motivated citizen. It is your dependent legacy that makes you human and accessible to others. A controlling manager without any sense of the dependent needs of self and others could come across as unfeeling, aloof, even cruel. Similarly, someone who strives competitively to be number one without any sense of compassion for others' feelings has a cold and heartless impact on the world.

At your worst you tend to be clingy, unable to risk, trapped in the situation you were born into, just like your father, just like your mother, or tolerant of mistreatment because you cannot risk being on your own. You are made uneasy by separations, jealous by inattention, fearful by silences, panicked by rejection, and devastated by abandonment. You tend to smother those you love and try to possess those people you should allow to be free. You can be passive and paralyzed when facing danger and are strongly inclined to give away control to anyone who offers the prospect of saving you from abandonment or being alone. You seem governed by the belief that you need someone else to be your best.

The Controlling Person

You are concerned with managing details, creating order, devising systems, streamlining procedures, putting everything in its proper place, devising backup systems, evaluating, analyzing, making a case, checking the law, being certain of the rules, the numbers, and the facts. You work behind the scenes regulating, organizing, measuring, restructuring, indicating what should be done, by whom, and when. You don't like to explain your actions, and you expect people to follow your directions.

At your best you are fair, balanced, in charge, and responsible, anticipating the shortcomings of others and correcting for them. You are also fastidious and have great deductive and analytic capacity. You are the great researcher, the punctilious scholar, the financial wizard who knows all the tax loopholes, the master clinician, the top lawyer, the supermechanic, the historian, the station manager, the group leader. You love reports, studies, charts, spreadsheets, maps, and graphs because they give you control over your environment.

At your worst you can be petty, aware of costs but ignorant of values, and interested in money for the power it gives you over others. You can be vindictive, bearing grudges for slights that others view as unintended trifles. You're hurt when rejected and discouraged by mistakes. A failure can take the wind out of your sails when it reveals a flaw in your system. Sometimes you're oblivious to the emotional effects of your actions on others, but when you're not taken seriously yourself you overreact and become resentful. You can blame others even when it's clear that you're the one at fault. In the face of a potential gain or loss of power, your ethics can be shallow.

The Competitive Person

You are concerned with performing, winning, being first, being best, achieving, being noticed, being famous, getting credit, and being rewarded. More than any other kind of personality you direct your energy outward into the world. Where a dependent person needs love and the controlling person needs obedience, you are looking for appreciation.

This search for praise drives you. You want to please as much as be pleased.

At your best you're the great doer, the celebrity in your own circle, the corporate raider, the supersalesperson, the great actor, the brilliant scientist, the media star, the popular artist, the fair-haired politician, the war hero, and the national ruler.

At your worst you can be conceited, selfish, petty, insensitive to the feelings of others, and a show-off. Concerned only with being number one, you have a capacity for ruthlessness and questionable ethics when you're desperate, that is, when you're clawing your way to the top.

You tend to make much of your appearance, feel insecure about physical flaws, and be especially ungracious about aging. Although you sometimes use your good looks as a commodity, you also resent being recognized only for your appearance. You want to stand out yet at the same time seem a little embarrassed when you do.

The Composite Type

There is no such thing as a pure character type. The most dependent people get their way by using their helplessness in a controlling way. The most controlling individuals have a strong dependent streak because they cling to their methods and need to rule others the way a dependent person needs to hold on to another person. The self-motivated athlete still depends on a coach and uses controlling discipline for training and practice. Without a mixture of traits from all three personality types, no one would be a complete human being. A particular character trait becomes a burden only when your actions become rigid and you feel driven and inflexible. You always have choices, and with the exercise of each free choice you grow.

You are your own unique type. You must find your own way on the road from dependence to independence, from controlling to allowing others to be free, and from being better than others to simply being your best. Your personality reflects your particular journey through the important issues of each developmental stage, and like everyone else you are carrying some unnecessary baggage from the past. Knowing what you're carrying and why will allow you to let go and move on.

Let us examine that journey and its legacy.

3

The Emotional Legacy of Childhood: How Your Character Developed

Why is it that when you are suddenly disappointed a wave of childlike helplessness sweeps over you? At those times when your weakness surfaces, you doubt yourself. For a moment you feel like a child again. As the old feeling recurs, your childlike perception—often just a vague feeling, a distant emotional echo—comes forward to overwhelm you. It's hard to tell whether you're recalling the pain of your past or actually suffering only from the present experience. For this reason all overwhelming experiences can make you doubt yourself and feel like a child.

You are a rare human being indeed if, when confronted with the loss of the person you love, you have not felt a childlike sense of panic, desperation, and emptiness take over your being, even if only for a moment. Of course, being mature and more experienced now, you intellectually understand why the other person is leaving and can reassure yourself that everything will be better soon. And yet in your heart you still experience disquiet, loss, the confusion of not knowing what to do and the sheer helplessness of the moment. The reactivation of old injuries makes you feel as if you are the same person you were years ago, when your weaknesses were predominant and your sense of self least secure.

Because of their vulnerability, all children are exposed daily to events they can interpret as deprivation, isolation, loss, and defeat. While being loved by a caring parent tends to minimize the impact of these everyday hurts, they still occur and shape your character and your pattern of response. So no matter how secure your childhood was, you can look back and find moments of sheer terror, overwhelming loss, profound abandonment, and spirit-crushing defeat.

It is, however, not so much what happened to you that matters but that you were exposed to injuries that had a lasting impact on you. The damage you suffered was all scaled up or down to fit your life. The loss of a parent by one child and the loss of a friend upon moving by another could easily have the same impact on both children. I have seen a man who lost both parents as a child during wartime come through it with renewed determination and also seen a woman who was kept back unfairly in second grade entirely lose her will to work.

Your character traits originated and were reinforced in the three developmental periods of childhood—the dependent, controlling, and competitive. In each of these periods you experienced losses, threats, challenges, victories, and defeats, all of which had the capacity to shape your attitude. Your attitude is the persistence of character traits you used to meet these stresses.

This chapter explains how your various traits and attitudes formed. Understanding the context in which they first appeared helps you understand the stresses that reawaken your memories and the style of your response to particular stresses so you'll be better able to modify those responses.

In our earliest years we all followed a particular path

from overcoming dependence to developing control and
learning to compete in the world. Understanding the road
map of this journey, its common dangers and challenges,
will help to reveal where your strengths and weaknesses
originated and how you became what you are.

WHERE YOUR ATTITUDES COME FROM

There are three key developmental periods that shaped
your character and taught you a set of attitudes. The context
in which these attitudes originated determines what kind
of situation reawakens them and the emotional quality they
bring to the present when activated.

The dependent period occurred when language skills
were absent. Your reliance on others was absolute; without
their loving attention the needs you could not convey in
words would hardly have been noticed. Thus, dependent
legacies persist as feeling states that are brought to the
surface again especially by rejection and abandonment.
When these feeling states resurface, they do so with the full
force of the original pain, often making you feel an old
need for another person, which complicates the present
problem, makes you doubt yourself, and robs you of courage.

During the controlling period language skills were rudimentary. Power was almost magically attached to words
while rules, possession, and compliance were the critical
issues of the period. When feelings from the controlling
period surface, they are likely to be triggered by issues of
right and wrong, and they tend to superimpose rigidity,
stubbornness, and a need to be right onto the present,
turning an insignificant issue into a tug of war.

During the competitive period, keeping up appearances
and performing for others dominated your responses.
When competitive issues in the present reawaken earlier
competitive attitudes, you experience fear of failure, the
need to please, and the childlike need to win at all costs.

THE DEPENDENT PERIOD

You do not want to be alone!

You want the approval and acceptance of others and to be considered lovable and deserving of being cared for. If you have evolved into your most independent, mature, and self-sufficient self, you have taken responsibility for getting what you want and meeting your needs yourself. When you're not your best and don't feel strong, you're ruled by your needs and depend on others for fulfillment.

Needs, not wants, determine what you are.

If you need another person to feel complete, that need determines all of your motivation, influences your judgment, and sets the standards by which you measure your happiness and fulfillment.

A person who *wants* another person can be happy without one.

A person who *needs* another person cannot be happy alone. Such a person is dependent.

Needing Another Person

Consider what you expect from your love relationships as an adult and how you are most disappointed by them. You'll find that dependent issues play an important part. The compromises made in the name of love usually violate personal freedom and substitute dependency for independence. While some dependency is natural and good, to have a complete relationship is to risk allowing each other to be independent and free to grow. Unfortunately, people who need a relationship to feel complete often give up a part of themselves to make the relationship work. The issues of dependency that affect a relationship do not suddenly surface when you enter the relationship but have been part of you from the very first days of life.

Your fear of being alone is a good measure of your dependency. But if you look at life honestly, you'll realize you're always alone. Even with someone you love intensely, precious little time is spent together, and when you are together you are still alone.

The closest you can ever get to another person is to be alone together. In the best relationships you are free to be yourself, the same person when the two of you are together as when you're apart. In fact a partner who complains of loneliness is really lonely for the part of himself he has sacrificed to be in the relationship. Resentment over this sacrifice undermines the relationship and is a source of conflict in years to come. What you give up is always what you end up needing most.

Understanding Your Dependent Ties to the Past

Dependency is a deep feeling rather than something you can put into words, for it developed in earliest childhood. Purely a creature of feeling, all you knew was pain and pleasure with no ability to judge whether something was remembered or imagined. You learned to distinguish real from imaginary through painful experiences, especially the pain of separation from your parents. Few of us are totally free from reexperiencing that old anxiety lying deep within us that can be stirred up by a feeling of separation or rejection. When these archaic feelings of terror are aroused, we fear losing control and like infants believe we need another person to be whole. The first step to self-mastery is to remind yourself that at least part of the terror is just a memory. These feelings are our dependent legacy.

Babies are not born entirely without prior contact to the external world. I remember, during my first days on clinical rotation in pediatrics in the newborn nursery, being struck by a hyperirritable three-week-old child who could not be consoled. The slightest noise would send him into endless screaming and thrashing. The only thing that would calm him was an electronic device that imitated the sound of blood passing through the uterine vessels. The device was placed next to the child's head and in a moment the child stopped crying, his breathing became quiet, and he fell asleep. Hearing the sound of the intrauterine environment apparently reawakened other memories of peace. This illustrates that an important psychological bond is made prior to birth.

What sensory forces contribute to the formation of this bond? In the womb the child is in total darkness, floating in a bag of fluid. Vision contributes nothing to the experience; nor does position sense, for floating nullifies the effects of gravity. The receptors that give information about taste, smell, and hunger are likewise dormant. The senses of touch and temperature are constant and thus transmit no information to the child's memory. The inner sensations of bowel activity are not yet activated. However, the sense of hearing is intact and, in fact, since sound transmitted through fluid is very much amplified, sound is heightened both in intensity and predominance as it will never be again.

The sound of blood passing through the uterine vessels is always changing. When the mother sleeps her heart rate drops to sixty beats per minute. When the mother becomes angry or frightened her heart rate soars to over one hundred beats per minute. The impression this makes on the unborn infant is indelible.

How Your Sense of Comfort Developed

Imagine the traumatic impact of birth, when a child is thrust from total comfort into a strange new environment. The senses that were dormant are assaulted by the full impact of reality. Sounds that had been predictable and organized are replaced by a cacophony of strident inputs. Light is blinding. The sense of touch is abruptly activated. The air feels chilly. Gravity, which had no effect in the womb, becomes a friend, holding the infant close to the pillow and the comfort of a firm surface. In fact, this early positive effect of gravity forms the basis of our lifelong concept of being grounded, at home, centered.

Conditions symbolizing comfort before birth can be reinforced afterward. For example, the remarkable calming effect of being picked up and held stimulates a recollection of the zero gravity condition of floating in the amniotic sac. The mother who holds and buoys up a child not only is giving love but is in a sense helping her child recall the comfort of the original intrauterine environment. The child is also soothed when held closely to its mother's breast, where her heartbeat recalls the sounds of the calm state once more.

In addition to the effect of her physical nearness, a mother's attitude and comfort level during feeding is also important. It is possible for a mother to be betrayed by an anxious heart rate that triggers restless feedings. A baby may pick up the mother's discomfort and frustration and be unable to find comfort. Having been exposed to the sound of its mother's heartbeat and responding to her stress hormones crossing the placental barrier, it is no wonder that the child is highly sensitized to its mother's feelings. Should the mother be plagued with anxiety, merely being held close to the anxious mother may reinforce a kind of conditioned response in the child where the child produces stress hormones of its own.

Because the newborn is totally dependent on others for its survival, the child who is well attended to builds a memory of being cared for and develops a capacity to endure the pain of inevitable separations and unavoidable discomfort. A happy mother, content with her mothering role, gives much to her child just by being happy. If, on the other hand, the mother has unfulfilled dependent needs herself, she may become withholding or overprotective, thus prolonging the child's dependent experience. Instead of being a stage, through which the child passes with ease, it can become a period of forced dependency and overindulgence in which the natural self-centeredness of the dependent child is exaggerated. The child may become so dependent and demanding even its own mother feels like rejecting it.

Mothers who had a difficult relationship with their own mothers, however, often try symbolically to correct the experience by participating in a healthy relationship with their children. The pain of letting the child go that such mothers feel is deepened by their memory of being let go "too soon," that is, before they were given enough nurturing. The mothering a child receives when love is genuine and the mother is comfortable with her role has a key impact on the development of the child's comfort level and dependent character traits.

The ease with which children cope with the discovery of their separateness from the parent depends on the loving care they experience. The origins of your fear of separation are derived from this time when you first became aware of the difference between self and nonself. Few people are free of the difficulties that persist from this time of differentiating between self and nonself. Our sense of emotional comfort as well as our capacity for unrealistic thinking and shutting out the world stem from this period. No period is more important to defining your sense of yourself.

Where Your Feelings of Panic Come From

We had our earliest emotional experiences even before we were born. When a pregnant woman is under stress, her heart rate increases, as well as the stress hormones circulating in her blood, which cross the placental barrier and enter her child's circulation. Thus when a mother experiences anxiety, her unborn child has the same feeling. This is probably the only time in life we completely share the feelings of another person.

A case of mine some years ago illustrates how distant intrauterine feelings continue to influence us. I was giving a seminar when a musician with the city's symphony orchestra and his girlfriend of several years asked to discuss their problem in front of the group. She had left her husband for the musician, but in spite of his earlier promises of commitment to her, he now had cold feet.

"Why did you back away?" I asked.

"I don't know. I didn't know how to handle her emotions."

"What does that mean?" I pressed.

"I get uncomfortable when she becomes emotional."

"What are you afraid of?"

"I'm not sure . . ." He looked away, found his calmness, and looked back.

"When she gets emotional . . ." I prodded.

"I don't like being around."

"Who died or abandoned you when you were a child?" I played a hunch.

"No one. But my mother was never there for us emotionally. She was in institutions most of her life."

"With what?" I asked.

"Severe anxiety attacks. She was the most anxious woman in the world. I couldn't be with her without getting upset. My father said my birth was the traumatic event that pushed her over."

"Well, she must have been anxious when she was carrying you."

"I, uh"—he smiled—"I think that's probably a safe bet."

Looking at this sensitive musician afraid to commit to a woman who loved him, I thought about the world he must have experienced prior to birth. "Do you know what a mother's heartbeat sounds like to her unborn child?" I asked.

He shook his head.

I held the microphone close to my mouth and imitated the sound I'd heard in auscultating the pregnant uterus. "Whoosh-whoosh . . . , whoosh-whoosh . . . , whoosh-whoosh . . . ," I intoned slowly and softly.

He looked at me, intrigued.

"But when you were inside your mother's womb and she was distraught, this is what you heard." I repeated the same sound, now louder and faster, imitating a heart rate of about 130 beats per minute: "Whoosh-whoosh! whoosh-whoosh! whoosh-whoosh!" After about ten seconds the musician suddenly grabbed his chest in fear and started to sweat. I had precipitated a full-scale anxiety attack by re-creating the sound environment that had shaped his first panic experience.

He "remembered."

His girlfriend's resentful attitude totally dissolved, and as she put her arms around him his fear subsided. He understood that she didn't want to hurt him and that while commitment was a little threatening, it was not as incapacitating as the anxiety he "remembered" about being close to his mother. He hadn't understood those powerful early feelings until that moment and was finally able to separate those memories from the stimulus that reawakened them.

When such a memory recurs, the old emotion is experienced as if it were real and actually happening in the present. It is not distinguishable as a memory. It is no wonder that when you are overtaken by the recollection of severe anxiety you do not think it is a memory but a new experience in its own right.

Our emotional capacity to distort is deeply rooted indeed. The persistence of painful memories from early childhood can leave us confused about whether something is real in the present or remembered from the past. This can overwhelm us with feelings of panic and helplessness.

The following sections discuss other bonds that link us to early feelings and attitudes. Under stress these old hidden pathways can open once more, putting us in touch with a "remembered" terror or bringing out the tendency to act stubbornly or selfishly.

The Origins of Denial: The Dependent Defense

Here is a scene most mothers can relate to. It is time for the 2:00 A.M. feeding. The baby has been crying for a few minutes. The half-asleep mother finally makes her way into the nursery to offer the baby the nipple. To her surprise, she discovers that the baby is no longer crying but instead is contentedly sucking away, already going through the motions of being fed. Sometimes if mother arrives too late, the sucking will have stopped entirely. The baby will have fallen back to sleep acting as if it had already been fed.

Consider what just happened. The baby experiences hunger, awakens, and cries. After a while the baby "remembers" being fed. The memory of being fed and the actual experience of being fed are indistinguishable to the baby, who cannot tell the difference between self and nonself. Thus memory and reality are inseparable. The baby accepts the memory as real. In a sense it hallucinates the nipple and imagines it is nourished merely by the memory of being fed.

When the child turns away from the external world and finds comfort in its own mental process in this manner, it is using denial, the most primitive psychological defense. This inner world, existing entirely at the bidding of the dreamer, has the potential to become a total escape from reality.

The child who has learned to tell the difference between self and nonself also realizes that he is powerless to get what he wants from the real world just by thinking about it and also that he is alone when others are absent. So the child either retreats into his inner world to avoid the discomfort of deprivation or voices his complaint and demand for service. When the demand is met, the child, through a primitive thought process, thinks that his crying created not only the bottle but also the hands that brought it. Not sure how this works, the baby is frustrated by delays encountered in the external world. The inner world's imagined or "remembered" rewards are quicker but less nourishing!

If the baby's discomfort is allowed to persist, the baby will eventually stop crying and turn inward and away from the pain, for lack of any other way of dealing with it. In later years we all have the potential to deny the reality of a distressing world by retreating within to a relief we "remember." People look longingly through photo albums at the faces of departed people, trying to hold on to what has gone before. If we cling too tightly to the relief found in reexperiencing a past moment, we lose touch with the real world. And when we release the comfort that the memory has provided, the shock of reality abrades us anew. Thus to depend too heavily on denial to provide relief is to set ourselves up for greater losses. Finding this balance is a lifelong struggle for dependent people who have a problem letting go.

How You Learn to Trust

Learning to postpone pleasure and tolerate pain without surrendering completely to denial is the lesson every child must learn to achieve emotional balance. The lure of re-treating within will seem irresistible if the pain becomes too great, but the love of the child's mother offers a strong incentive to tolerate the inevitable little frustrations of the world. Again, the rewards of the inner world are quickly won but not nearly as satisfying as the reward of mother's love.

The mother who freely gives that love is instilling trust in her child. The child has made a bargain—to put up with pain as long as mother's love is given in return—and see-ing the bargain kept by mother allows the child to extend that trust to others in the adult years.

Several results may ensue when that love is not forth-coming. In some cases the world comes to the child's rescue, and the child is able to join together the patchwork of various people's affections and shape it into a sense of being loved and lovable. But not all children are so fortu-nate. The dependent child, needing love, is vulnerable to misinterpreting *any* attentions, no matter how inadequate or harmful, as love and thus can end up being manipulated or even abused.

At the very least the child denied parental love becomes confused. The child is hurt by the rejection but feels inhib-ited in expressing resentment for fear of appearing even more unlovable and lessening the chances of being cared for. That withheld anger soon becomes guilt. Such children often grow up not knowing whether they are doing things for their parents out of guilt or out of love. They tend to seek out rescuers to provide what they have been denied, but only end up disappointed again. These false starts prolong the process of discovering their independence and belief in themselves, the basic lesson of the dependent period.

Your Earliest Emotional Debt

What happens to the unrelieved hurt that a child experiences in the early months? As with an unmet physical need such as hunger, some of it is alleviated mentally. One method of mentally handling this pain is dreaming, through which the child works out the unexpressed problems of the day in symbolic form during sleep, thus processing the emotional residue. This is especially important during early life, when feelings cannot yet be expressed symbolically through words.

Even so, some hurt probably remains unexpressed. The more hurt, the more neglect, the more is stored up. Stored hurt is called *anger*.

Expressing anger requires a target, the conception of which depends on a more completely developed sense of self and nonself. It requires intention, the ability to state yourself in relation to the statement "I am." Thus it seems likely that every child has stored up some unresolved hurt. This old hurt causes irritability, the first manifestation of withheld anger and frustration. The child who becomes cranky, who is a poor eater or sleeper, or who develops colic may also be expressing such stored-up hurt. A child who has continual difficulties managing hurt will move from the period of dependence to the period of control with a storehouse of anger. This persistence of anger explains a good deal of the contrariness of the so-called terrible twos. How this anger is expressed and the way its expression shapes character will be discussed later.

The Origins of Your Imagination

The young child's capacity to turn inward to fulfill needs is both the basis for all unrealistic thinking and the source of creativity. If help in relieving pain or meeting needs is not forthcoming from the outside world, the child may retreat into fantasy. If mothering is inadequate or the child is severely deprived, the child may begin to get lost in a fantasy world—a pattern that is difficult to break once established. This can lead to negative effects in adulthood. When we are desperate, we are able to believe in what we need to believe in rather than what actually is.

Our need to be loved makes us especially susceptible to wishful thinking. Who has not imagined finding a desperately needed love or exaggerated its sincerity or completeness? It is no small wonder that we experience so much disappointment later in life when our hopes are dashed by reality, but it is truly remarkable that our capacity for imagining does not cause us to set ourselves up for more unrealistic expectations and to suffer even more. The miracle is that we have the resilience to endure deprivation and rejection and are still able to push forward and risk again.

I recently saw a woman who had survived Auschwitz with her mother. In the camp the mother became obsessed with protecting her daughter and involved her in complicated fantasies. With people starving and being brutalized all around her, the mother insisted on pretending to make apple strudel and would send the daughter on "errands" to the "corner store" for ingredients, admonishing her, "Get the biggest raisins and the stick, not the powdered cinnamon. Make sure he doesn't cheat you and look for worms in the apples." At first the daughter was totally bewildered and would sheepishly walk around the death camp with her mother's detailed instructions running through her mind. At first she was reluctant to play along, but gradually she gave in to her mother, first to appease her and then because it was something to do. "Do you know after a while I could smell the strudel and even taste it?" she remarked.

Of course Auschwitz continued to be a horror, but the mother diverted her daughter from every awful perception.

As a result this woman emerged from the camp with an undiminished capacity to feel joy. In the camp she had reunited with her mother at the level of allowing her mother's feelings to take precedence over her own, returning to the dependent bonds of childhood to sustain her. Of course when the mother finally died forty years later she was forced to mourn not only the loss of her mother but also the loss of the buffer that had shielded her from pain.

The relationship that existed between this mother and daughter before Auschwitz was not excessively dependent. It was in all respects normal. In fact, had the early period of nurturing been overprotective, it is likely that the regression that occurred in Auschwitz would have become more like a psychosis and much more difficult to give up.

In an effort to make our feelings comprehensible to others, we use our ability to take the unique world we perceive within ourselves and project it outside, giving it form and substance. That is the heart of the act of creation. The same capacity to hide from reality and imagine an inner peace is also the ability to dream the dream of a better world, make tools, build civilizations, and create a more just social order. Creativity, the most profoundly human gift, is born of your most fragile human weakness, your utter helplessness as a child. In a sense you spend your life trying to create a part of the world that gives you comfort. Your motivation for creativity comes from this dependent period, in which you experienced deprivation and compensated for it with your imagination. Your pain leads you to create a better world.

The Lessons the Dependent Period Teaches

The way a young child learns to feel secure being with its parents has an impact on how the child learns the lessons of the later stages of childhood. Fortunately, children show flexibility in adapting, relearning, and discovering for themselves the truth of a situation. Although your early experience prejudices you, your life still has the potential to be a corrective relearning experience. Your dependent experience teaches you the solace that closeness to another person can bring. It also reveals its dangers—namely, rejection and disappointment. All the seeds of growth and evolution as a person are sown in the dependent period. What follows only refines the dependent wish.

Dependent issues remain with you throughout life. You develop new abilities and prove new strengths, but you still must deal with your need for others and your loneliness. It is desperation over being alone that fuels most mistakes in later life, such as choosing the wrong mate, giving in to peer pressure, and abandoning good judgment.

Except for the early part of the dependency period, the stages of childhood development are not discrete, and dependency issues appear again and again. The period of control starts as soon as you begin to master the rudiments of speech and mobility, when you first begin to assert your will on your environment. Controlling and dependent issues coexist. The child with dependent and controlling needs soon finds himself in the competitive stage, vying with other children and siblings for love and control. These competitive needs appear, combine, and develop along with the others. Each child shows a different rate of growth in dependent, controlling, and competitive traits. The stages may overlap, but the dependent stage leaves an indelible mark on all of us.

Life, fortunately, offers continual opportunities to grow and perfect our strengths.

THE CONTROLLING PERIOD

The controlling aspect of your character probably begins to take shape much sooner than is conventionally thought, somewhere between three and six months of age, when you first willfully take action to control your environment.

Developing the ability to determine distance between self and an object, reach it, grasp it, and take it into the mouth may seem like modest achievements, but they signal the development of the child's ability to intend an action mentally and bring it to completion in the world. They not only imply the development of consciousness and choice but also herald the evolving individual's sense of personal agency. Achievements like standing, walking, and talking are greeted by the parent with enthusiasm and delight and thus reinforced. Parents measure their children's progress and compare it to that of other children. It is a source of parental concern as well as egocentric pride. Parents also imagine their children's future by the way they master these skills, often investing their own frustrated aspirations in the strides their children make. They perceive the hands of a surgeon dissecting a stuffed bunny, the fingers of an artist scribbling with a crayon, the legs of a ballerina bouncing to a music box, and the arm of a major-league pitcher hurling toys from the crib.

How You Learned to Control Others

The achievements that get the warmest reception are usually those that parents perceive as solidifying parent-child bonding. At first the child smiles at people, teddy bears, and balls with equal delight, but only people smile back. Returning the parents' smiles melts their hearts because the act suggests a sense of recognition and belonging.

The parents' positive response registers in the child's memory and reinforces his growing use of physical mastery to affect another human being's reaction to him. Of course being egocentric and having only rudimentary reality-testing skills, the child easily comes to believe he can control his world with a smile, a word or two, or a gesture. When his powers fail, he feels frustrated and may try to use physical force to get control.

More and more the child becomes a creature of control. As he moves into the second year, language skills well under way, every utterance he makes creates a stir. He gets his way merely by pointing at objects, causing the magic hands of his parents to retrieve toys from shelves and bring them closer. Years later it's no surprise that when we're frustrated or don't get our way we point angrily. The magic of pointing has deep roots, connoting the power to control others.

During this period the child's dependent needs still press for fulfillment while the ability to control advances. As the child gathers strengths and skills, he still measures his parents' responsiveness to his demands. People become controlling to ensure that their dependent needs are met. Control is the magic dependent people yearn for to secure love.

It is natural for a child who is dealing with achieving control to continue to be treated in a dependent fashion by his parents, and sometimes to act dependent and at other times controlling. The ability to deal with issues of dependency and control at the same time indicates health and fluidity.

Why and When You Regress

A child who is under stress, ill, confused, or frightened by changes in the environment typically exhibits features of a younger child by becoming more dependent. Little regressions in the face of fears, the unfamiliar, new faces, or new situations are characteristic of all children and often involve acting clingy in a new setting. When an uncertain situation occurs later in life, you utilize the same regressive pathway, act needy, and look to others for help.

A controlling child who appears well adjusted but who may have denied his dependent needs by growing up too soon may be prone to regress dramatically in the face of a severe setback later in life. This is especially true when much of the so-called growth was really a kind of flight into maturity to avoid dependence on an unreliable parent. Delinquent juveniles often wet the bed when they are first incarcerated, almost as if signaling their captors that they are not thugs but helpless children who still need to be taken care of.

Our regression to more childish behavior is common.
The controlling defense of making an excuse requires a
logical and verbalized thought process, and so does the
competitive defense of pretending. On the other hand, the
dependent defense of denial requires neither logic nor
verbalization. It shuts out pain instead of explaining it
away. In adult life, when faced with overwhelming stress,
we tend to regress, using denial to block the pain and spare
ourselves the burden of blame and explanation. We just
hide.

Discovering the Power of Words

A child in the controlling stage can react to stress not only
by regressing but also by becoming obsessively neat and
attempting to place his room, thoughts, and words in order
to assert symbolic control over the rest of the world. This is
an extension of the child's belief in magic: not only can
imagined things be taken for real, but real things can be
controlled by imagining to do so. A symbolic tool is all that
is needed. In the make-believe world of children a fake gun
can kill, a magic wand can transform, and an orange crate
can land on the moon. And the right magic words, properly
spoken, can do anything. Words come to have the same
power as tangible things.

The year-old child, developing language skills, quickly
learns about the powerful effect of speaking a person's
name. The child begins to equate uttering "Mommy" or
"Daddy" with conjuring up the parental figure and basking
in his or her love and removing the child's loneliness. In
doing so he is laying the groundwork for an entirely false
system of belief and for mistaken expectations about being
able to control the environment. He begins to place faith in
the word-deed, the concept by which a spoken word initiates or completes the desired action.

The word-deed concept perfectly suits the power-hungry
child, who wants to control the magic of the universe. Of
course what the child really wants is the power to keep

from being abandoned and left in a position of total dependency. Every time we seek power as an adult, we are motivated in part by the old fears of being helpless, powerless, alone, isolated from love, and unable to improve our lot or save ourselves. The power-hungry adult is really a fearful child. And children who are habitually rejected when they call Mommy or Daddy are most likely to become power-hungry adults, still seeking more power so they can control a loved one's response to them and minimize their risk of being rejected.

How You Learned to Protect Yourself with Words

Language skills form the basis for the child's evolving psychological defense system. During the dependent stage the child silently turned inward and away to avoid painful events. Such denial did not require any language skills. The child of the controlling period uses excuses as a defense to explain the pain and limit his responsibility and thus reduce his guilt and shame. Excuses require logic and language to reason away the injury. The capacity to make excuses develops at an opportune moment. After all, the child in the controlling period, bent on exploration, disassembly, miscellaneous violence, and wanton destruction, is making a lot of mistakes.

Sometime between the establishment of denial and the development of the child's ability to make excuses appears a transitional defense, which the child utilizes almost immediately upon learning to speak. It seems to develop as an imitation of the parents' first attempts to set limits, to help the child define a sense of boundaries and understand right and wrong. A powerful word is introduced into his vocabulary. It is intended to inhibit all activity, and from the child's point of view it has power and magic.

It is the word *no.*

No, a negative controlling response to a disagreeable reality, is a case study in the corruption of power. The scene is familiar. The family is gathered for a meal and the child is being difficult. When the spoon approaches his lips the child turns his head away. Another adult takes over, confident in her mothering skills, and converts the spoon into an airplane coming in for a landing.

"No." The child resists with a confidence beyond his years. The spoon approaches the landing field again, disguised this time as a butterfly.

"No" is the engaging response. Another adult coaxes from the side.

"No." Another attempted landing is waved off. A lively discussion ensues.

"Come on!"

"No!"

"Please."

"No!"

In a variety of situations the child uses *no*—over and over again—to hold his own against a team of dedicated adults. They have language skills, education, experience, motivation, even his welfare at heart, and still he defeats them with a single word. The power and effectiveness of this primitive communication are not lost on him. He gains attention and power if he continues to say no. The power he has discovered is intoxicating.

Resistance and refusal are the first ways the child learns to control his environment verbally. When his language skills improve, empowered with this negativity he will develop additional language excuses that will make him a formidable adversary indeed.

The Origins of Negative Behavior

Is the development of power always to be accompanied by its abuse? Is learning to speak always tainted by the need to resist? Does the ability to think using words always result in making excuses and blaming others?

What is the source of this negativity?

A good argument can be made that the child is carrying over negative feelings from his dependent past. It is common to suggest that adults have emotional baggage. Since children's defense systems are not nearly as sophisticated as those of adults, it is not unreasonable to suggest that children, even young children, have unresolved emotions from the past.

Put yourself in the position of a child. A two-year-old child reacts against any feelings of helplessness, angrily resisting any restraints that limit his autonomy or his ability to act in his own behalf, to move freely or do what he wants. In this controlling period his physical and verbal flaunting of power is in part an expression of anger over his old dependent vulnerability, and while he may not be able to put the old hurt into words, he "remembers" it with every fiber of his body. When he is obstinate, the two-year-old is declaring his freedom from dependency. He is shedding old emotional baggage.

As his language skills develop, he is able to give words to his demands. He is able to say, "No, I don't want to." Such assertions of power should not immediately arouse feelings of conflict in a parent. Bear in mind that what the child is so defiantly saying and doing to assert control also means, "I want to show I am not helpless."

This pattern persists into adulthood in controlling people. This is why trying to oppose a negative person by sheer brute force only makes him feel more like a helpless child and increases his negativity.

Controlling adults often feel like stubborn two-year-olds when their power is questioned and their rules ignored. They become physical, pushing and shoving and demanding obedience. They are motivated by the same issues that concerned the two-year-old, the fear of being weak and isolated, the dread of admitting their vulnerability. Almost like a replay of the terrible twos, controlling adults, now armed with formidable powers of logic, exaggerate the wrongs others have done them and blame their hurt on someone else's disinterest or disobedience to justify their own angry response. Sometimes it seems as if nothing has changed but the person's age.

Self-Doubts

You begin to understand that there are limits to your ability to control, yet you never completely give up your dream for power or your belief in magic. You discover you cannot always control your own feelings. You learn you cannot control the feelings of another person. When you try to keep someone from leaving you, the person pulls away at the first opportunity. So what's the point of trying to control anything if you cannot control anything that really matters? Why do you even try? Because you cannot accept your weaknesses and are trying to conceal them. You control because you want to hide your self-doubts.

These self-doubts originate in the controlling period and persist just below the surface in all of us:

- Am I lovable?
- Am I good?
- Am I strong?
- Am I smart?

Why We Make Excuses: The Controlling Defense

As infants we depended on our passive lovability to survive, but as controlling children we had to take specific action to obey and please our parents. Because such autonomy implies responsibility, we had to make excuses to explain our shortcomings and justify "bad" behavior to remain in our parents' good graces. We wanted to ensure our lovability, our biggest self-doubt.

As we grow, we're judged "good" or "bad" according to our performance when earlier we were considered good just for being ourselves. We make excuses to deny our vulnerability and fear of rejection and to prove we are blameless, that is, deserving of love. The defensive objective is to correct unacceptable actions and so adjust an unlovable self-image and become lovable again. We make excuses to placate self-doubts.

Unlovable Self-Image	Plus	Excuse	Equals	Lovable Self-Image
I'm bad.	+	You made me do it. You're unfair.	=	I'm good.
I'm wrong.	+	I got poor directions. I was tricked.	=	I was really right.
I lost.	+	You cheated.	=	I really won.
I'm weak.	+	The work load was too heavy. No one could do this.	=	I'm really strong.
I'm angry.	+	You hurt me first.	=	I only protected myself.
I'm stupid.	+	You withheld facts and distorted information.	=	I'm still smart.

The above model shows how and why adults use controlling excuses as an attempt to manage reality with logic.

Excuses range from a simple explanation of what went wrong to "They're out to get me." An excuse may be a highly intellectual argument in response to the question "Why won't you commit to marriage?" or simply blaming your tools for a bad job.

Your excuses originate from when you first began to
point at things. When you learned the concept of "not-me"
and began to point at what you wanted, you also learned to
point the finger and blame others, saying "It wasn't me."

The essence of growing is to learn that what feels good
is right and what feels bad is wrong without having to make
excuses. To do so you must trust yourself and your intrinsic
goodness, even if you sometimes mess up or do wrong.

Your Wish to Be Perfect

A controlling adult's wish to be perfect stems from the
childhood wish to be blameless. Since real growth means
embracing your faults and examining your weaknesses,
controlling people run the greatest risk of becoming rigid
and failing because of their insistence on always being
right. They need to feel they are beyond criticism so that no
one will have a good reason for withholding what they
need or rejecting them. They believe they need to be perfect just to be safe, so admitting even small imperfections
makes them uneasy and self-doubting. If they can be imperfect in one way, they reason, they could be imperfect in
others. Since being imperfect is a fact of life, acknowledging themselves honestly is a continual threat to their self-
esteem. Even slight criticisms compel them to refute others'
logic and testimony.

Controlling adults tend to minimize the importance of
feelings because feeling implies being vulnerable just as
weakness and imperfection do. This is a tragic flaw, for it is
precisely this unwillingness to be emotionally open that
causes other people to push them away, bringing about the
very rejection their control was designed to prevent.

Intellectualizing—Misusing the Power of the Mind

Probably the least satisfying activity you can pursue with
the human mind is to try to use it to feel. It simply cannot
be done. You can make sense of your emotions, but you

don't feel with your thoughts alone. You feel with your body and mind together, acting as a connected sensory unit. You sense emotions bodily. Your mind merely helps identify the emotion your body feels and connects it to the event that caused it, the fulfillment or the loss.

Your mind can only act as a safety valve when it comes to dealing with feelings. When your mind attempts to deal with emotions, it manages the overflow by reasoning rather than by resolving the original source of the feeling, often resulting in obsessive or compulsive behavior. Relieving the source of hurt by facing the loss directly and feeling the pain is what is required.

All emotions are related to body states. Your first experiences of feelings are not with words, but with physical sensations. If you do not feel emotions physically, you are living in your head. You cannot love with your head. Only when you feel from the heart do you feel deeply. The emotions are physical feeling states that are understood as a special language by the mind:

- When you experience loss, you feel something drop within you. You feel emptied, as if something has been torn away from you.
- When you feel anxious, your muscles tighten, your heart races, and your head pounds. You sweat. You tremble. You have trouble breathing. Your teeth may chatter. You are more alert and are easily startled, the runner in the starting block ready to jump the gun.
- When you feel angry, your body tenses. You feel pressure building within you. You sense a willingness to combat the enemy. Your jaw tightens. You make a fist. Your nostrils widen as you hunger for additional air to meet the demands of your taut muscles.
- When you feel guilty, you feel as if a weight has settled on you. You try to conceal angry feelings. Feelings of worthlessness weigh on you, push you down, make you tread with leaden footsteps.

• When you are depressed, you feel sluggish, listless, and weak, as if your energy has been drained from you. Inside you feel a cold fire consuming you. The outside world does not interest you.

The mind that is out of touch with physical feeling is a stranger to reality. Controlling defensive systems isolate feeling from physical experience. This is the source of many emotional problems, for a feeling in your head is a feeling that does not resolve.

The more you depend on symbolic, intellectual means to express your hidden feelings, the less in touch you seem with the world and the more neurotic you appear—that is, driven by emotions that you wish to hide.

Controlling people who intellectualize are fighting a losing battle against the emotional course of their own history. Their goal should not be to control their feelings but to be free to express them and allow others the same right. Motivating all of their actions and excuses is the one feeling they cannot isolate or correct for—isolation itself. At the heart of controlling people's fear is the dread of being alone. The paradox is that their defensive isolation of feelings, while allowing them to think they're perfect and providing them with a ready excuse for everything, only increases their sense of loneliness by more firmly establishing residence in their minds, separated from physical feelings and contact with the outside world.

Being isolated from your own feelings is the deepest loneliness of all. The risk of admitting hurt and dealing with the pain of the moment in vulnerability and simple honesty is the only real solution.

To feel fully is to live fully.

Feeling less is living less.

THE COMPETITIVE PERIOD

The competitive period starts sometime before the age of two, when the child begins to express a sense of self by asserting and performing. Competitive traits such as assertiveness, confidence, and initiative develop in the struggle for survival among siblings and friends and form the building blocks of pride and responsibility. While dependent people rely on their neediness to inspire others to care for them and controlling people, also motivated by their dependent needs, use control to keep from being abandoned, competitive people try to make others love them for their performance. Competitive people are willing to work for others' praise and esteem.

Like the other two personality types, the competitive character needs to be loved and needs to have control over other people's love but is also motivated to do or be something to win that love. Compared to the controlling character, the competitive character is free-spirited and more willing to risk losing the praise of others. Others view the competitive person with a mixture of envy and admiration, wishing they had the same courage or talents. People are impressed by what a controlling person owns or controls, while they admire the competitive person's style, charm or grace, beauty, or brains.

HOW YOU LEARNED TO COMPETE

If the childhood periods of dependency and control were well managed in a loving relationship between you and your parents, you should have come to feel that your acceptance at home required only being pleasant and obeying the house rules. In the outside world, and this is what competition is about, you found a harsher set of standards. You were compared to other children. Now you had to prove yourself worthy to a new audience.

Your outside performance also seemed to influence how your parents felt about you. Even if they tried to disguise it, they appeared a little disappointed when you did not compete well, perhaps adding to your sense of failure by pushing you to try harder or to do better. If you hadn't felt loved before, now you felt you had to be the best at everything to compensate.

No matter how talented, you could not escape this need to prove yourself worthy. Other kids seemed better endowed and braver merely because they had done what you had not yet attempted. They had the edge. You defined your deficiencies in the mirror that your playmates provided.

Not only did you meet other children who were more experienced, stronger, smarter, faster, better looking, better dressed, more popular, and more confident, but you also began to learn in school about great men and women who were brilliant at a young age. Discovering that Mozart wrote a symphony when he was eight years old filled you not only with wonder but with tormenting questions about your own self-worth. Where did you fit into this enormous, terrifying world? That question persists through life.

Learning to Pretend: The Competitive Defense

Almost as soon as you saw other people doing things you could not, you tried to imitate them. A small child going to the piano and pounding on the keys when an older sibling is playing is a familiar sight. The result is usually noise, but the child is convinced that he is actually making music. As a child, whether you were playing ball, moving chessmen around the board, or painting a picture, just being there and pretending were enough to convince you that you were doing the same thing as the grown-ups. At first the quality of effort didn't matter. Your imagination filled in the deficiencies and made it all even. This early imitating activity formed the basis for your faking in later years, that is, being there and just going through the motions.

Later, when your efforts were measured and corrected, you encountered harsh comparisons between the ideal you were striving to emulate and your actual work. You recoiled from being judged and may have shied away as soon as someone tried to instruct you on the correct way to play the piano or paint. You wanted to do it your way. You wanted to play and pretend your efforts were real, good, and worthy. The world began to place more demands on you, and in school you compared the houses and trees you drew to your classmates' work. If you discovered that you could not draw as well as they did, you pretended that the way your work came out is exactly the way you intended it and that you liked it that way.

When you were disappointed by your school and athletic performance, you may have denied your discomfort, made excuses for your efforts, or more than likely pretended not to care, saying that you just weren't interested enough to give your best. Actually you were afraid of being measured, trying to preserve your belief that you were as good as you pretended. Imagining yourself as a success, winning the prize, the applause, and the adoration of a stadium of fans, became a common mental image. Sometimes it acted as a guide to help you visualize success; other times it was unrealistic and set you up to reach too high and fail.

If you pretended too much, you ran the risk of living in an imaginary world, fantasizing success instead of working to overcome your shortcomings. Concealing your deficiencies and disappointments by pretending they didn't exist or you didn't care about them, or escaping into fantasy, forms the basis for the pretending manner in which you deal with your shortcomings later in life as well.

Learning to Please Yourself

In the competitive period, if you were lucky, you learned from your parents' example how to be happy with yourself even if you are not a celebrity or a genius. Your parents' acceptance of themselves, even though they weren't perfect, gave you confidence. You learned that it is OK to love yourself just as you are. However, if your parents were unsure of their own worth and tried to make you achieve what they could not, you would have felt great pressure to perform, not merely to prove yourself but also to please them, satisfy their frustrated yearnings, and hopefully win their love in the process. At the back of your mind you may still hope your success can make your parents feel better about themselves, which is a perverted wish to please others, because even when you win, something is missing.

You began to establish your identity by observing your parents, believing they were powerful and smart, the kind of person you hoped to evolve into someday. As you grew older, you realized you may have exaggerated your parents' worth. This is usually a time of great disillusionment, because in recognizing your parents' limitations you fear you may have foretold your own.

When Your Parents Aren't Happy

If your parents were healthy, they wanted you to have a better life, avoid mistakes they made, take advantage of the opportunities they provided, and learn the lessons they paid so dearly to learn. However, you can learn only so much by example or instruction. You have to learn your own lessons through your own experience. Healthy parents during the competitive period provided consistent support that allowed you to fail without losing belief in yourself or your parents' love. You were able to risk with confidence, without being distracted by the need to please others.

Everyone pays a price for their parents' career failures and life frustrations. Your parents' sense of success and failure has a lasting influence on your own sense of fulfillment. Your parents may be envious of the very support they provided for you if they lacked parental support and blamed their failures on what they were denied. Such parents may try to take credit for your efforts or diminish your accomplishments. They may also claim they would have done better than you, given the same opportunities you had. If your parents' lack of self-love limits their ability to love your accomplishments, the situation creates frustration, resentment, and emptiness in you, especially if you still wish to prove yourself and please your parents.

How your parents *feel* about their own accomplishments, not what they have actually accomplished or what you have created, determines their attitude toward you. Leopold Mozart, a third-rate composer but arguably the greatest violin teacher of his time, announced to anyone who would listen during young Wolfgang's concerts, "I am the father," as if his son's genius was proof of his own. Wolfgang compensated for his father's withholding attitude by becoming a braggart and show-off, determined to get for himself what his father would not give. Characteristic of the competitive type, he openly lavished on himself the praise he believed no one else had the taste or sensibility to bestow on him. You would think a man of Mozart's legendary talent would be secure enough to be generous, yet his need to put other composers down reveals the residual insecurity he felt at the hand of his unhappy controlling father and the urge to put down his father along with them.

Accomplishments alone are not enough to give you self-esteem, but build on and confirm your earlier sense of being loved. No amount of applause from without can ever quell an inner feeling of self-doubt or fully compensate for an unloving parent. Until you declare you are lovable, good, and worthy by your own standards and decide to love and accept yourself for yourself, you vacillate. You need to learn you are lovable not merely because someone else loves you but because you love yourself. Learn to see each of your accomplishments in its own right with an identity of its own, apart from yourself, as a job well done, then move on to the next task. No work or achievement, however great, can confirm your lovability if you do not first love yourself and forgive those who did not love you enough.

Self-Esteem

Establishing self-esteem is the goal of the competitive period. But especially when you are young, it is far easier to attach esteem to external trappings than to a belief in your innate self-worth. Society, peer groups, advertising, and your own lack of self-esteem drove you to acquire material symbols of success to feel good during this pe-

riod. When you were a child those might have been better
toys, a trip to Disneyland, or expensive sports equipment.
As a competitive adult you picture yourself driving a fancy
automobile or living in a grand house, sporting a fancy
watch, or wearing the right clothes. This is really a contra-
diction, because appearing like everyone else is exactly
what you do not want as an adult. As a child you wanted to
be accepted, but you didn't want to be seen as inferior or to
be excluded for being different. You didn't feel confident
enough about your differences to develop, show, and prize
them as your uniqueness. When you doubted your specialness, you tried to hide by fitting in, seeking symbolic
acquisitions and peer acceptance as easier standards to
reach than defining your own excellence. If you're a competitive adult, which most of us are, you still do so.

This fear of defining yourself is the crisis of the competitive period. Failures in this period, because they were the
first failures you knew, could have had a devastating effect.
You wished to hide from the truth that you believed your
failure confirmed about you. You mistakenly believed that
you had proved yourself worthless, rather than simply
learning the lesson of your mistakes and acknowledging
that you still had work to do. Seeing bright children around
you succeed with apparent ease, without understanding
the work and preparation that went into their success, you
falsely believed that success should be easy, that a genius
does not have to work, that if you had a gift it would do it
all for you. The real lesson you needed to learn was that
everyone struggles and it is the struggle that defines your
gift and shapes your style. At this time some children go
into hiding and lose their identity by fitting in, adopting
easier peer standards, looking for safety from this dangerous exposure of self. There is a seductive attraction to
mediocrity at the very same time there is enormous incentive to excel. When and where do children find the courage
to take the risks of exposure, test their real worth, and
hazard losing their belief in themselves? The question lives
on within all of us.

Fluid Choices

As we've seen, dependent and controlling needs are present throughout childhood and continue to exert influence in the competitive period. Your use of the three major defense types is generally fluid throughout childhood, depending on the threats you face. You hide from the pain of a loss of love with denial, you manage a loss of power by making excuses, and you avoid a loss of esteem by pretending. How rigidly you maintain your defenses depends on your willingness to take responsibility and risk, which in turn depends on your self-confidence, your belief that you are loved and safe. In short, you need to feel you won't lose everything if you fail.

The rapidity and ease with which a child can change defensive postures is remarkable. The child tests out competitive defenses when he feels brave and resorts back to controlling or dependent defenses when he is less certain. This fluidity is the most important factor in growing up healthy, a process of experimenting to find the most comfortable emotional shoe.

Not long ago my wife and I accompanied another family climbing Dunn's River Falls in Jamaica. The oldest child, Sabrina, was nine and full of enthusiasm, wanting to run ahead of everyone to the top. Two-year-old Talya stayed on a path with a babysitter, content to identify people by name as they came into view.

Mallory was seven and, looking up at the falls from the beach, seemed intimidated by the rushing water and not at all sure about the wisdom of making the climb. Mallory mentioned that she might accompany her baby sister Talya and climb the stairway back to the top. "I don't know about this," she said, looking at her feet. "I don't know if I can do it. It's too hard for a kid."

We invited Mallory to climb with us. We explained how to climb on the rocks, where the slippery parts were, and how to find sure footing. We explained that if she planned her steps and picked her way one step at a time she would do fine.

Mallory seemed encouraged by having a method to master and cautiously followed us, stopping every so often to ask a question. She took each new instruction to heart, and after a few hundred yards of climbing she seemed to have the knack of it. In fact, she started to outdistance us, expressing glee. As she climbed, instead of asking for reassurance she would tell us what danger she had just mastered, although it was obvious that she still felt some insecurity. She was a perfect example of a child developing mastery, entirely typical of her age and developmental stage. No excuses! She was learning how to control a difficult situation.

Mallory suddenly caught up with her older sister and, feeling emboldened by her recent accomplishments and brimming with a newfound sense of power, she challenged Sabrina to see who could get to the top of the next rise first. It turned out to be an especially difficult climb, but Mallory was off like a shot. She pulled herself through the very same torrents that only a few moments before on the beach had caused her to doubt herself. Sabrina pushed Mallory, nudged her off the best footing, and "accidentally" managed to step on her foot when she got too close. But Mallory, being smaller and perhaps offering less resistance to the water, pushed ahead, and the race ended in a dead heat.

"I won," called Sabrina, clapping her hands and jumping up and down.

"You cheated," Mallory answered. "You pushed me."

"Sore sport. You lost," retorted Sabrina.

"I did not and I'll prove it." Mallory pointed to the falls just above. The two girls raced to the top. Ever the diplomat, I declared the contest a tie and we waited for the girls' parents to arrive. A series of languid pools and flat terrain, by far the tamest part of the climb, awaited us ahead. When her mother arrived, Mallory suddenly feigned helplessness and anxiously reached for her mother's hand as she pretended to climb with great difficulty over some flat dry rocks at the edge of the pool. "Help me," she called, full of staged terror, acting totally dependent and playing her role so convincingly that she seemed overcome by her own helplessness and lost her footing on level ground. This was the same child who, moments before, had raced headlong, climbing upward over slippery rocks through a torrent of water.

Her original fear of the falls caused Mallory to have a dependent wish to avoid danger and be like her younger sister. Her desire to master her fear of the falls led her to a controlling solution. The presence of her sister prompted her to race competitively. And finally, the presence of her mother evoked a mock dependent helplessness. All of these responses were fully embraced by the same child within a span of fifteen minutes.

What parent has not had the experience of speaking earnestly to an eight-year-old and been delighted at the child's sensitivity and mature understanding and, only a few minutes later, being called to rescue a younger sibling from the same child's bullying and cruelty, and then in a moment seeing the child whining sullenly because he feels no one loves him?

The period that precedes adolescence is a mixture of the three earlier periods. The behavior a child shows is determined as much by the stimulus for the behavior as it is by the child's character, a kind of situational definition of character type. Thus when a particular situation makes a child fear abandonment, the child is likely to act dependently. A child who is made to feel powerless makes excuses to control the situation. A child whose self-esteem is lagging in math class becomes competitive in the school yard. Of course it may all change in a moment.

Finding Yourself

The competitive period is about learning to define and pursue your own gift, beginning the search for your own identity, for your uniqueness and specialness. Developing this identity is necessary so that you no longer rely on other people to feel good about yourself as a dependent person does, nor must you control others to give you a sense of power.

This is a lifelong goal that merely begins in the preteen years. Parents and schools often encourage children to achieve uniqueness by being the one at the top, the best. And while striving for the best has merit in its own right, the quest is easily tainted if it becomes a substitute for finding yourself.

The problem of this period is that it is always easier to be better than another person than it is to be your best. Being your best, after all, means risking to find out just how good you really are. This is the fear of all competitive people. They compete for the place at the top of the ladder rather than looking within to find their unique talent. They become adults who accept the "best salesperson of the month" award flushed with the momentary fullness of being recognized, but soon find that the glory is passing. When you don't fulfill yourself, the substitute goals, like an addiction, have only ephemeral satisfaction.

The only lasting feeling of fullness comes from giving your gift from within, tolerating the limitations of that gift and still being willing to share it in its incompleteness and imperfection, evolving in the process of giving as you do.

GROWING UP

Your ability to grow and be open with your feelings continues to depend on your dedication to truthfulness and your willingness to take responsibility for your life. This is never easy to do. Initially the sheer energy and vitality of youth are often enough to keep you on the road to success, without having to examine your life. If you've had a difficult time growing up, you're likely to bring with you a well-formed penchant for using a particular defensive system under stress.

The way a particular defensive style is activated in later years depends on the kind of losses you experience and your willingness to confront problems directly. Having lived through all three developmental periods, you have the potential to act in a dependent, controlling, or competitive way. However, one particular emotional response, typical of your character, usually predominates under stress. But even if you are well balanced, mature, and in touch with your feelings, a particular loss still has the power to reawaken unresolved old feelings and defensiveness:

- A loss of love awakens feelings of dependency and leads you to deny your pain and doubt your ability to help yourself.
- A loss of power or influence activates your need to control. You blame others and make excuses for your failings.
- A loss of esteem makes you feel defeated. You seek easy victories to assuage your hurt and save face and to pretend that things aren't so bad.

Usually when the danger is over you regain your balance and greet the world evenhandedly, telling the truth, at last, about the situation you just endured, admitting your responsibility to friends and to yourself, and finally you grow from the experience and move on. Sometimes it takes many mistakes to come to understand that you are responsible for what happens to you, but reality is patient and continues to provide examples until you learn. It can take years, decades, a lifetime. Courage!

YOUR CHARACTER TRAITS IN ADULT LIFE

Thus as you get older, when you are under stress, traits from each period of development reappear from time to time, grow prominent, merge, and fade. When you are a young adult, dependent issues such as being loved, being in touch with family, establishing roots, and making friends are especially important. Controlling concerns, such as developing a sphere of influence, attaining security, and establishing financial independence become more important in the years that follow. In your thirties and forties, as you strive to win success and esteem, risking failure, giving up the familiar to find yourself, your competitive traits surface. In later life fears about losing control and power rise to prominence once more as retirement becomes a reality. As you grow older, you begin to depend more and more on others, and dependent concerns take over again.

Each of the three personality types also experiences distinct reactions to the passing decades, outlined in the chart on the following three pages.

CHANGING AND GROWING

You are always going to be the same character type. When you change for the best you will initiate more of your behavior from your strength and less from your weakness. Although you may grow toward being your best, you never completely shed the potential for acting in a defensive way under stress.

How do you correct your character deficiencies to make a whole person of yourself? How do you begin to grow and develop a sense of maturity and independence that allows others to be free while you strive to be your best? You need not be trapped in past patterns of negative responses. You can learn to function as a spontaneous person and become free.

You do so by becoming aware of the stresses that can cause you the most damage, by learning to understand your feelings, and by expressing them honestly. Only in this way can you avoid crippling emotional debt.

Understanding how each stage of your development contributed to your personality has already started you on the path to emotional freedom. Now you need to accept the

Decade	Usual Landmarks	Dependent Landmarks	Controlling Landmarks	Competitive Landmarks
Preteens	Identity defined by belonging, achieving, or industry. Changeable, fluid; up and adult today, down and childlike tomorrow. Boys in wolf packs hiding from girls in social clubs.	Apron strings too tightly held out of fear of being on one's own or offending parents. Wonders, What if . . . ?	Early signs of rigidity: takes rules, grades, religion too seriously. Fears punishment for anger. Perfectionism. Eating disorders begin.	Wants to be first at everything. Losing is devastating. Hates shortcomings and hides them.
The Teens	Rebellion begins, testing identity, self vs. the peer group. Risking in sports, jobs, relationships.	Rebellion minimized; hides at home or seeks security in love; anxiety limits risking.	Attracted to grades, work, anything that conveys a concrete way of measuring worth.	Plays for applause, popularity, to please others, afraid of showing real self.
The 20s	Rebellion subsides. You finish school, test your worth, try life out on your own, fall in love, marry, aspire, climb, push, upgrade résumé, redefine goals.	Postpones leaving home or may marry prematurely. Still under another's rule. Parents and security too important.	May overtrain, stay in school too long. Goals: perfection, a system that works, influence and security. Wants to be in power.	Full steam ahead; material goals; energy is high. Overwork. Seeking the high of life. Fickle.

Decade	Usual Landmarks	Dependent Landmarks	Controlling Landmarks	Competitive Landmarks
The 30s	You want more meaning and success. Financial burdens sharpen your goals. Ambition and drive peak. Feelings matter. You begin to resolve old mistakes.	Family and security issues dominate and inhibit growth. They also bring resentment. Anxiety common, obstructing growth.	May marry weaker partner to feel in control. Postpones real risks, builds power base instead. Money talks and rules.	Led forward by victories; neglects all for the career. It's about success, fame, new worlds to conquer.
The 40s	You get comfortable. Responsibility increases. First illnesses remind you of your mortality, slowing you down. You stop fooling yourself. You're more honest, focused on reality.	Family matters and security issues intensify. Spouses and kids may break away to be free of smothering and may finally rebel.	May take unrealistic risks. Rising to the top, holds on to power. Demands respect. Children's autonomy poses a threat. Building a dynasty.	Winning still important, but energy not what it used to be. "What's it all about?" Looks within for goals. Feels cheated. Still a little lost.
The 50s	Real emotional growth. You know what you have to do. Your opinions matter. Economy, friendship, decisiveness rule. You lead; others follow. Support parents and kids. Family responsibility peaks.	Difficulty letting children go, empty nest. Kids resist contact. Can be a time of depression. May start to take risks to find self and define independent identity.	Trouble releasing control over family. The need to break away to be free. Suffers from loneliness. Stress-related illnesses. May take desperate risks to prove strength.	Energy not what it used to be. Has to focus and be more introspective. Bigger acquisitions when successful, stressed out when not. Real purpose?

Decade	Usual Landmarks	Dependent Landmarks	Controlling Landmarks	Competitive Landmarks
The 60s	You lose friends to illness, budget time better, enjoy self and travel, give your opinion more openly. False beliefs fade.	Dependency shifts to kids. High potential for depression, regrets.	Becomes rigid in face of change. Holds the helm, knows best, stays the course.	Looking over one's shoulder at younger competitors. Wonders why.
The 70s	You abandon meaningless struggles, smell the flowers, care for others. Empathy increases.	Kids asked to run affairs. Dependency increases.	Control masks waning strength. Fears dependency. Won't turn over the helm.	Talks about what could have been, if only there had been more time, luck.
The 80s	You try to stay healthy and independent. Each day matters.	Total dependency, resisted by kids.	Set in your ways, argumentative.	Talks about the good old days.

person you are. Chapter 4 will help you recognize your character strengths and weaknesses and make you aware of the emotional prejudices that undermine your journey of growth. To make the most of this information you need to accept everything that has happened to you. It took all of it to bring you to this moment. Part II of this book will then show you how to rid yourself of the emotional debt of your character weaknesses and act from your strength with confidence.

In the end, emotional freedom means feeling good about yourself—feeling lovable, strong, worthwhile, and capable. The process takes a lifetime, but each step you take will give you new optimism and assurance. You have already found the right road.

4

Understanding Your Character Type: Examining Your Strengths and Weaknesses

"I can't believe I acted that way—again. When will I ever grow up?"

There is nothing as painful as realizing you have hurt someone you love, lost control, or made a fool of yourself. Letting yourself down is the most painful disappointment, and no prison holds you more firmly or dismays you as much as believing you are hopelessly trapped in the weakest part of your character.

The ultimate truth is, if someone is going to do you harm, mess up your life, interfere with your love relationships, or keep you from succeeding in your career, it is most likely to be you. The hidden negative inclinations of your personality do more to spoil your chances than all your enemies combined.

It doesn't have to stay that way. You can stop giving in to the automatic responses that get you into trouble. You can make a choice to do what you really want. You can become your best.

The purpose of finding emotional freedom is to break this self-destructive cycle of acting in the dark.

It should be clear by now that most of the habits that get you into trouble are remnants from the early stages of development. You can't change the way you were brought up, but you can gain more understanding of who you are and what your weaknesses are. This chapter explores the strengths, and particularly the weaknesses, of each character type to make you aware of what keeps you from succeeding when you pursue your goals. Examining these character traits honestly, with your eyes wide open, will help you set realistic, attainable goals for lowering your defenses and attaining emotional freedom.

Childhood is a preparation for coping with the stresses of adulthood. Each of the three stages we have all passed through has left us with issues whose resolution continues throughout adult life. And each stage has taught us valuable life lessons:

- The period of dependency creates the groundwork on which you later build relationships and determines how you learn to value other people. Obviously, even if you got through the period of dependency without difficulty, learned to trust, and formed close personal ties, you are still not immune to pain when a person abandons you later on in life. You will, however, be better prepared than someone who had poor parenting during the dependent stage and will be much less likely to become overwhelmed when faced with losses of relationships.
- If you achieve balance mastering controlling issues, you learn to feel good enough about yourself to allow others to be free. You will still experience frustration and feelings of powerlessness later on when struggling with financial reversals, but you will be more flexible about the experience than someone who has already developed rigid, controlling attitudes.
- In the competitive period you learn that you must compete for recognition and attention. If you took

the competition of later childhood in stride, you may still find yourself trying to keep up with colleagues in later years, but you will be far less concerned with winning merely to beat others than someone who had suffered severe humiliation during the competitive period and now has to win at any cost. You will, of course, also be more realistic about taking risks.

YOUR POSITIVE AND NEGATIVE POTENTIAL

You have the capacity to initiate your thoughts and actions from a position of strength and confidence, of truthfulness and self-acceptance, rather than from your weak character traits. Operating at its best, each character type has many worthwhile assets. An independent, warm family person and team player may still be a dependent person at heart, but one who has grown into his positive potential. An organized businessperson who motivates others to do their best may still be a controlling person, but one who has developed enough belief and confidence in herself to be able to encourage others to act freely. Finally, a self-fulfilled creative performer is still a competitive person, but one who seeks his best by competing with his best.

You also retain some legacy of negative traits from all three developmental periods. Some negative potential for acting dependent and denying reality, for controlling people and making excuses for your shortcomings, and for competing with others while pretending not to care remains with you even when you are successful and happy. What follows will help you become aware of what brings out these negative traits. Failing to acknowledge and understand your negative traits prevents you from being free.

To remove the obstacles from your path to emotional freedom, in this chapter you will examine your strengths and weaknesses, your blind spots, and the buzzwords that define each character's dynamics. As you read, bear in mind the character type that seemed to fit you best in Chapter 2.

Your Dependent Traits

Strength	Weakness (Understated)	Weakness (Overstated)
Supportive	Undermining others when threatened. "I should never have depended on you. You always hurt me."	Overestimating the worth of those you depend on. "I know you'll *never* let me down."
Loyal	Fickleness in the face of danger. "This isn't what I signed on for. I'm out of here."	Goes down with the ship. No independent thought. "I can't leave."
Nurturing	Giving away too much. You set up others to use and reject you or act helpless to control others.	Smothering, overprotecting, inhibiting autonomy, infantilizing others.
Loving	Clinging, won't give the other person space to be.	You live only for the other person and lose yourself.
Tenacious	You let go when afraid of rejection.	You hold on to the known rather than take a risk.
Team player	You're always complaining, measuring deficiencies of the organization. You feel unappreciated and tend to overestimate self-worth.	No independent thought. You follow rules to a fault, tattle, are a nuisance, try to get on leader's good side.
Confident	You exhibit pervasive self-doubt, continually asking for reassurance.	You demonstrate childlike overconfidence.

DEPENDENT STRENGTHS AND WEAKNESSES

Your dependent character strengths and weaknesses all relate to your ability to bond with people. Your dependent strengths lead you to become part of a family or team, to be concerned with establishing security and consistency. Your dependent weaknesses reflect your belief that you cannot stand alone and that you need another person to make you feel complete, to keep you from being lonely, or to be safe and happy. Your dependent character strengths are realized when you assume independence and contribute to the well-being of others. Your dependent weaknesses predominate when you have unrealistic expectations, such as a need to be taken care of, or rescued when you feel abandoned. At such times dependent yearnings surface, and you wish to possess others. Then you tend to focus only on the failure of others to meet your needs and forget that you are an adult and can take care of yourself.

The chart opposite not only presents strengths and weaknesses but also points out pitfalls to be mindful of. The underlying requirement for acting from your strength is simply believing in yourself, even when things are not going your way.

CONTROLLING STRENGTHS AND WEAKNESSES

Your controlling strengths make you valuable in organizing and completing complicated tasks that require long-term management and discipline. Without the supervisory capacity of the controlling character type, the business of the world would come to a halt. Dependent workers would have no leaders, and the creative competitive types would have no one to organize their plans and direct their inventions toward completion. Your controlling strengths are, of course, balanced by corresponding weaknesses. You may control too tightly when you doubt yourself and insist on being right or you may act out of control and then become surprisingly passive and paralyzed when your highly organized system seems to falter.

Your Controlling Traits

Strength	Weakness (Understated)	Weakness (Overstated)
Orderly	Others get lost in your system. Only you can find things.	Your system is too rigid; neatness matters more than content.
Group leader	You lead by the book, blame the rules, but follow them anyway, often mismanaging priorities.	You demand obedience, belittle and publicly criticize offenders.
Follows orders	*Your* way is better, but you seem to make up the rules as you go along.	You follow orders too rigidly; compassion and empathy fade.
Reliable	Unreliable	Inflexible
Responsible	Irresponsible	You take over everything but the blame.
Analytical of details	You're overwhelmed by the forest; problems in focusing.	You're overwhelmed by the trees, focus too narrowly.
Organizes well	You can't leave well enough alone. You overorganize.	You lose human touch, use rules to punish and control others.
Understands the facts	You can't grasp the obvious.	You slant evidence to prove you're right.
Respects the law	You secretly cheat.	Rigid enforcer of the letter of the law.
Knows the price of everything	The value of things escapes you.	Pricing things is your only enjoyment.

COMPETITIVE STRENGTHS AND WEAKNESSES

Your obvious strength is your competitive spirit. You are a self-starter and a go-getter. Your competitive weakness is that you can become overly competitive and, in being so unwilling to accept a failure, throw good energy away on useless projects just to prove you're a winner. Conversely, in the face of defeat you can prematurely abandon the cause and give in, pretending not to care, just when you should give your best.

Your Competitive Traits

Strength	Weakness (Understated)	Weakness (Overstated)
Good, driven competitor	You give up too easily after losing the lead. Easily discouraged by unexpected failure.	You never give up and waste energy trying to prove yourself.
Expansive, outgoing	Self-doubting, constrictive	World's biggest braggart
Popular	You need adulation and attention to work.	Spiteful if ignored, no one's true friend.
Proud of specialness	You blame tools for your failure.	You abandon faith when losing, may cheat to win.
Imaginative, creative, inventive	Lack discipline. Impulsive, you fall back on routine and get trapped in ruts when creativity fails.	You want to reinvent the wheel rather than learn the ropes.
Self-starter	Need to be driven when you lose faith in yourself.	You put cart ahead of the horse and let the project run away from you. *(continued)*

Strength	Weakness (Understated)	Weakness (Overstated)
Leader	Your self-doubt causes you to lose direction in a crisis.	You demand blind allegiance from followers; need to be believed in.
Good performer	Inconsistent; you look for easy victories.	You can humiliate others when clawing for recognition.
Visionary	You break promises when overwhelmed.	You reach too high.
High self-esteem	Masochistic	Narcissistic
Strong individual	You masquerade as reluctant when not in spotlight.	Your grandstanding undermines team effort.
Hero	The wimp, claiming you were cheated in defeat.	Backbiting, unsporting in victory.
Clever	You retreat into fantasies; you're superficial.	You're scheming when mean-spirited.

UNDERSTANDING YOUR BLIND SPOTS

True strength of character depends on understanding the weaknesses that are potential spoilers of your talents. Believing in yourself enough to get your weaknesses out of the way of your strengths is often enough to carry the day.

Our blind spots reflect a lack of awareness of our weaknesses.

To a greater or lesser degree, all three of the following patterns of blind spots are found within all of us. A particular blind spot may be transient and appear only under severe stress, such as bragging to cover faults when passed over for recognition, or it may be pervasive, such as always expecting the worst to happen.

Blind spots can keep us from seeing either the bad or the good in a situation. We can believe all is well or all is lost just as easily (and unrealistically). Their purpose is to weigh the scales so the conclusion we draw is slanted to give us comfort, to make us appear right, good, or smart. This prejudiced point of view also causes us pain because it delays our dealing with reality.

Try to recognize your tendencies as you read the following descriptions.

Your Dependent Blind Spots

Your dependent blind spots incline you to:

- weight the positives heavily and disregard the negatives, leaving you wondering later why all your wishful thinking hasn't added up to a happy life
- believe the sky is falling when one bad event happens, see the loss in every event, define a person as bad based on one flaw
- distort the worth of a relationship and ignore all of your partner's flaws just so you can stay right where you are
- minimize your hurt so you won't need to stand up for yourself when someone has wronged you *or* exaggerate your hurt to control others by making them feel guilty about injuring you
- believe you have an obligation to anyone who ever expressed love for you and give losers, hurters, controllers, and mean-spirited people the benefit of the doubt just because they promise love
- try in vain to rekindle a love that has been hopeless for years
- accept being mistreated as better than being ignored

To overcome dependent blind spots, you need to know that nothing comes from nothing. Life is hard work. Everyone is alone, and you are capable of getting through the night by yourself. The part of you that wishes to be rescued should never be allowed to take over the part of you that can rescue yourself. When you believe that someone is going to make it better for you, you only set yourself up for disappointment. *You* are the only one who can really take care of you.

Your Controlling Blind Spots

Your controlling blind spots incline you to:

- waste energy to prove you're right or perfect long after it has ceased to make any difference
- prove others wrong when you could just as well have ignored the problem
- argue a case passionately just to convince yourself that you are smart when you really don't care about the issue
- get lost in complicated logic when admitting a simple feeling of fear, hurt, or anger would immediately clear up the situation
- confuse neatness of presentation with feasibility of result, orderliness with worth, and appearance with substance
- argue with vigor the parts you can understand while depreciating the importance of what you don't know or fear you can't grasp
- undervalue kindness and overestimate the worth of cleverness
- believe in power and try to buy your way out of all problems
- assume that there is a price for everything, that people can be bought, and that when they are bought they should feel obligated, not resentful
- assume people owe you for what you have given them
- interpret independence as rebellion and seek to punish people for growing, which you see as betrayal

- believe you are invincible and then blame others when you suffer a setback
- bear grudges

To overcome controlling blind spots, you need to accept your humanness and remember that you might be wrong. Seek out worthy teachers who will point out your mistakes so you can learn from them. Remember that if what you give is not given freely, it is given to manipulate. Risk feeling hurt and admit it.

Your Competitive Blind Spots

Your competitive blind spots incline you to:

- believe you must always be best
- believe if you don't win you fail
- value praise more than performance and so encourage flattery
- be vain
- engage in wishful thinking and believe in your own dream when it is only an escape
- hide defects while exaggerating strengths
- insist that the people who love you be your audience and believe your audience loves you
- find some way to get to the center of every stage
- distance yourself from the parts of your life and history—old friends, family names, place of birth, or level of education—that may embarrass you by showing you are merely human

To overcome competitive blind spots, you need to believe that your success is increased by acknowledging your failures or humble beginnings, not hiding from them. You need to accept that people will identify with your struggle, since you show by revealing your hard work that it is possible for others to win as well.

BUZZWORD EXERCISE

Since you think in words, it is only logical to examine the
words that have special impact on your personality type,
the words that trigger defensive responses, the buzzwords.
A buzzword immediately evokes an action, a feeling, or an
attitude.

The words and phrases in the following lists are defined
to approximate the prejudicial viewpoint of each character
type. You will find yourself defined by the words that
provoke you the most.

Take your time going through the words. Read each one
aloud. Close your eyes and feel its emotional impact. If you
get a strong reaction, the term has special meaning for you.
Open your eyes and read the definition. Does the definition explain your emotional reaction? Does it reveal your
underlying concerns? Go through the three sections in this
manner. Some words are defined in more than one context.
Pay attention to the meaning that applies to you most.

Dependent Buzzwords

Abandonment: The greatest threat in life; implies having to face life alone.
Acceptance: A continual quest for external endorse-
   ment; self-interests are initially gladly sacrificed
   for it, but later the sacrifice is resented.
Appreciation: Sought from others as proof of lovability; when absent, results in sulking and self-pity.
Belonging: Desired condition, main source of comfort,
   during which signs of rejection are nonetheless
   still anticipated.
Contact: The more insecure you feel, the more contact
   with others you need.
Desperation: Belief that you are inadequate to make it
   through a crisis alone.
Fear: Anticipation of rejection, disapproval, or the
   withdrawal of love; the basic dependent feeling
   state.

Growing up: Not necessary yet, so long as supply lines are still open and others still fulfill your needs, someday a possibility, but faced reluctantly.

Happy: Having the people you need around you.

Holding on: The best way to avoid a potentially worse situation.

Indulgence: Asking to be accepted and be given to *because* you are needy and to be forgiven for your weakness and excused from having to act responsibly.

Letting go: To be avoided at all costs. Implies the threat of the unknown.

Loneliness: Motivator for desperate action.

Love: Your reason for being, an end in itself. You become disappointed when you do receive it. You always need more. Often withheld by others to control you.

Loyalty: What you offer and demand from others, often an extension of your neediness. You're loyal so long as you're provided for.

Possessive: Holding on to people as if they were the only barrier between you and emotional ruin. Intensity of possessiveness rises and falls inversely to your self-confidence.

Protective: While seen as overprotective by others, to you it's only exercising reasonable caution to safeguard those you love.

Rejection: Second only to the fear of death as your greatest fear.

Risk: Why risk anything ever?

Security: You'll pay or do anything to achieve this.

Self-esteem: What you have when you feel loved.

Self-pity: If others only knew how you suffer, they would never leave you or make trouble for you.

Separation: If permanent or involuntary, the hurt can push old unresolved resentments to the surface and precipitate a depression.

Trust: The unrealistic hope that the key people in your life will never fail to come to your rescue, a continual source of disappointment, leading you to conclude mistakenly that you can't depend on anyone.

Understanding: If you feel loved, no understanding is necessary. If you do not feel loved, no understanding makes any difference.

Controlling Buzzwords

Abandonment: A potent threat, but the hurt is immediately covered with anger rather than expressed as hurt.

Anger: Your only easily expressed feeling, even then rarely shown in a straightforward manner, but with justifications and explanations, blaming and self-righteousness.

Anxiety: Your hidden but underlying feeling since you fear everything is continually on the verge of going out of control.

Argument: Friendly, helpful discussion.

Criticism: Of others—a more socially acceptable form of anger often disguised by being called "constructive." Of yourself by others—unfair, unfounded, slander.

Encouragement: Available from you to others at a price, subject to being replaced with deprecation should the other person disappoint you.

Enemy: One who disagrees with you.

Excuse: Logical explanation of and payment in full for all social expressions of negativity or insensitivity.

Happiness: Being in control.

Hurt: To express hurt is dangerous because it reveals weakness and may invite attack. To withhold hurt is to fantasize about retaliation. To release hurt is disadvantageous because forgiving others is relinquishing power over them.

Important: Whatever you are presently concerned with.

Injury: Seldom revealed in a timely manner, but brought up again and again as justification for mistreating others or withholding from them.

Logic: Often influenced by and used to justify a hidden feeling, weakness, mistake, or other shortcoming.

Loneliness: Acceptable only when you decide to isolate yourself from others. Dreaded when it is the result of rejection and forced on you.

Love: A commodity valued more in its conditional and measured bestowal than in being given openly; often equated with currency.

Manipulation: Helpful coaxing.

Mind: Mistakenly believed to be the center of all power.

Obedience: Expected behavior of anyone with less power.

Paranoia: Showing a reasonable interest in others' motivations, especially those who might hurt you.

Pessimism: Being realistic about life.

Possession: Nine-tenths of the law and all the excuse you need to hold on to whatever you want.

Punishment: Justifiable correction in the other person's best interest.

Respect: The prerequisite attitude others must show for you to take them seriously.

Special: What you secretly doubt you are, which makes you want to remove all opportunity for others to reject you.

Syntax: Thought and speech patterns reflecting your need to manipulate: "Don't you think that . . . ?", "Isn't it true that . . . ?", "Don't you really mean . . . ?", and "Aren't you saying . . . ?" Such phrases are used to control others' responses or provoke an argument for which you have a ready response; for example, "Don't you think twenty is too young to get married?"

Threat: Anyone else's strength.

Weakness: Major flaw of *other* people.

Competitive Buzzwords

Acceptance: The esteem of others, sought continually in every action and comment.

Beaten: A misinterpretation of the facts; besides, you did not give your best effort.

Comparing: Defining your value by relating it to the worth of others, especially when you feel insecure.

Courage: Never really felt until victory is securely in hand and then likely to be exaggerated to dispel the existence of previous self-doubt.

Creativity: What you feel is your most underrated and unrewarded strength.

Detached: How to appear to anyone who tries to get close to you or wants to know what you feel.

Discipline: Avoided until absolutely necessary. You improvise until then.

Disorganization: Camouflage to keep from being judged.

Escape: Typical response in the face of an unfavorable result, best made good before a disappointing conclusion is obvious to others.

Failure: An inconclusive and probably unfair test of abilities.

Fantasy: The best part of reality.

Feign: Doing what must be done to get your way.

Followers: Other people.

Friendly: A dangerous ploy because others may react to it as a come-on.

Honest opinion: Demanded from others, but objected to when given freely.

High, the: (1) Feeling of success at the moment of realization that winning is at hand. (2) Reason for living. (3) Anything that erases self-doubt.

Imagination: What other people lack in understanding you.

Insecurity: Arriving at the party unnoticed.

Insincere: Getting away with as much as you can.

Invention: Easier than research and doing homework, sometimes an avoidance of discipline. Follow-through always a problem.

Leadership: Positions coveted for their privileges, avoided because of their responsibilities, and, when attained, tend to overwhelm you with boring details.

Lose, to be a loser, loss: Worst nightmare come true.

Loyalty: What have you done for me lately?

Phony: Secret self-appraisal admitted only after a failure or in isolation.

Play: What work is expected to be like.

Prestige: Prestige will do nicely.

Quit: To avoid judgment.

Rank and file: Where you'll never find the competitive person smiling.

Security: A good plastic surgeon, a patron with endless loyalty and wealth, deafening applause, headaches from photographers' flashbulbs, a good review, fan mail, flowers from total strangers, envy, and recognition from others.

Selfish: Merely taking full advantage of the opportunities that naturally present themselves.

Sincere: Doing what is right for you.

Success: Winning while others lose. Sometimes avoided when it is at hand for fear of losing or not being able to hold on to it.

Truth: What you always tell.

Win: When recognition is as big as the success.

As you complete this exercise you should have a clearer sense of yourself. If some of the terms seemed unflattering to you, remember that they represent only your negative character potential at your worst. You need to consider how your strengths and weaknesses, blind spots, and buzzwords interact to stimulate your behavior. In the next chapter we will examine the key that links all three of these features together—the underlying defensive system of each character.

CORRECTING YOUR NEGATIVE LEGACY

As you read the following goals, think of them as positive directions that balance and correct your weaknesses. Don't be surprised if you find helpful reminders in each category. Be open and read each goal slowly. If any goal speaks to you, write it out on a separate 3" × 5" card. You can post the cards where you will see them or carry the stack of cards around with you to remind yourself of your intentions.

Goals to Help You Overcome Dependency

Your goal is to become independent. Dependent questions such as "Am I loved?" and "Am I needed?" and "Who is there for me?" will arise in every struggle for independence you undertake. To achieve true independence you must give up your dream of being rescued by anyone except yourself.

No matter how independent you become, a splinter of dependent yearning may pull at you when you feel alone, rejected, or discouraged. When your worldly enterprises are failing and your courage has failed you, it is easy to give in to the notion that you can't make it on your own and need to be saved. Dependent people come to this realization *whenever* threatened or forced to confront or reveal themselves. At such times they look outside themselves for help. They need to look within.

The following corrective life goals point the way to achieving independence.

You need to:

- remember that life is not always fair and that every rejection or insensitivity does not need to be taken personally, reacted to, or be made into a major disaster. Most injuries are unintended, simply thoughtless actions.
- understand that no relationship is all good or all bad.

You ignore the negative parts of a relationship at your own peril. It's better to face problems as they appear than expect them to go away.

- avoid acting out of desperation and realize that when you are desperate you look for a relationship merely because you need to be in any relationship.
- realize that you are enough, that you are complete as you are.
- create a life of your own that pleases you.
- take responsibility for getting out of harm's way instead of expecting others to protect you.
- accept that the way things are right now is the way things are supposed to be. This is it. There is no more.
- accept your solitariness as a natural state and use it to your advantage, rather than filling it with yearnings for people who are not present.

Goals to Help You Overcome Your Need to Control

You control to keep from feeling powerless to avoid rejection.

You need to:

- allow others to be free to speak their minds, live their lives, disagree, leave and enter your life when they want.
- assume responsibility for your failures as well as your successes.
- accept your limitations with grace.
- give up on the impossible, cut your losses, save your assets and energy for another day.
- understand that it is only human to be afraid and hurt.
- accept the imperfections of others as reflections of their humanness and not use them as a justification for attacking or criticizing them.
- remember that the things that make you angriest are

the truths that you don't want to accept.
- accept your weaknesses with humility and learn to empathize with others who share your weaknesses rather than putting them down for what you will not accept in yourself.
- understand that the way things are is largely the way you have caused them to be. It took the sum total of everything in your life for you to become the person you have become. So accept all the parts of yourself to be free of deceit.

Goals to Help You Overcome the Competitive Trait

You pretend not to care to save face.
   You need to:

- seek your best self and stay on the path that promises the greatest personal, spiritual, and emotional development and remember that early success and money can be a deadly trap.
- be your best at whatever you have talent for and see that you are using your talent as much as possible.
- risk failure and still give your best efforts when the tide turns against you.
- be willing to commit to what you love.
- be willing to give your career a rest and not make every minute of every day be about you.
- be willing to act and do good anonymously and still feel rewarded for your best effort.
- teach in a giving way and help someone else get there too.
- learn to forgive other people for not recognizing and celebrating your worth. After all, it took you a while to believe in yourself. You don't always have to be a big star just to have a little worth.
- realize that if you feel you have to prove your worth all the time, nothing you do will ever prove you are worthwhile.

- define your own standards, invent your own methods, follow your own instincts not out of rebelliousness, spite, or to show others, but because your talent points you toward its own goals and suggests its own methods. Remember this when you fail. Remember it even more when you succeed, for success by other people's standards may have caused you to abandon your own.
- remember to be grateful.
- realize that if you achieve the biggest of all successes it is still likely that no one will remember what you did, but if you please yourself doing what you love, it will be enough.
- let go of past victories and move on.
- let go of past failures and move on.
- take time to walk in nature and realize the true scale of things, to sense your own insignificance and the awesomeness of the Milky Way.
- be generous to yourself and take time to celebrate the good.

POINTS TO REMEMBER

You deserve what you accept.

You can always find someone to blame for hurting you, undermining you, lowering your self-esteem, but the way you turn out is still your own doing and your responsibility.

People are always going to be more interested in themselves than in you. It's a fact of life—the nature of survival—and shouldn't disappoint you. You should be interested in yourself first as well.

The person who truly loves you will respect your right to say no and to be your own person, to have your own opinions, and to live your own life. If you have to give up your personal rights to be with another person, you will eventually end up without yourself or the other person.

Disappointing another person is not the end of the world. The person who overreacts to your free choice is trying to control you.

The person who rejects you for telling your true feelings has rejected you long before this, does not love you, does not belong in your life, is not your friend, will never give you anything worth keeping.

You get better by expecting to be better.

You always have more power and more strength than you realize.

You can always be a little braver.

PART II

WHERE YOU ARE NOW

5

The Feeling Cycle:
Understanding Your Emotions

The difference between a happy person and an unhappy person is not that the unhappy person has more negative feelings but that the happy person deals with negative feelings more effectively, resolving them at the time they occur. Some people who have had significant losses can still be joyous and creative, act lovingly toward their families, and work with passion. Unhappy people carry each new loss around with them, adding it to the pack of unresolved problems that weigh them down, waiting for the next injury, and wondering if it will break their back. A person who is in emotional debt—who is storing unexpressed feelings—is an unhappy person.

Being happy is liking the way you feel.

Being unhappy is not liking the way you feel.

Before you can begin to free yourself from emotional debt, you need to understand how your feelings evolve. This chapter explains what feelings are, the cycle through which they develop, and how we all use our defenses to avoid feeling pain—the very tactic that leaves us in emotional debt.

THE FEELING CYCLE

While character type determines which hurts we are most sensitive to and our defenses determine how we avoid expressing them, our feelings evolve in a predictable pattern common to everyone.

There are only two feelings: pain and pleasure.

The way you experience pain and the name you give it depend on when the pain occurs.

Pain in the present is experienced as hurt.

Pain in the future is perceived as anxiety.

Pain in the past is remembered as anger.

Unexpressed anger, redirected and held within, is called *guilt*.

It requires energy to redirect anger. This depletion of energy is called *depression*.

Hurt is the only completely real negative feeling. It is the feeling of being injured right now by events that just happened.

Hurt is experienced as sadness, the realization of loss or disappointment. A dependent person often feels rejected, betrayed, and worthless when hurt. A controlling person tends to feel powerless, stupid, or undermined. A competitive person tends to feel defeated or like a loser.

Generally a little anger is revealed whenever hurt is expressed. In fact a little anger is necessary to get the hurt out and protect yourself. For this reason expressing hurt can be troublesome to people who fear injuring others. This can also be a difficult problem because people generally wish to hurt others most when they have been hurt themselves. Expressing hurt requires bravery, self-esteem, and the willingness to risk being rejected by revealing the anger that goes with the hurt.

Anxiety is hurt that is anticipated. It is most real immediately before an injury is about to take place, when it acts as a warning signal to prepare you to avoid the pain or to defend yourself. It is least real when it takes the form of obsessional worrying over meaningless details or of

phobic or panic reactions. A dependent person feels anxious when expecting rejection. A controlling person becomes anxious when his power base is threatened. A competitive person feels stage fright when his self-esteem and
self-image are on the line.

Anger is the recollection of being injured, hurt removed
in time from the loss that caused it. Even a small amount of
unexpressed hurt can fuel a great anger. The more anger
you withhold, the more likely you are to have an explosive
outburst and with minimal provocation. That is, in fact, the
very purpose of anger: to stimulate expression of pain. The
anger you feel is often out of proportion to the hurt that
caused it because anger stored is held in a common pool,
not sorted neatly and compartmentalized by its source.
When anger over a particular old hurt is finally expressed,
anger from other such hurts tends to leak through, distorting the volume of the protest and sometimes creating confusion.

When anger is stored up over a long period of time, it
tends to lose its connection with the hurt that caused it and
becomes free-floating, seeking expression whenever it can.
Such anger recruits the service of the mind to its defensive
purpose, giving rise to recurrent angry thoughts and a
feeling of disquiet or brittleness. Sadly, the angrier you feel,
the angrier you become. Being angry becomes an excuse
for being angry. It is only when the hurt is understood and
expressed that the anger disperses.

THE EMOTIONAL RIGHT-OF-WAY

When we examine how feelings are expressed, we see that
some feelings take priority over others. When people say
they have mixed feelings, they mean that they have both
positive and negative emotions at the same time, and their
negative emotion is blocking the expression of the positive
one. Negative emotions cause pain. Positive emotions
cause pleasure.

All positive feelings have to give the expressive right-of-way to negative feelings. You are familiar with the way even a trivial irritant can momentarily defeat intense feelings of love. As soon as the negative emotion is expressed, the positive feelings usually return and can be expressed again.

It is important for the emotional pathway to be clear to permit the expression of love, not just in interpersonal relationships but also in your work. You put aside the passion for life when negative emotions are stuck in the expressive pathway. If your work cannot be infused with your passion, your self-esteem drops, a sense of monotony takes over, and you perform automatically.

When the emotional expressive pathway is closed down, the mind tries to explain the situation on either side of the emotional traffic jam. Awareness does not produce relief, but merely directs you toward the hurt you must resolve.

The Emotional Rules of the Road

- Only one type of emotion—either a positive or a negative feeling—can be expressed at a time.
- You can express a negative feeling and a moment later express a positive one.
- You can express hurt and anger together, especially since the purpose of anger is to energize the expression of hurt.
- You can be anxious, hurt, angry, and guilty all at once, but the feelings become difficult to differentiate and you seem confused.
- You can express hurt and anger from several sources at the same time, but when you are unaware of the origin of your feelings, you do little to resolve them.
- An extreme feeling tends to crowd other emotions out of the expressive pathway, making you unrealistically negative or positive. Overwhelming the expressive pathway in this manner is a defensive act.
- Shock, sudden massive denial, numbs you to reality,

blocking out all other emotions. Thus, even in the face of certain death, people in shock may not protect themselves, their self-preserving fear apparently disabled by their denial.

- A feeling of panic is likely to prevail over all other feelings.
- Overwhelming guilt, especially over a specific misdeed, acts as a continuous blocking force in the emotional expressive pathway until it is resolved. Such guilt directs you to seek symbolic punishment until it is resolved, possibly even causing you to walk into danger intentionally.
- When the overwhelming urges to kill or commit suicide occur at the same time, psychosis is often the result. The emotions are trapped in the expressive pathway and emotional blocking results. The internal feelings cannot be expressed and the external world cannot be honestly perceived.

UNDERSTANDING YOUR DEFENSES

Defenses dampen pain, shielding you from awareness to allow you to function in the face of danger or loss. The same defenses that conceal pain also keep pain from being resolved. Being vulnerable and feeling the pain is the only way to resolve it.

Everyone defends against the pain of reality. We all need some buffer to protect us from the direct onslaught of life's cruel mischief. It is the fluidity of your use of defenses and, finally, your willingness to give them up and resolve your pain that determines your flexibility and your capacity for happiness. Those who are emotionally free are not without defenses but rather are aware of them and have a minimal need to maintain them. They accept pain, get beyond it, and move on.

Most people employ a unique combination of denial, excuses, and pretense as their protective screen. No two people are exactly alike in their defensive structure. Your childhood experience shapes not only your defensive style but also when and how intensely you use your defenses. Still, you always have the potential to outgrow your sensitivities to particular losses and learn to deal with them honestly rather than give in to a fearful automatic response.

Your personal style and temperament reflect the kind of defenses you use most, and your choice of defenses reflects your personality. A rigid person automatically depends on one particular defense. The well-adjusted person is flexible, more willing to relinquish denial, excuses, and pretending to feel the pain, move on, and be at peace.

YOUR CHARACTER TYPE AND ITS DEFENSIVE STRUCTURE

Defenses can act anywhere in the feeling cycle to provide distance between you and your anxiety, hurt, anger, or guilt.

In a sense, a defense is a lie. Its purpose is to give you a little more time to cope with a frightening threat, a little more time in innocence before totally accepting the loss. So a defense allows you to act as if the loss hasn't fully occurred. It's a temporary shield that lets you buy time until you get your forces organized. When you're ready, you lower your defenses, face the threat or loss, permit yourself to feel the full impact of the injury, and deal with it.

Defenses are activated not only when the threat is real but also when it is imagined. The imagined threat is likely a product of emotional debt, originating from both past unresolved feelings and character type. For example, when you're frightened, you imagine a recurrence of the kind of loss you suffered most recently. Also, you tend to imagine the type of loss that your character type is most sensitive to. A dependent person typically imagines being abandoned, a controlling person imagines losing power, and a competitive person imagines being defeated. It is when you least believe in yourself that you are most likely to act defensively and therefore imagine the danger you most fear.

There is a self-fulfilling quality to defensive behavior in that it can alienate others and bring about the very loss most feared. Constant attempts to protect yourself can ensure that the loss will occur. When you have limited knowledge of your defenses and are reluctant to take responsibility for creating your own problems, you become what you resist most. For instance, no one likes to be constantly badgered by an insecure person, to be asked over and over again, "Do you love me?" "Will you stay with me?" "Where have you been?" "Where are you going?" Such defensiveness becomes a prison that anyone would try to escape from by pushing the insecure person away, the very thing he or she most dreads.

The feeling that is defended from experience is also kept from resolution. As is discussed beginning in Chapter 6, there are several natural ways to resolve an incompletely expressed feeling: verbalization, dreams, fantasy, and creative enterprises such as work and symbolic acts of commemoration. All of these are part of the process of working through, a form of mourning. Feelings that are not worked through are bound behind defenses and hidden from your awareness.

When you recognize and allow yourself to experience a feeling, you can lower your defense against it. The defense you use to hide a feeling is usually much broader than the pain it is designed to contain. Thus when you're confronted with a feeling you're afraid to feel, your fear of releasing your defenses can be more painful than the original injury itself.

Under stress each of the three character types tends to revert to a typical defensive behavior pattern. The dependent person will appear desperate, searching for security and protection by someone more powerful. The controlling person will tend to become rigid in his beliefs and actions and insist that he is right. While competitive people represent the most mature adaptation of the three personality types, they can still appear to be childlike, pouting when they fail or don't get their way or pretending, in the face of failure, that they didn't really try or care.

While we can't change our basic defensive style, we can learn to be more direct and honest about the pain we experience so that we don't need to protect ourselves so rigidly. Willingness to face the truth allows us to be open and to grow. Emotional freedom is based on believing in our own worth. The more we invoke our defenses, the less self-confident and less willing we are to examine our shortcomings. Real self-confidence is not believing in being right all the time, but rather remembering that we're good even when wrong.

Denial: The Dependent Defense

The dependent person uses denial to protect against abandonment, the loss of love, or the threat of injury. Denying reality makes it difficult to deal openly with life's problems. Because the defense of denial originated earliest in life as a helpless child's way of shutting out discomfort, it is the primary defense of dependent people. Unfortunately, continually using denial to deal with life's stress obscures the problem, making it more difficult to solve, and thus aggravates feelings of helplessness and hopelessness.

The following common expressions of denial are listed in order of increasing intensity. The farther down the list the defense is, the more the feeling is denied and the less aware—and therefore the less free—the person using the defense is.

Examine this list closely and ask yourself how you've used each form of denial. What do you defend against in this way and when? What hurt do you want to avoid?

Anything you do to turn away from a painful reality falls into the category of denial. This turning away echoes the young child who does not have verbal skills turning his head away from a painful stimulus. The purpose of any of

The Range of the Defense of Denial

Defense Form	Dynamics
Hoping	Expecting to be rescued by external forces
Procrastinating	Postponing facing unpleasant or difficult tasks
Diverting	Leading others away from painful feelings, either theirs or your own
Generalizing	Avoiding all dogs because one dog has bitten you
Being late	Resenting where you find yourself in life
Losing focus	Inattention to anything that might lead to a painful truth
Lying	Misstating reality to avoid pain
Not knowing	Repeating "I don't know," wishing not to know
Misplacing	Avoiding painful events by losing items needed to deal with them, such as car or house keys, directions, telephone numbers, documents, receipts, etc.
Not hearing or seeing	Missing the obvious remark or road sign altogether because you do not want to deal with what it may lead to
Being confused	The obvious facts don't make sense, because their painful meaning is too frightening. Also, creating disarray to conceal the truth.
Forgetting	Interruption in the recollection of a specific painful memory or anything symbolizing it or leading to it, ranging from a momentary lapse to a total inability to recall
Making slips of speech	Similarly, a hidden feeling can be triggered symbolically, momentarily overcoming denial to intrude inappropriately and out of place as a sudden memory or expression.

Blocking	Broad disruption of the thought process to avoid pain so that not only the specific painful event but also much benign reality is shut out. Words may be heard, but their meaning is scrambled—a regressive posture by which you assume the perspective of a younger child, when the meaning of words was unknown. You focus on parts of words rather than their meaning. Words in turn lose their ability to convey ideas and painful feelings.
Global denial	This is denial of psychotic proportions. What is painful is not accessible to awareness. The price paid for this insulation is to live in an unreal world.

these various forms of denial is to keep from feeling the full impact of a feeling. You use denial most when you fear losing someone you care about. Denial keeps you from feeling.

To grow you need to feel.

Excuses: The Controlling Defense

As we've seen, the basic structure of controlling defenses is the excuse, the attempt to blame other factors or people for our mistakes. Everyone has a natural tendency to use some controlling defenses under circumstances that threaten to diminish personal power. When the situation improves, the reins are loosened and the situation is allowed to flow freely. However, the controlling person uses controlling defenses automatically, whether or not the situation calls for them. A person who uses excuses extensively cannot admit mistakes and therefore cannot learn from them.

Controlling people rely on excuses to superimpose external order on the world and conceal their self-doubt. If you are a controlling type, you explain your defensive posture as necessary to do something correctly, and you are the one who defines what *correctly* means. Each controlling trait, weakness, or defense in the chart is followed by the controlling person's explanation or hidden motivation. While these defenses are the tools of an organized person, they become problematic when they take on a life of their own rather than contribute to attainment of goals.

In examining the following controlling defenses, try to identify the ones you use most and see how you use them. What responsibility do you avoid? What feeling do you fear?

The Range of Excuses

Defense Form	Dynamics
Neatness	To look professional, to be in proper uniform, thus to escape criticism, to be in order.
Scheduling	Ostensibly to be able to keep appointments but also to manage others, cut them off, and limit stress.
Criticism	To maintain order and standards by measuring others and keeping them in line.
Greediness	To acquire external means and thereby to enhance symbolically the value of the inner self, especially when self-worth is in doubt. To acquire enough power to keep others from leaving.
Inflexibility	To get others to comply because the perfect plan demands perfect obedience.
Explanations	To maintain belief in one's infallibility.
Magical thinking	To reason that if a certain thing happens, a particular consequence will occur or be prevented from occurring. A way of attaining symbolic control over what seems uncontrollable.
Excessive orderliness	To create external order and thereby avoid facing internal disarray, another symbolic way to manage hidden anger and self-doubt.

Undoing	An extension of magical thinking as action; to balance and thereby cancel an unacceptable thought or wish through a corrective symbolic act. Generally the thought or wish involves being angry and hurting a loved one. E.g.: A mother who secretly resents her baby for tying her down to the house but can't admit it (the hidden feeling) worries about the baby smothering (the unacceptable angry wish) and so checks in on the child 25 times a day (the ritual that undoes the anger).
Reaction formation	To assert bravery instead of admitting weakness; e.g., climbing mountains while fearing heights or raising money for charity while being greedy. Another form of undoing.
Renunciation	To give up all of your wicked ways, especially in the face of being caught and punished: conversions under stress, turning state's evidence, deathbed confessions, drastic life changes, without fully accepting responsibility for what you've done, giving only lip service to remorse.
Intellectualization of feelings	To avoid vulnerability by using the mind to feel, reasoning away hurt and rejection. "Who cares whether others like me? I don't need them."
Rationalization of actions	To avoid guilt from hurting others by reasoning that under the circumstances what you did had to be done and someone had to do it and that is that!
Blaming	To place responsibility outside yourself to maintain the belief in your goodness and integrity.
Projection	To ascribe to others the painful feelings and shortcomings you cannot accept in yourself, a form of blaming; but where blaming involves one event at a time, projection is a general style of ascribing responsibility away from yourself to the point where you see your negative feelings more in others than yourself.
Paranoia	To abandon reality, believing that the reason that you failed or are afflicted is that outside forces have plotted to do you in. Projection carried to its extreme.

The person who uses controlling defenses often seems to be in better shape than people who employ denial or pretending because controlling defenses create the impression of order and structure. It is not uncommon to see seriously disturbed paranoid people who are still able to run a business, rule a country, or manage huge sums of money. They wield their power rigidly and appear strong to the weaker people around them. Such so-called strength is an illusion, really based on their discomfort in expressing any vulnerable feeling at all.

Pretending: The Competitive Defense

The defensive legacy of the competitive period is to pretend not to care about your work or loved one when threatened with failure or rejection. The essence of pretending is to act as if the value of the thing lost is unimportant and so diminish the impact of the hurt. Pretending protects your self-esteem but also limits your success by keeping you from doing your best and giving your full attention to solving problems.

Like everyone else, if you are competitive you need to accept your own feelings and admit when something hurtful matters to you. You need to be able to declare your emotional vulnerability without posing as indifferent. You need to lower your facade, reveal your heart, and allow the world to see you as you are. To do this you need to accept that you have value. Unfortunately, competitive people often live as if they are only as good as their last accomplishment and therefore believe they can be redeemed or doomed by their next risk. It is no wonder that they pretend it doesn't matter when they fail, saying they weren't really trying, committed, or involved. Much of the fear of commitment that bedevils relationships is based on the fear of not being good enough, for competitive people would rather break loose than commit, get close to another, and be seen without pretenses, that is, as they are.

We all need to come to terms with our capacity to pretend, to find a balance between the ability to dream and create and the tendency to use imagination to conceal our problems. Competitive people need to learn to risk being accountable for failures in order to learn from them. If we pretend we weren't really trying, we can never be satisfied with what we've done.

The following defenses, presented in order of increasing intensity, reflect the competitive tendency to be governed by pride, to save face at all costs. As you examine these defenses, consider when you employ them. What failure do you fear? How realistic and honest are you?

The Range of Pretenses

Defense Form	Dynamics
Comparing	Defining yourself by what others are doing or have acquired
Pleasing Others	Earning others' praise to make up for your own lagging self-acceptance
One-upmanship	Putting someone down to feel better about yourself
Bragging	An overcompensation for feelings of low self-worth over your accomplishment, usually because the accomplishment was too easy and could not answer the question "How good am I?"
Exaggeration	Making more of an accomplishment to make it seem as meaningful as the risk you *should* have taken
Game playing	Minimizing stress by devaluing the meaning of emotions, stating that life is only a game and insisting that you were only playing *(continued)*

Keeping a stiff upper lip	Pretending all is going well in spite of obvious setbacks, keeping up appearances, acting invincible
Playing emotionally dumb	Pretending the pain went over your head, the competitive adaptation of denial
Wishful thinking	Living emotionally in the belief that things are better than they are
Faking	Acting as if your wish were reality, often leads to your embarrassment when you are confronted with reality and you get caught.
Role playing	Acting like the person you would like to be, especially common among adolescents trying out new identities. Role playing gives you a slippery emotional quality because you can act out either side of a conflict without really being involved. Typical roles: the scapegoat, know-it-all, fool, spoiler, crisis monger, aristocrat, prima donna–star, hypochondriac, Don Juan or siren, high risker, critic, fierce competitor, people pleaser.
Depersonalization	Feeling as if you aren't yourself. It serves to distance you from situations that overwhelm you. Commonplace in adolescence when your identity, physical body, hormonal balance, and ideals are placed in crisis all at the same time. The feeling is one of drifting, light-headedness, of not being you. You can believe that you're going crazy.
Splitting	A variant of role playing in which emotions are split off from your awareness of a painful event and replaced by an attitude of "So what? Who cares?" The fact that you really do care is readily apparent to others. You seem brittle.
Dissociation— amnesia	An even more serious form of splitting in which part of your awareness or memory has been split off along with the unacceptable feelings.
Multiple personality	A form of amnesia (*not* schizophrenia) in which painful experiences and feelings have been split off from memory and have given form to discrete personalities.

No matter how far you evolve, how mature and open you become, you still have the potential to react according to your particular style of defenses. Knowing how you hide feelings is the first step in discovering the feelings you're hiding.

Remember, you have choices, and even in the most overwhelming situations you can act and feel more honestly. The way to a happier life is simply to feel the hurt as it happens and get on with it. The feelings you avoid eventually rob you of your life.

DEFENSES AND EMOTIONAL DEBT

If you had no defenses, you would have no emotional debt. You would be free. You would show your hurt when you felt it, perhaps with a touch of anger. Others would stand back and give you room, cease to love you, or continue to love you. If they chose not to love you because you spoke out, you would let it be their problem.

You would not dread what you could not control or prevent but would face life with a sense of self-confidence and respect.

You would experience pain in a totally visceral way, without the intervention of your defenses.

You would express your hurt and anger without feeling you were bad.

You would react to your anxiety as a signal to get ready to defend yourself and not be paralyzed by fear.

You would not feel shame. You would make your mistakes, accept responsibility for whatever damage you caused, and move on.

When You Delay Expressing Your Feelings

Feelings that are not expressed as they occur are stored in emotional debt. There are several stages of emotional debt:

1. Reactive emotional debt is a momentary delay between an injury and the expression of hurt.
2. Recent emotional debt is a longer delay during which additional hurts may occur and be combined and stored as resentment.
3. Remote emotional debt includes unresolved hurts from years ago, including childhood hurts that have influenced the development of your character. These remote feelings are activated by painful recent emotions that remind you of the past.

Here's how the three types of emotional debt are incurred:

You experience an emotion with your body even before you are aware of its identity or meaning. If you don't push the feeling away, it resolves quickly. You simply ask yourself what hurts and why and deal with the problem. This is reactive emotional debt, the preoccupation with an immediate emotion just before it's expressed. Your discomfort in holding in the feeling is what propels you to come forward and let it out as soon as possible.

If you push the feeling away, time elapses, your mind takes over, and your feeling is internalized and grouped together with other stored feelings in recent emotional debt. Its meaning becomes less clear, and it is hidden behind defenses and combined with other older emotions. Confusion increases, so you often cannot understand what is troubling you. You are upset for "no apparent reason" or "due to some unknown cause." Holding in feelings of anger eventually erodes your self-worth. You question whether you should speak up. You worry about the consequences. You feel closed. Most of the time, however, you don't even know why. You just feel an emotional inertia, the effect of your defenses consuming your energy.

Habitually delaying expressing feelings results in remote emotional debt. Any new hurt produces an exaggerated defensive response, and so it is not dealt with directly and tends to be stored. Your feelings build to an explosive point until from time to time they break free of defenses and are expressed out of context and out of control. Others cannot understand or sympathize with your exaggerated expressions, leading to further alienation and loneliness and a sense of helplessness. Whenever you try to make emotional contact, you're rebuffed because you hurt others. The process feeds on itself, producing even more anxiety, hurt, anger, and guilt.

Being Open to Your Feelings

Being open to your feelings and expressing them is the way to avoid emotional debt. Feelings are most real when dealt with the moment they occur.

Experiencing anxiety directly, without hiding it, motivates you to face the potential danger and manage it. However, if you use your mind to handle anxiety, your defenses interfere, and precious time is lost. You may analyze the potential danger, dissect it, discuss it with friends, write about it, reexperience it again and again, but you don't manage it, and it intensifies. After a while you become afraid of things that *might* happen, exploring long chains of possible events. Worry replaces logic, and you become confused trying to discriminate between real and imagined threats.

When you allow yourself to feel the pain, your anger passes quickly. When you do something wrong or disappoint yourself, you feel regret, not guilt, and use that feeling to motivate yourself to set matters right. You admit your humanness, take responsibility for the harm you've done, seek amends, and learn your lesson. Your self-worth quickly resurfaces and allows you to forgive yourself. Whatever pain you feel soon subsides.

Defenses, the very devices that give you room to adjust to reality, also lead you to lose touch with reality and distort the world around you, prolong your pain, and cause you to suffer.

There is a delicate balance between protecting yourself and being open.

Understanding the Unconscious:
The Path to Insight

Understanding the relationship between a physical feeling and its cause is called *insight*. Insight also involves understanding how your feelings motivate your actions. You develop insight most easily when you have nothing to hide. When you hide feelings, it's difficult to separate current feelings from old feelings coming to life again.

This confusion about what you feel is called the unconscious.

Like a photographic plate, insight depends on how sensitive you are, that is, how long an exposure to pain it takes for you to form an understanding of a feeling impression. After each emotional experience you must be free to move on to the next frame of reality. If you hold on to feelings, you form confused multiple images in which the ghostly context of the past persists, and your view of the present is compromised by superimposed emotional double exposures. You're not sure if the feeling you're experiencing is real or memory.

The unconscious consists of feelings you have not yet named.

Another way of saying this is that in a sense there is no unconscious, only a lack of understanding of what you feel.

What is commonly labeled as unconscious are those motivations for which you do not wish to accept responsibility and feelings that seem beyond your grasp. To an anxious swimmer who is in water only a few inches over his head, the bottom seems miles deep. Similarly feelings that are beyond your grasp feel equally remote and frightening. They seem unknowable or deeply buried, inaccessible to your understanding, especially when you're afraid of knowing their meaning. It's the nature of defenses that what they conceal feels deeply buried but in truth is only partly hidden, just out of your reach. The same mind that uses defenses can also put them aside and allow you to make a connection with these hidden feelings.

Most people don't take the time to notice their feelings, to pay attention to their emotional response to the world. Instead they wait too long and notice feelings only when they are stored up and threaten to escape. These unnoticed feelings are also the unconscious. Any activity that takes place out of our knowing can be called unconscious. Much of what we call unconscious is simply not paying attention, a form of denying again.

Simply paying attention to what you're feeling will bring much of the unconscious into the realm of awareness and therefore into your control. If you truly want to know the truth and are willing to see yourself as you really are and believe that nothing you can discover about yourself can hurt you, you can know everything about yourself. It's when you fear the consequences of admitting a feeling or taking responsibility for an action that you turn away and its meaning becomes hidden.

Feelings are continually passing from the light of your awareness to the protective shade of your defenses into that realm of inaccessibility called the unconscious. These feelings are continually being called forward into awareness by situations in the present whose emotional content mirrors the feeling concealed behind the defense. When these hidden feelings come forward, they jar your memory, catching you by surprise. Insight is a sudden realization of the connection between your actions and feelings or between a feeling in the present and a feeling in the past. The realization feels new and powerful. Of course you were aware of the truth all the time but were just too afraid to look at it directly.

Once a hidden feeling and the event that caused it are understood, the insight makes them seem obvious and somehow uncomplicated. There is nothing quite as transparent as the hindsight of an emotional illumination.

Hidden old feelings often come forward with a greater than expected intensity, creating a sense of release and surprise, as if turning on a light in a darkened room. You're exposed to a truth you have not yet adapted to. At such

moments the truth seems compelling and profound. The
healing process, working the feelings through, allows them
to take on their ordinariness once more.

Some people who spend their lives trying to acquire
insight are really looking for a sense of power that is
missing in their lives and that they hope some therapy,
religion, cult, self-improvement, or motivational technique
will supply. These courses usually have an initiation level
that points out the psychological or spiritual shortcomings
of the candidate and offers a series of steps for addressing
these deficiencies and attaining mastery. While they may
experience some evolution through these avenues, most of
it would have happened naturally had they just been honest. What they acquire is mostly fluency in the language of
a system as well as a dependency on it, a sense of being
accepted and understood, and, finally, considerable financial expenditure. The knowledge that these people ultimately seek is that they are all right just the way they are.
Their motivation for seeking it is their fear that they are
not.

Of course there is always more you can learn about
yourself, but much of such knowledge is analytical background noise, not really necessary for personal mastery.
True mastery is freeing your mind from its defensive
burden. The purpose of attaining insight and of understanding your feelings is to be able to be at peace with
yourself so you can be fully available for the events and
people in your life, without the need to distort. To do this
you need to know and accept that you are good, lovable,
smart, and strong. If you believe this with enough confidence to admit when you are not good, when you are less
than lovable, when you are not acting intelligently, and
when you are weak, you know what you need to know to
live your life with insight.

Typically when old feelings come forward, they exaggerate your response to present events, usually the ones that
awakened them. This exaggerated response is called *neurotic*, that is, driven by hidden feelings. The older the

feelings involved, the more neurotic—that is, exaggerated—your response.

Some people seem to greet every stressful situation with a prefabricated emotional response that has minimal relation to the ongoing reality. Wherever they go, they find signs of betrayal or abandonment or evidence that they are being cheated or treated unfairly and then react as if what they have found is intentional. Expressing these prefabricated feelings never completely releases their original hurt because they vent only with noise, without understanding.

When it intrudes, the neurotic emotion is distorted and can draw others into irrational battles. Others experience its expression as overreacting, and the person expressing the old emotion feels out of control. The more you try to conceal such feelings, the more obvious they appear to others. Most of your insecurity comes from the dawning awareness that you are unable to keep your feelings secret. You're not even sure what it is you're trying to conceal. You're afraid to look. This fearful ignorance only reinforces your self-doubt.

There are two kinds of feelings: those you want to know and those you don't want to know.

The feelings you don't want to know can be called *unconscious* as well.

Again, the more you try to contain your feelings, the less stable you feel. It's a losing battle.

When you allow feelings to come to the surface, look at them, and identify their source, the sense of being overwhelmed gives way to understanding and relief. The unconscious becomes knowable.

THE ULTIMATE SOURCES OF YOUR PAIN

Like everyone else, you seek to define your personal worth. You want to know if you're lovable, strong, and worthy. These basic questions, which reflect the predominant concerns of the three periods of character develop-

ment, are continually posed throughout life and represent
the emotional debt of your character.
  Dependent questions:

  • Am I good? Am I bad?
  • Am I lovable? Am I unlovable?

Controlling questions:

  • Am I strong? Am I weak?
  • Am I smart? Am I stupid?
  • Am I right? Am I wrong?

Competitive questions:

  • Am I worthy? Am I unworthy?
  • Am I a (real) man? Am I a (real) woman?

  You often ask these questions through your actions and
choices alone without even being aware of them. When you
receive an unfavorable response, you're often crushed
without fully understanding why. These questions explain
much of your unfathomable behavior. Don't be misled by
their simplicity. If you had the answers you wanted, you'd
be happy and have high self-esteem. It's as simple as that.
  In fact, all hurt can be seen as receiving a negative
response to any one of these questions. The same loss can
mean different things for different people. Your personality
type interprets the answer according to its own characteristic terms. A dependent person who is abandoned takes it
to be a confirmation of being bad or unlovable. A controlling person who is abandoned feels out of control and
takes it as an indication of weakness or stupidity. A competitive person loses face and interprets abandonment as
the consequence of a lack of personal worth and desirabil-
ity as a man or woman.
  While each personality type will interpret a negative
response to any of these questions as a loss, the dependent

person will always be most sensitive to the issues concerning lovability and goodness and will tend to read these issues into other questions. The dependent person who feels stupid will also feel unlovable. A controlling person will react to rejection in the same way as a dependent person but, in addition, will be concerned that weakness and stupidity played into it. A competitive person will suspect he wasn't important or famous enough to win the rejecting person's favor.

DEFENSES, EMOTIONAL DEBT, AND THE FEELING CYCLE

Any defense can create emotional debt by obscuring any feeling in the feeling cycle. The chart on the next three pages summarizes how this happens.

The chapters that follow will explore the individual emotions in the feeling cycle and provide ways to work through those not yet resolved. The object is to help you live in the moment fully and honestly.

Stage in Feeling Cycle	Effects of Denial	Effects of Excuses	Effects of Pretending
Anxiety— Pain in the Future: I may be hurt. I'm afraid.	"Everything's fine. No problem."	Too ready to blame others: "Their mistakes will hurt me."	"What, me worry? I don't even care."
Emotional debt created	Fear goes within, becoming a vague apprehension of pervasive danger. Now anything overwhelms.	Misplaced focus. Lack of responsibility allows damage to extend. Buries fear in meaningless details.	Failure to risk results in self-doubt, and lack of belief in the worth of anything. Generalized stage fright.
Hurt— Pain in the Present: I am hurt. I'm sad.	Pain is delayed and overstated, deepening hurt and creating anxiety about future hurts.	Gives reasons for not being hurt: "I'm so strong and smart I'm invincible." Loss is explained as others' fault.	Pretended indifference. "Don't be ridiculous! How could someone like you hurt someone like me?"
Emotional debt created	Little losses are perceived everywhere until the original hurt is admitted and resolved. Anxiety is now felt because expressing the hurt is seen as risking further injury: i.e., rejection.	Excuses are inadequate to contain the injury, and the hurt rapidly evolves into anger, which is seen as a less vulnerable feeling state to admit. Preoccupied with convincing self of strength, much rationalizing.	In minimizing injury the person also devalues himself. Lowered self-esteem may prod him to seek a symbolic victory to offset the loss. If all losses can be replaced, nothing seems to have meaning. This undermines motivation.

Stage in Feeling Cycle	Effects of Denial	Effects of Excuses	Effects of Pretending
Anger— Pain in the Past: I resent being hurt. I'm angry.	Unwilling to admit anger, the person smolders and pouts, holds in resentment.	Obsessed with fantasies of retaliation; tends to punish others, alienating them.	Pretense of not caring gives way to explosive outbursts of unguarded anger in which various targets are subjected to overkill.
Emotional debt created	Self-esteem is lowered so much that the person cannot express anger and ends up feeling victimized.	Excuses made for retaliating. The obsessing mind now acts as detective, seeking out evidence of others' guilt. Plans punishment but fears taking action.	Tends toward retaliatory and compensatory behavior to express the anger and hurt supposedly not felt, which embarrasses the person, who did care after all!
Guilt— Inward Anger: I'm to blame. I feel guilty.	Denied anger tortures the person with self-doubt: "I deserved this. I'm no good" rather than discrediting the person needed.	Blames others for making him feel bad. Justifies angry position: "If it weren't for me, they'd have suffered. Some gratitude!"	Callousness toward self increases as pretending not to care gets out of control. Doubts self-worth. "Nothing matters. It's all an act anyhow."

Stage in Feeling Cycle	Effects of Denial	Effects of Excuses	Effects of Pretending
Emotional debt created	Self-punitive behavior. Beats others to the punch by hurting self to relieve guilt.	Blames self for trusting others, who failed him. Yearns for absolution but can't confess mistakes, didn't do anything wrong.	Moments of remorse alternating with self-destructive behavior. Motivated to make histrionic reparations.
Depression— Withholding Anger Depletes Energy: I'm drained. I feel depressed.	Displays helplessness as if to prove he had no role in all that led to this. "Why did this happen to me?"	As a sense of responsibility trickles into awareness, believes he brought all of it on himself and secretly wonders if he is evil.	May admit depression but pretends that it is the result of something unrelated to what he really cares about and overreacts to a minor problem.
Emotional debt created	Tendency to be rigid, clingy. Adheres to the role of victim.	The mind used to blame others now incriminates self with full force. Only he knows how bad he really is. May seek revenge on all if he projects.	May precipitate a loss he feels safe in mourning rather than admit how he failed and what that failure revealed about him.

6

Understanding Hurt: The Mourning Process

Being present for this moment is everything.

If you're not present in this moment, you're not fully alive. The persistence of old memories and the preservation of old anger and grief rob the present of its innocence and charm. When you're feeling old and worn with fatigue and the ways of this world, you grow nostalgic, and the present serves mostly to remind you of the life you once lived, bidding you to recount your losses and victories.

Sorrows age you prematurely. When you're in emotional debt, you're pessimistic about the future and, even in your green years, long to return to the past to remedy the shortfalls of love and opportunity you suffered. Sometimes you yearn for more caring, for more time with someone who is no longer here, for a chance to speak your mind and release your emotional burden or just to resolve your confusion by finally discovering what really happened to you. You can speculate, you can lament, you can yearn, but as much as you may wish to return and round off your emotional experience, you can never go home again.

Your real home is in this place, at this time. The present is for action, for doing, for becoming, and for growing. The

123

past is only commentary. What happened to you in the past, no matter how painful, is only a memory. The pain may have been excruciating in intensity, but it is gone now. In a sense the future is also commentary because it reflects how you interpret your past. So it follows that you can be free only by living in the present, because it is only in the present that you have the power to act.

You do justice in the present to those you loved in the past not by reliving the pain of their loss but by remembering the joy of their lives. If you were hurt, you redeem your honor not by exacting revenge but by growing to find victory on your own terms. If you were damaged in the cruel contests of love, you restore yourself not by living in endless pining but by relinquishing the lost object of your yearning and looking within to find a lovable self.

The purpose of processing emotions in the present is to release old hurt from the defenses that hold it, mourn the loss completely, and end your suffering. There is nothing more hopeless than something whose time has come and gone. It is trying to hold on to what has passed that hurts you the most.

When you keep the past alive, you create unrealistic expectations for the present. You display the wrong feelings at the wrong time. Others find you difficult to understand. Your life feels confused, and your actions seem inexplicable. This emotional inaccessibility keeps others at bay and perpetuates your emptiness.

You must learn to discriminate between the memory of an old pain and the experience of a new loss. If the old memory still hurts, the issue has not been fully settled. A remembered pain that has not been resolved feels like a new pain just being experienced.

To free yourself you have to live in the moment. The past is memory; the future is fantasy. Being in the moment is the source of your strength and peace.

This chapter is concerned with learning how to stay in the moment by dealing with hurt as soon as it occurs so that no residue persists. While this chapter focuses on the loss of a loved one because it elicits all of the stages of mourning, the process applies to all losses but with less intensity. It is all about hurt.

The feeling of hurt ranges from disappointment to dissatisfaction, feeling injured or wounded, abused or cheated, disconsolate, sad, unhappy, aching, sorrowful, disillusioned, like a loser, anguished, grieving. It is an active feeling, reflecting what is going on right now.

In essence mourning is dealing with hurt.

If you mourn well, you live well.

If you can't mourn fully, you mourn all the time.

When I come home my cocker spaniels often crowd around and get in my way, and occasionally I accidentally step on a paw. I invariably pat the dog, telling it that I didn't mean it and that I think it is a good dog and that I'm sorry. I do not know if such verbal apology has any meaning, but the dogs seem entirely willing to drop the matter and move on. They do not feign limps or whimper with each step or sulk or turn their heads away. The dogs are happy to see me and don't hide it. They are totally caught up in the moment and just want to play ball. I am willing to conclude that my dogs bear no grudge. I imagine if I had abused or tormented them they would snarl and recoil in my presence. However, with no such angry past history between us, any and all injuries I cause them are quickly forgotten and, in some dog sense, forgiven.

Being human and having verbal skills makes us much more sophisticated than my dogs, but it also allows us to hide our emotions behind defenses and so gradually become less open. The dog looks at the world as it is. We imagine what it could be, remember what it was, are reminded of what we felt when it was different, and wonder if what is going to happen next is going to be a repetition of the painful past. Our intellect frees and burdens us at the same time. To regain our sense of immediacy and our ability to be present in the moment we need to be unguarded, open, and aware of our feelings. We need to be accepting of our past to be fully alive in the present.

MOURNING AND CHARACTER TYPE

The stages of childhood development are recapitulated in the steps of mourning. Any severe loss has the capacity to initiate a mourning process that progresses from the dependent use of denial through controlling excuses to the competitive habit of pretending everything is better until acceptance is reached. In dealing with an overwhelming loss you return to your most primitive defensive posture and work through progressively more mature defenses. Your personality type has an innate propensity for a certain defensive response, so your ability to move forward through the stages of mourning will be limited by the persistence of your particular defenses. In addition, each personality type is especially sensitive to particular kinds of losses, which are most likely to initiate the mourning process and elicit its characteristic defensive response.

Dependent Losses

Dependent losses symbolize the loss of the parent's love or support and so bring to the surface an infantile sense of helplessness and powerlessness, doubts about the ability to survive without the love of another person. Dependent losses include:

- the loss of a loved one or the loss of an important person's love
- the loss of the belief that you are lovable
- the loss of self

Because dependent losses have such early roots, they have the capacity to evoke the helpless feelings of childhood. If a childhood loss is not completed, mourning in adult years is increasingly difficult, for old unresolved feelings of hopelessness intrude into the present and convey not merely loss but the bottomless depression of a helpless person as well.

Controlling Losses

Controlling losses symbolize the loss of control over people you depend on for love or a sense of power. What controlling people are ultimately trying to control is the love of others. Remember that down deep the controlling person is really dependent.

Controlling losses include:

- the loss of power or position, influence, seniority, authority, or access to these sources of power
- the loss of money, work, financial success
- the loss of physical strength, youth, health

An adult experiencing a loss of control tries to undo the loss by making amends, excuses, promises, and bargains and by rationalizing.

Competitive Losses

Competitive losses symbolize the loss of self-esteem, personal excellence, and personal worth. Just as the school-age child uses pretenses to avoid embarrassment, you try to hide your sense of failure by pretending that whatever you suffered doesn't matter to you. Unfortunately, this pretending not to care becomes a giant stumbling block because it is difficult to mourn and release something or someone you pretend never mattered.

Competitive losses include:

- the loss of self-esteem, worth, or stature, whether social, intellectual, or romantic
- the loss of success
- the loss of reputation, image, appearance, social or professional standing

A competitive person who loses someone close is likely to feel the loss of the praise and appreciation that person provided. If you made pleasing others rather than yourself the most important part of your success, you experience their loss as a loss of your direction and purpose. You have to remember that your goal is not to please or win but to evolve as your best.

CHARACTER TYPE AND THE STAGES OF MOURNING

The stages of mourning are not discrete plateaus. There are a wide variety of responses at each level, depending on individual and character types. People also move forward when they feel better, only to revert back when a wave of pain overwhelms them. It is also common for people to have moments of acceptance even in the midst of severe grief.

The following stages describe the evolving mourning process. Each person's grief proceeds in a different way, depending on the symbolic meaning of the loss, character type, and defensive system.

I. Initial Shock—Immediate Denial

The universal first response to the harsh reality of loss is the most primitive form of denial: "No!" The event has such terrible implications it seems like the end of the world, so it must be questioned: "How can this be true?" "This can't be so." Fainting is an act of denial, totally shutting out consciousness.

The *dependent person* tends to practice denial as long as possible, drifting between the horror of knowing and the anxiety of accepting.

The *controlling person* tries to sort the painful information as reasonably as possible. As if saying, "Wait a minute, let me make sure that the loss has really taken place before I commit to feeling any pain," he focuses on details and choices to keep from feeling powerless.

The *competitive person* may pretend that there is no surprise at all, that he knew something was going to happen, because this makes it possible for him not to be hurt as much by the loss.

II. Later Denial—Initial Impact

The next response is to test the depth of the loss and try to feel the emptiness it has created. "I can't believe it" gives way to "I don't want to feel it" and then "I can't bear it." During this testing you continue to slip back into more complete denial, asking "Is this really true?" or "How can this be?" And you seek information to explain the unacceptable.

The *dependent person*, overwhelmed by a sense of free-fall, panics now that his support is gone and feels guilty: "Am I a good person despite being so selfish, so self-involved, and so angry?"

The *controlling person* tries to impose order on the chaos—handling the funeral arrangements and being "too busy" to cry—to minimize the pain. His intellectual attempts failing to produce peace of mind, he chokes on powerful swells of emotion and wonders if there is meaning in any of his efforts.

The *competitive person* can feel detached, superficial, almost glib, which can alienate others. Besides causing people to reject him when he needs sympathy, his defensive indifference makes it impossible for him to mourn. Later on, splinters of grief pierce through his facade.

III. Understanding the Loss—Undoing

As the realization of the loss sinks in, you begin to evaluate the situation to see if it is at all possible to limit the damage. You distance yourself from your feelings and use your mind to comprehend the injury, entertaining even irrational explanations merely because they offer hope in an otherwise hopeless situation. You wish to undo any harm that your own shortcomings may have caused, and you negotiate and plead with the deity. You'll offer yourself up as a substitute, lead a chaste and sober life, rededicate yourself to the high path—anything to stop the pain.

The *dependent person* analyzes the loss and reasons how unfair life is to him.

The *controlling person* has been analyzing the loss from the very beginning and may well get stuck at this stage of the mourning process. He relives the scene of the loss, reviews the motivations of the participants, second-guesses fate, perceives plots and hidden agendas, and discusses the loss endlessly from every point of view but the emotional.

The *competitive person* seems brittle, proudly fighting back tears and insisting he's already gotten over the loss when he is actually just starting to feel it. He may scold family members for displaying emotions, which embarrass him because they are too close to his hidden truth, or may engage in total hysterics, merely acting like a person in mourning.

IV. Blaming

You begin to reconsider everything you did that could possibly have had a role in the loss, imagining "If only . . ." as you begin to blame yourself and others for shortcomings and lack of understanding. You retrace your actions and wish to go back in time to change your behavior and edit your comments. You can carry this to an extreme and blame yourself into virtual paralysis. You reason if you could be to blame for what went wrong, perhaps you do have some power after all, and maybe you can still work magic and correct the situation. The obvious futility of this position leads you to test reality and eventually allows you to give up your blaming position and accept the finality of the loss.

The *dependent person* is likely to use anyone who ever opposed or hurt the person he has lost as a target for his displaced anger. He may deeply regret the way he burdened the other person. On the other hand, he may blame the other person for abandoning him and so runs the risk of playing the role of victim.

The stage of blaming may totally preoccupy the *controlling person*. He seeks to blame others while being tormented by self-accusing thoughts. To keep his feelings secret he frequently becomes closed and tough, appearing as a lonely citadel of angry sadness.

The *competitive person* continues to have great difficulty mourning because he is still trying to pass off the loss as having minimal meaning. He may pretend to be busy and already back on the right course. Going about business as usual, he may act out feelings of guilt by creating a failure that allows him to mourn a safer symbolic loss. He may blame himself for the safer failure and thus get through this stage by proxy.

V. Pretending

Pretending prepares you for acceptance of the loss. You try to pull your life together and carry on as before, but with some realization that you are still mourning. You try to imagine yourself coming to terms with the loss and claim you are all right because you can see yourself being all right someday. Unfortunately, this projection into the future often gives way to profound feelings of emptiness as the realization of the loss breaks through.

The *dependent person* focuses on the changes that the loss has inflicted, anxiously imagining a future life alone. The loss of an important person also presents the dependent person with an opportunity to grow by learning to accept it fully and discovering his ability to survive.

The *controlling person* leaps back into life's routine with intensity, often becoming obsessed with work to avoid pain. Being away from the routine overwhelms him with lonely thoughts, which trouble him, because isolation is the only feeling the intellectual defenses of blaming and excuses cannot push away.

The *competitive person* has been pretending everything is fine again for some time. Unfulfilling diversions raise the question "Why doesn't anything seem to matter?" Thus the loss continually recurs in symbolic ways because he has only pretended to get over it.

VI. Acceptance

There is no such thing as complete acceptance. When you can remember a loss with a little distance and much less pain, you have accepted the loss and mourned it fully. You accept that life is different now and move on.

Even when achieving acceptance, the *dependent person* feels some yearning for what was lost. For years there are moments during the day when the loss catches up with him. A deep sigh releases the sadness, and the mood gradually fades, but the feeling of missing the other person persists.

The *controlling person* can spend years mourning those lost because he fights his feelings of vulnerability. Until he finally accepts, he stays busy and reestablishes control by devoting his energy to work.

From time to time the *competitive person* yearns for the praise the person lost might have provided. He also sees the meaning of life reduced by the amount of pleasure he got in pleasing the other person. The feeling of loss of the other person is sometimes so self-centered that it embarrasses him.

THE DYNAMICS OF GRIEF

The following chart summarizes the stages of grief, the feelings that prevail at each stage, and the typical reactions of each of the different character types.

Mourning Stage	Common Dynamics	Dependent Dynamics	Controlling Dynamics	Competitive Dynamics
Initial shock	"No! It can't be. What? I can't (don't want) to believe it."	"Please don't make me face this."	You ask what happened, when, where, who, why, to avoid feeling the pain.	"I knew something was going to happen."
Denial	"How, where, and when did it happen?"	"What will I do?" Hopelessness alternates with fearfulness.	May get caught up in details and arrangements to have a sense of control over helplessness.	"Well, it's all for the better somehow." You smile through the tears.
Explanations	You try to understand why, to undo the loss, to bargain. "We were just about to celebrate his birthday."	Self-pity. You focus on the unfairness of life. "This is the worst thing that has ever happened to me."	Preoccupied with understanding rather than feeling. You mourn in lonely "lapses."	Apparent lack of sadness alienates others. "No one knows what I'm going through."
Blaming	You externalize the pain. "If only . . ."	"Why am I always a victim?"	You initiate vendetta against "guilty" parties.	You erupt with anger or sadness.
Pretending	"I guess I'm doing OK." "I'm fine."	"I'll never be the same. Nothing will."	You work obsessively to block feeling the grief.	"Everything's perfect again."
Acceptance	"It's different now." "Your dad would have been proud of you."	"I still miss him/her."	Little waves of mourning intrude to sponsor bursts of controlling behavior.	"I could have used that person now."

WORKING THROUGH

These stages of mourning are experienced not only when you lose someone dear to you but to a lesser degree when you experience any loss. This process of coming to terms with a loss, called *working through*, is one of the most important of all mental functions. Working through is the main concern of psychotherapy, in which the unmourned loss is identified, its effects defined, and its pain liberated from the defenses that bind it so it can be felt and accepted.

The process of working through is what living happily is all about. If you could not work through your hurt, and live in the present, you would be a rigid, vengeful, disorganized person whose mind was totally recruited in the service of defending against the truth. Working through is not forgetting the pain but feeling the pain, testing your ability to live with it, and, finally, allowing the pain to subside.

Working through is dealing with the disappointments of life as they occur so that hurt is not stored in a reservoir of anger waiting to overflow and disrupt the balance of life. Working through is not suffering but in fact the only cure for suffering. You suffer most when you try to contain an old hurt. When you feel the hurt, allow the tears that have been held in to flow, accept your role or forgive others, and let go of the pain, you have worked through the feeling.

Working through is not a passive process but one requiring the active expression of hurt. It necessitates coming forward with your pain, making it known to the person who needs to know about it most. Working through, in short, requires taking a risk.

When a pain is not worked through, it seems to have a life of its own, creating problems that seem unsolvable, inexplicable, and confusing. Pain not worked through has the capacity to intrude on an otherwise pleasant situation and superimpose a feeling of despair and hopelessness. Instead of enjoying those who are present at a family get-together, for example, you focus attention on who is missing.

Some people who have not yet completely worked
through their loss are catapulted by a passing remembrance
into the full turmoil of the mourning process again. It is a
common experience to be suddenly overwhelmed with a
powerful feeling of loss or nostalgia when going through
the belongings of someone we once loved. This is not a
relapse to the previous state of mourning but a continua-
tion of the process of working through the unmourned—
that is, unfelt—feelings.

When you mourn, you continually find yourself catching
up with the new reality and slipping back. Having lost the
job, you find yourself taking the route to the old workplace.
When a favorite restaurant closes, you still make a sugges-
tion to go there. You find yourself driving past the old
house after you have moved. Working through is in a way
breaking the old habit of expecting reality to be a certain
way. It is a relearning experience.

The Persistence of Unmourned Pain

When a pain is not worked through, it persists as a sad
memory, as a nostalgic or an angry mood state, or as a fear.
The strength of an unmourned loss's capacity to influence
your present feelings and thoughts is remarkable. Evelyn, a
seventy-six-year-old woman, made the following call to my
radio program. It illustrates the power that feelings not
worked through can exert over an entire life.

> *Evelyn:* I am married (*clears throat*) to a very fine man
> (*clears throat*) for fifty-four years. I have very great
> feelings of anxiousness and insecurity. I'm afraid he'll
> die if I let him out of sight to walk the dog. . . . I think
> it could stem from the fact that when I was born my
> grandmother, who only spoke German, raised me
> because my parents had to work. We all lived together
> . . . She died suddenly.
> *D.V.:* How old were you? From what years did she raise you,
> from birth to when?
> *Evelyn:* From birth to five days before my third birthday.

She died of pneumonia. I went into a depression. I not
only lost my grandmother, but I lost my communication because I was not allowed to speak German after
that.

D.V.: So you were all bottled up with your grief at that time
and had no way of expressing yourself.

Evelyn: Very true.

D.V.: Especially since the feelings you had about your
grandmother would have been in German.

Evelyn: Yes, true. Umm, I have been told that I never cried
at any time after this. Now, Dr. Viscott . . .

D.V.: Hold on. Because you know . . . you see, when you
talk to me, Evelyn, the feeling that you give off is of
someone who is under pressure. You feel like you're
always under pressure.

Evelyn: (*clears throat*) Very true.

D.V.: What, are you coughing? Do you have a cold?

Evelyn: No, I . . . just from excitement.

D.V.: Is that the way you are all the time, coughing? Something stuck in your throat?

Evelyn: Yes.

D.V.: See, that's the feeling trying to get out. That's the
inhibition that's present in your life, and you feel it,
uh (*mimicking clearing the throat*) as something
down deep (*mimicking a hoarse voice*).

Evelyn: Yes.

D.V.: That's the feeling of wanting your grandmother. What
did you call her?

Evelyn: I just called her Mommy.

D.V.: Did you call her something in German?

Evelyn: German. Mutter? . . . Mutter.

D.V.: Mutti?

Evelyn: Mutti (*powerful sense of recognition*)!

D.V.: Mutti. Do you think of Mutti?

Evelyn: I think of her all the time.

D.V.: All the time. And do you see her picture?

Evelyn: (*sighs*) I don't have a picture of her.

D.V.: In your mind.

Evelyn: I have it in my mind, yes.

D.V.: And what is it you see in your mind?

Evelyn: I see it . . . I see her as very kind eyes looking at me
with wrinkles, with a wrinkled face and a love of me
that's very great.

D.V.: Do you still speak German?

Evelyn: Uh, I can. . . . I can understand some German, and
I can speak some, but not fluently.

D.V.: OK. If you would talk to me as if I were Mutti, in
German, what would you tell me? If you could say
some words to me, now. *Was wollen sie sagen?*

Evelyn: (*very great emotion*) *Mutti, ich liebe dich.*

D.V.: *Ich liebe dich.* How?

Evelyn: Uh . . . so deeply, I'm . . . (*choking*) . . . and I'm so
afraid I'm going to lose my husband.

D.V.: Now you're bringing up the sensitivity from the old
loss and attaching it to the present.

Evelyn: Yes. I'm so worried about losing my husband that I
can't even let him go out of the house to walk the
dog. I'm so worried he won't come back or that something will happen to him.

D.V.: See, it's that fear again, of being completely powerless
as a child, that's coming to the surface.

Evelyn: Yes.

D.V.: Part of what you're afraid of with your husband is the
fear of losing Mutti. You see, all of it's come through.
You have lived your life as fully as one lives a life.
You've had all these good things, but what you
haven't had is the release of the loss of someone you
haven't been able to say good-bye to. That's made you
feel frightened.

Evelyn: (*with recognition*) That's right.

D.V.: You have to say good-bye to Mutti.

Evelyn: Yes.

D.V.: Can you say that?

Evelyn: Yes, I could say good-bye to Mutti.

D.V.: Tell me.

Evelyn: Good-bye, Mutti.

D.V.: *Kannst du auf Deutsch sprechen?*

Evelyn: *Ich . . . Ich . . . kann.*

D.V.: To Mutti. *Zu Mutti sagen.*

Evelyn: Pardon me?

D.V.: Speak to Mutti in German.

Evelyn: Mutti, I *kann nicht* German *sprechen,* but *ich liebe dich,* so much.

D.V.: And farewell.

Evelyn: And farewell!

D.V.: What are you feeling?

Evelyn: I feel better. I feel lighter, and I shall do that. I shall bid her good-bye in German. I'll be able to think of the words more clearly when I'm off the air.

D.V.: I know you will.

Evelyn: I'll bid her good-bye.

D.V.: And that's what has to happen, so that you can spend the time with your husband without worrying about losing Mutti and placing that on him.

Evelyn: Thank you, Dr. Viscott.

D.V.: Ich liebe dich.

Evelyn: Ich liebe dich.

This call touched thousands of people who recognized themselves in Evelyn. The transcript cannot convey the emotional release that occurred when we spoke in German. In a very real sense your feelings that haven't been worked through own you, hold you in their grip, direct your thinking, and limit your happiness. The grasp Evelyn's defenses held on her feelings was especially great because her ties to her relationship with her grandmother were in German, and because her parents prohibited her from speaking German after her grandmother died she was even further isolated from the awareness of her loss. As we have seen, denial is the only defense that operates without words. When Evelyn's language was taken away, only denial remained.

Working through feelings, mourning them with open acceptance, is as important to living as breathing.

Feelings are the breath of the soul.

Now let's define the key skills for dealing with hurt as it occurs.

7

The Skills for Working Through Hurt: A Handbook

With the mourning process as your model you can understand how to work through the simple hurts and losses of everyday life more effectively. Everyone has difficulty dealing with hurt. There is no set script for the process. Some people pass through denial in a moment and come directly to acceptance, especially when they have had a series of losses. A fresh loss merely fits into the ongoing mourning process, but at the same time it can also overload the person's ability to cope. People who have experienced multiple losses—due to the AIDS epidemic or during war, for example—either become numb with the continuing horror or go into a state of protracted mourning where they feel disengaged from the real world and trapped in an inner landscape of mourning.

While severe losses are likely to get the most attention, it is the minor losses—social slights, the failure to be acknowledged or appreciated—that end up causing you the most difficulty. It is precisely because these smaller losses elude your attention that you tend to exclude them from the mourning process and go about your life as if nothing has happened while within they build up imperceptibly into emotional debt. The poet Wordsworth wrote, "The world is too much with us." The hectic pace of work, daily events, and the media are intrusions that limit our ability to process the simple feelings of life.

Sometimes it's difficult to find time to reflect, to prioritize emotions, to hold on, to maintain your equilibrium. You hold back feelings and experience stress, the pressure of unexpressed feelings seeking release. Additional emotional debt is caused by the frustrations of traffic, slow elevators, and endless credit checks and the growing realization that you lose your dignity and value as a human being when you are viewed as a statistic, a consumer, a working ant. You want your individuality back. You want to matter. You want to be yourself and have an identity in a world that does not seem to care that you exist.

To live fully in a world that encroaches on you at every turn you need more than ever to be emotionally free. The key is to be able to speak your piece and release your minor personal hurts when you feel them so that you do not develop a callus of emotional unawareness merely to survive or carry such emotional debt that you explode in response to the impersonal world.

FEELING THE PAIN

The most effective way of dealing with pain is to experience it as it occurs and to continue feeling it just as long as it is present. There are of course many factors that influence how long you feel pain or keep it alive.

Try this simple test:

Clap your hands as hard as you dare.

Feel the feeling of hurt. Your hands sting, and your fingers feel full. After a few moments you may notice tingling or burning and some minor pain at those spots where the greatest contact was made—where a ring impacted or where you might have bumped your hand when you clapped. After a few minutes you have the faint sensation of pressure being lifted, and you may feel ready to go on with the next paragraph.

Wait a moment before you move on. Just sense the pain again. You have to heighten your sensitivity to pick it up, but it is still there, getting fainter every moment. If you had an old injury, it may be reactivated and drown out the pain from clapping.

Now it is so faint that you have to search to feel it. Is it real or is it memory? Your resolution of pain determines how you see reality, for if your pain lingers you see a hurtful world.

Now imagine that you just hurt your hand in an argument with a lover. You had pressed for an answer about your lover's intention and in a manner totally uncharacteristic he or she took a swing at you with an open hand, which you defended against by holding up your hand, and then ran out of the house in embarrassed rage. Imagine you're sitting in the kitchen looking out the window. Now feel the residual pain in your hands as if it were the result of warding off your lover's attack. Even though it may be extremely faint, it's there. Find it. Focus on it. It's where you were just hit by someone you love. When there is an emotional component to physical pain, it can still be felt even when only a memory.

If you had decided to hold a grudge against your lover for hitting you, you would confuse the memory of being slapped with the residual emotional pain you still discern and would exaggerate the pain to fuel your grudge. When hurt is used to keep anger alive, the hurt is very slow in resolving. It requires forgiveness to stop hurting.

The following techniques will help you learn to express feelings in the moment so that no matter who hurts you or when or under what circumstances you can discharge the feelings as they occur.

LIVING IN THE MOMENT

Everything happens in the moment. Life is now. Growth is now. Happiness is now. Feelings are real in this moment. Everything else is fantasy.

The moment is a period of time in which you can hold a single idea, in which you feel a feeling before any resonant emotional recollection takes place.

The moment is brief, a few seconds. Here is one moment: the time you spend reading this.

Now it is gone, and you are in another moment.

Moments come and go, and the feelings contained in them age and slip out of reach of your emotional grasp. You then remember rather than experience them. It is customary for people to wish pleasant moments to tarry awhile so they can grasp their loveliness. You take photographs to preserve the moment. The artist struggles to capture the gesture or the telling detail and, by a perfect rendition of part of reality, to recapture the feeling of the whole and bring it to life. Art is all about keeping the moment alive, making it visible, cherishing it, delineating it, seeing its essence. The moment well depicted in art not only tells you about the moment that exists now but also relates it to the moment that came before and the moment that is coming next.

All of your aspirations are really about the moments you live, the moments you cherish, savor, and dream about. You yearn for the moment of victory, triumph, conquest, success, and for your entire life you work to live out moments that seem to justify your struggle. These moments pass. So do the moments in which you heard of the loss of your loved ones and the times you accepted failure.

The ultimate moment is the moment of accepting yourself without the need to do anything to prove your worth but merely to be yourself. This moment lasts.

It is impossible to keep any moment alive, that is, to make the present last. All moments are fleeting. Hurt only lasts a moment before it begins to turn into anger. So it is important to learn to be as spontaneous as possible in expressing the hurt in the moment it occurs. This allows you to express your hurt in its most simple and understandable form, when it makes the most sense to others. You put yourself at an unfair disadvantage when you allow hurt to age into anger, because when you finally express your hurt feelings with anger, you are likely to hurt the other person. Then that person will probably get defensive and will not be especially sympathetic to your pain. If you wait too long the other person may not even remember the incident, and you find yourself exaggerating or acting like a wounded child to make your point.

Voicing your hurt as it occurs is the only way to be alive in the moment.

Perhaps you feel you need the other person's approval. Perhaps the other person is your employer and you are afraid of losing your job. Perhaps the other person is your lover, and you are afraid to discover that your lover does not care about your feelings. Whatever you fear losing becomes the reason you are not open to expressing your feelings in the moment, and not reacting in the moment ultimately makes matters worse.

Techniques for Being Alive in the Moment

The following dynamic techniques are critically important to being alive in the moment so you can resolve hurt rather than store it as emotional debt. Do not take them casually. While I have simplified and translated their dynamics into unassuming language, they represent twenty-five years of helping people tell others that they've been hurt *when* they hurt. I discovered that this was difficult for many people to do. People often don't even realize that they have been hurt. They need some way to extend the length of the moment of injury so they can get their bearings and discover what they are feeling. Also, hearing that you have hurt someone is a painful experience. The expression of hurt is often perceived as an attack, making the injured

Defensive Reactions to Hurt

Denial	Confusion, delay in realizing that the injury has taken place. As the bad mood builds, sullenness increases. When the feeling of hurt is felt, it is often not attached to the event that caused it. When the hurt is finally identified, "How could you?" and "I can't talk about it" and "You're killing me" attitudes prevail in an attempt to punish from a passive position.
Excuses	Knee-jerk response to try to control or punish the injuring party, accomplished with an air of self-righteousness. "Now you've done it" attitude belies the long-standing existence of a hidden grudge and preparation to respond to any attack with overwhelming force. While this hidden agenda is generalized, it leads to overreacting and specific attacks, criticizing and undermining the attacker. Overkill weakens the case. Victim becomes villain.
Pretense	"I don't care. It doesn't matter. What do you expect from someone like that? So what? It's nothing, a scratch, a flea bite. I didn't even pay attention. I must have missed it."

party into the villian. The chart above shows how the three defensive styles respond to hurt.

You can overcome these defensive operations in an open, undefended way by learning some key verbal techniques. These are comments to be made openly when you first feel the pain and when there's the best chance of correcting the misunderstanding and maintaining good relationships with people you care about.

As you make a comment to get the attention of someone who's hurt your feelings, proceed to the next comment that most directly expresses your feeling of hurt. Then explain your injury in specific terms. Even in the presence of intimidating people by whom you feel inhibited, these are the simplest techniques for bridging the gap between your hurt and inability to risk disclosure. Try to master the first few so you can deliver them in a natural, comfortable style.

1. "Excuse me. I didn't hear what you just said. Please repeat it."

This statement has great power because it puts you in immediate control of the situation. Whether you know perfectly well what the other person said and maybe even why or you think you may have misheard the comment, this statement gives you an opportunity to check your perception. The other person may not be aware of his remark, possibly because some unresolved negative feeling entirely separate from you has intruded and motivated it. After all, other people also have problems with emotional debt. The hurt may actually have little to do with you; it may be symbolic.

Saying "Please repeat that, I didn't hear what you just said" opens up a new perspective for the other person. First, by claiming not to have heard, you've offered a shield for that person to hide behind. Next you've given him a chance to reconsider what he said. Recalling the comment, he will almost certainly be uneasy. When the comment is repeated, pay close attention to how it is edited. The injury or put-down has probably been omitted. You should at once accept the correction without comment and make some positive sign. You have let go of the hurt. Now you are in a position of strength. You're being kind and understanding, and the other person will appreciate and respect you for it.

If the original comment is repeated and the insult intended, remain silent or move on to one of the following techniques. If the other person refuses to repeat, merely reiterate that you did not hear, but be aware that the other person is resisting disclosing a feeling. You now have the option of pressing forward if you choose or letting it go, now knowing more clearly with what you are dealing.

If you feel that you have missed the opportunity to express anger by acting in this conciliatory way, you are reflecting your own problems. Your emotional debt is intruding. The correct tactic is to express the concerns you have before they become a problem, not to start a fight, when old anger is called to the surface.

2. "I don't understand what you just said. Please explain."

Ask for clarification. The assumption is that you did hear the remark and are ready to quote it to the other person. If you do repeat it, say "I thought you said . . ." and be prepared to be told that you misquoted the other person or that he or she misspoke. Again, accept any correction and allow a retraction. Your object is to bring the issue to light in the moment, rather than bury it or go to war.

3. "Is that so?"

This is a wonderful comment. It should be made simply, without elaboration or embellishment, when you've been told something hurtful, critical, or negative. Don't react; just ask "Is that so?" By doing so you offer the person a chance to correct himself while creating an atmosphere of tolerance in which a correction will be accepted. Add "Is this true?" or "Really!" to intensify your meaning.

4. "What just happened?"

Use this technique when the other person resists responding to the previous comments. It indirectly probes the person's reaction to your attempt to clarify the situation. This is the kind of comment to make to someone you're familiar with rather than to a relative stranger, because it asks for the other person to explain the reluctance to be open.

Act puzzled but without hurt. Remember, you don't understand enough yet to be hurt. When someone is resistant to confrontation, any display of hurt can push the situation into an argument.

Remember, you're trying to understand.

The Skills for Working Through Hurt   147

5. "This doesn't make sense to me."

This technique is more confrontational, for it implies that the remark was irrational. Still, by claiming that the remark doesn't make sense to *you*, you're the one asking for assistance. It also allows you to express some negativity in a safe manner. You can ask for elaboration by adding "Maybe I missed something" or "You'll have to run that by me again." The advantage of this approach is that it clearly keeps the feeling alive and on the table before it can be forgotten.

6. "This doesn't feel right to me."

This is a good way to introduce feelings of hurt into a situation in which your injury is definitely the result of the other person's action. It declares outright that you don't like the way the present situation feels. It also presents your position as differing from the other person's, since most people in our society use the words *feel* and *think* interchangeably.

If you permit another person to establish a position that hurts you without timely opposition, the other person will take your delay as tacit agreement. Later, when the pain has built up and is converted to anger, your resistance will seem out of place and overblown. The longer you wait, the more likely this is to be so and the greater the chance that when your reaction does come it will be unnecessarily hurtful to the other person.

7. "I'm not sure."

This simple comment, delivered with a shrug and a look of doubt, is an effective way of slowing down the emotional transaction of the moment and demonstrating that you're not pleased with what's going on. It does not disclose your emotions specifically but opens the door to more open discussion. It works well when someone is trying to force you or control you. If they don't get the hint, make a more forceful statement.

8. *"I'm not comfortable with this."*

Here is a straightforward declaration of your discomfort, although it involves some risk. By making this comment, you put your feelings on the line and may run the risk of discovering that the other person doesn't care how you feel. To love another person is to care about his or her feelings the way you care about your own, so a person who is isolated from his or her own feelings can hardly be expected to care about yours. Since self-love is the limiting factor in loving others, people who are hesitant about expressing their hurt to others are afraid to discover that they are dealing with someone who does not have the capacity to care for them.

Once one gets beyond the fear of discovering the truth, this technique is a good way of initiating meaningful communication. Knowing the truth may be painful, but it is always the beginning of healing and growth.

9. *"I'm having trouble dealing with, or accepting, this."*

Now you're putting the problem on the line. You're stating that you're not in agreement with the situation. The other person is being asked to look at your concerns. You're opening the matter up for discussion right now.

Again, you run the risk of being ignored or rejected, but you are being an adult.

10. *"This hurts" or "You just hurt my feelings."*

This is the most direct statement of injury, and in a relationship between two open, mature adults it is probably all you need. However, people have difficulty making such an open declaration of hurt because they don't want to discover that the other person hurt them intentionally, nor do they want to create a conflict. Yet when you avoid an external conflict when another person injures you, you only sow the seeds for conflict within yourself.

Some people will take your declaration as an accusation. Controlling people especially do not like to hear others complain and often become more controlling and punitive. It is as if they are saying I'll teach you to complain about my hurting you. For this reason it is useful with controlling people to begin with a less direct declaration of your hurt.

No matter what tactic you start with, the end result is the same, expressing your hurt in the moment. By stretching out the time in which the awareness of a feeling decays, you can provide yourself with the room to make a declaration of your feelings. When you finally get to a level of understanding at which your feelings can be stated, it is important to say "Well, that's what I thought you said. It hurt my feelings." This is needed to take the conversation to the next level of truth so that the feeling of hurt can be resolved.

11. "I want to" and "I don't want to."

Declare your intentions and desires simply and without fanfare as soon as you are aware of them. These two comments may appear to be more suitable to a manual on self-assertion, but learning to use them properly can save you a lot of discomfort and confusion in the future. They are the two best and only explanations for your actions that you ever need to give.

When you want something, say so. People who say what they want get what they want. Once you've passed age two, no one is even vaguely interested in trying to read your mind. Sitting in silence, expecting people to give you what you want or avoid what you dislike, is another way of testing people. It is bound to meet with disaster.

Likewise, if you don't want to do something, say so immediately. When we do something we don't like, it's common for us to expect others to be aware of our sacrifice and make up to us for it by granting us indulgences. Unfortunately, we're difficult to be with at such times, and instead of feeling grateful, people get irritated at us for being in a bad mood and just want to get away from us.

Indicating what you want and not going along with what
you don't want are not selfish acts but rather acts based on
knowing yourself and the limits of your giving. When your
actions are not based on that self-knowledge, you end up
resenting everyone and feeling used because you don't
stand up for yourself.

RESOLVING THE HURT

Feel the hurt. Don't be afraid. Once the injury of rejection, disappointment, betrayal, embarrassment, or failure
has taken place, you only make it worse by avoiding it. Feel
the hurt. Healing begins when you admit the truth of the
pain. Until you do, you suffer.

First, accept that you've been hurt. This may be hard to
do because to you it may mean you're not cared for, you're
weak, or you're not as good as you thought you were. You
need to know the truth no matter what. It is better to find
out sooner than later.

Your greatest hurt probably will not be inflicted by an
enemy but by someone you love and counted on, someone
whose injury was compounded by betrayal—violation of
your openness, innocence, and trust. If you're hurt, it's
likely because you let your defenses down; you had an
understanding that was violated by the other person.

It is not suggested that you become cold and defensive as
a way to avoid this. In fact people who shut down because
of hurt do more damage to themselves than anyone ever
does to them. The idea is to be flexible, open, and resilient
and to be able to express your hurt with immediacy. That
way you can defend yourself when you need to, still being
free to love and trust again and to work with uncluttered
spontaneity and unclouded judgment.

Few hurts have the sting of discovering a truth about
yourself that you did not want to know. It's painful to see
yourself as flawed, less than you hoped to be, unkind,
stubborn, selfish, greedy, or uncaring. Be open to these

self-realizations as soon as possible. Understand that you're no different from anyone else in having these shortcomings. It's your knowledge of your weaknesses that gives you real control, not trying to give an impression that you're always strong or perfect. In fact it's when you try to maintain a saintly facade that you're most susceptible to sudden losses in self-esteem, a hurt for which you set yourself up.

PRACTICAL REMINDERS

If someone else has hurt you, express your hurt as soon as possible.

Reach an understanding of the situation that allows you to let go of the hurt.

Forgive the other person by declaring that you no longer hurt and have let go of the pain.

When you discover the other person has hurt you on purpose, due to some old hurt of his own, it's important to be as open in hearing his hurt as you expect him to be in hearing yours. Remember, although held-in old anger seems exaggerated, it feels appropriate to the person feeling it, so the other person may sincerely feel entitled to hurt you back.

Sometimes the other person denies or forgets having injured you, especially when there's been a long interval between injury and your bringing it up. It is not proof that the other person is a villain or evil. You too have hurt people and are still not aware of it. Whenever a distance suddenly widens between you and another, you can safely assume one of you has been hurt. Much of the time the person you've hurt has remained silent out of embarrassment for being so weak or sensitive. He may have been afraid of offending you and may have been further aggravated at you for not noticing that you hurt him. Remembering that you're not always innocent and the other person isn't all bad goes a long way toward making peace.

If you're someone who's easily hurt, you may hurt others by appearing so fragile that they fear expressing their own feelings. They may feel that discussions always focus on your hurt feelings and avoid theirs. People whose first reaction to everything is to act deeply hurt manage to offend others.

Don't use your pain as a weapon.

If disclosing your hurt creates an unpleasant situation, immediately ask "What just happened?" and be mindful of the techniques we've discussed for working through the difficulty step by step.

- Don't play the victim.
- Ask questions. If the other person seems bent on hurting you on purpose, say, "You're not feeling good about yourself, you sound hurt," and listen to the response without reacting to it. Just listen.
- Don't let frustration cause you to give up.
- Be persistent, but keep your distance.

- Become the observer and watch the interchange unfold.
- Feel your hurt in the other person's presence. If you run from it, it will grow.
- Keep comments simple.
- Don't play shrink.
- Don't exaggerate or overplay your hand. Someone who is resistant to hearing your story will focus on the part you exaggerate to refute your charges.
- Don't be afraid to show your injury, but don't make a public display for the sake of embarrassing or punishing the other person. This is only hurting back.
- Don't go behind the other person's back. The politics of vengeance are complicated and will create even more emotional debt.

Be direct.
Be brave.
Be immediate.
Tell the truth.
Tell it now.

Expressing hurt reveals how much things mean to you, so it is always a personal disclosure. Holding onto hurt only makes you suffer in smoldering anger. Expressing your hurt brings relief even if it is not completely received. To be able to tell the person who hurt you, "I feel better now," is the essence of letting go. And when you admit your own hurtful behavior, you can begin to correct it.

There is nothing like feeling better to feel better.

8

Understanding Anxiety:
The Anticipation of Injury

Anxiety is the expectation of loss. It anticipates pain in the future, pain that hasn't happened yet, pain that is not real.

Anxiety manifests itself in feelings ranging all the way from curiosity, wondering, qualms, concern, distrust, misgiving, worry, apprehension, trepidation, and fear to phobia, dread, horror, panic, and terror.

Anxiety *feels* real, but you have actually suffered nothing. You have merely anticipated a loss or an injury. Your imagination is attempting to make sense of something you *expect* to take place.

Anxiety serves you well by protecting you from threats of danger. It allows you to anticipate where injury may come from and prepare to defend against it by using your heightened state of awareness to make good your escape.

At its simplest and most straightforward, anxiety is constantly at work in the animal world. For example, a sea gull will avoid resting on a beach house roof where a dummy owl is displayed. The sea gull will not check out the dummy to see if it is real even after the dummy has remained motionless for a long time. The visual image of the feared object always evokes the avoidance response. So whenever the visual danger signal is received, the bird flies away. If you need additional proof, try to approach a sparrow.

In humans, however, it is the context in which we perceive a signal that gives it the power to trigger the anxiety response: we fear what we have come to believe is to be feared. We even fear whatever *reminds* us of something we're afraid of, and we can generalize our fear. The sea gull fears only the owl, but we might also come by association to fear the beach house and perhaps even the sea. Also, our ability to react to language as if it were reality allows us to fear the symbol of a thing as much as the thing itself. We can easily become conditioned to react with fear to the mere mention of a feared person's name, especially if we're still concealing the hurt that person caused us.

Anxiety serves as an effective emotion when we pay attention to its signal as soon as possible, recognize its meaning, and act on it in a way that ensures survival. However, no one can survive long in a state of heightened awareness without draining emotional reserves.

Attaining emotional freedom does not mean avoiding feelings but dealing with them directly in the most economical way so that you have the maximum energy to pursue your work. Because unresolved anxiety diverts your focus from constructive work, it intrudes on your performance and lowers your confidence. By failing to pay attention to details, you make mistakes and so bring about the very loss you dread. This is the paralyzing effect of anxiety.

HOW YOUR ANXIETY THRESHOLD VARIES

The very advantage of anxiety, the head start on reality it provides, is also what gives us problems. People who are so spooked and alert for danger can misinterpret anything as imminent danger. Soldiers expecting an attack, for example, will shoot at a falling leaf merely because it is moving. When danger is real, the feeling of anxiety is valid. When the danger is imagined or remembered, anxiety is a distracting burden, like a false alarm.

Imagine that you lived below a dam. During a severe drought you probably would not think of the dam failing, but you might begin to wonder about the dam when the water was high. You would certainly worry about the dam if there had been a recent report of seepage, the water level was high, and you were in the midst of a torrential rainstorm. If you had been hurt by the dam's failing in the past, you might worry whenever the forecast called for a chance of rain, even in a dry season. Thus your recollection of an injury would inflate your concern over the present danger, reducing the amount of danger needed to sound the alarm and make you anxious. This could be called learning life's lessons, but some of us hold on to these lessons so tightly that we are in an almost constant state of anxiety.

Much of the trouble that people suffer with anxiety comes from the unknown as much as the unreal. The unknown makes us feel helpless to protect ourselves, which in turn reawakens feelings of dependency and prompts us to use denial to shut off our fears. Unfortunately, this leaves us afraid but still unaware of what it is we're afraid of. In a vicious circle, our sense of helplessness increases, and the unknown is made even more fearsome.

When anxiety is a feeling about a fantasy or a feeling about a memory, it reflects such concerns about ourselves as "Am I good, safe, lovable, smart, strong, worthy, doing the right thing the right way?" If you fear you're inadequate, it's easy to interpret innocent events and comments as dreaded criticism or proof of your worst fears. In this way anxiety tends to become generalized and leads you away from the real issues you're concerned with.

You need to accommodate to your feelings—that is, to adapt to and deal with stimuli and not react to them with an automatic flight. In a sense you have to learn to reset your awareness level. People from the country, for instance, learn to accommodate a much noisier background so they can learn to sleep in the city.

In a similar manner you accommodate to personal feelings of anxiety by expanding your experience. Just think of how differently you drive a car now than during your first driving lesson. The road is just as fraught with danger now as it was before, but you no longer worry about each hazard; mostly you don't worry about your ability to drive. You plan a course through the traffic, generalizing a safe path without worrying about every object. You work from a few set points to be sure you have clearance. This is the function of learning to drive, believing in yourself and developing a familiarity with the stimulus level of the streets.

The Persistence of Past Fears

We stop accommodating to reality when our defenses shield us from threat so that instead of adjusting to a danger we hide the threatening feeling and live with a false sense of security, denying, making excuses, or pretending that the danger doesn't exist. Of course the thing we fear still lies hidden behind our defenses. From time to time some hidden anxiety is triggered and breaks loose. This is startling since our defenses have led us to believe all was well. The release of old anxiety can be provoked by the actual occurrence of a similar threat in the present or by something symbolic of a former threat, a kind of emotional déjà vu.

The liberated old fear attaches itself to the present fear, exaggerating it out of context. If the old event was an especially important one, even a mild stimulus may provoke a maximal anxiety response. The old source is difficult to recognize, because the new threat gets all your attention. Thus your reaction makes little sense to you.

To illustrate, it would be like becoming afraid of any red car, whether it is a threat to you or not, simply because you were once hit by a red car. The expectation that a red car is dangerous leads you to drive unsafely. Thus the very feeling of anxiety that was originally designed to protect you now endangers you.

Anxiety also comes from the fear of accepting what has happened in the past. When you feel pain in recalling an injury, it is a sign that you have not completely accepted the old hurt. This battle between the feeling and the defenses that hold it in place gives you the sensation of losing control. The release of negative feelings from the grip of the defenses also frightens you because it is accompanied by the escape of unsettled doubts about yourself. So when you have a sudden, fearful recollection, you fear for your worth as much as for your safety.

Whenever a hidden old loss breaks into awareness, it feels real, as if it were happening right now. Through the mourning process, painful feelings are gradually brought into awareness until they are fully accepted and resolved. Until resolved, the partially hidden feeling amplifies similar feelings in the present, letting you know you still have unfinished business to take care of. It is this anticipation of the release of this remaining portion of pain that causes most anxiety.

Until you fully mourn them, painful events hold you in this fearful grip. Filled with anxiety, you come to doubt your emotional integrity itself. Understanding the source of your anxiety almost always reveals a loss that you don't want to face, but it gives you relief both from your symptoms of fear and from your suspicion that you're crazy. Facing the fear by understanding the loss increases your self-esteem and reveals a truth that you were partly aware of all along.

THE DAMAGE ANXIETY DOES

Anxiety that has ceased to be of the useful variety manifests itself in many damaging ways. As chronic anxiety it builds and accumulates, keeping you in constant stress. It can paralyze you, preventing you from taking the risks you need to take to move forward. And it can lead to debilitating paranoia.

Chronic Anxiety

Chronic anxiety develops as a result of continually repressing negative feelings. Lucy, a severely troubled woman, obsessively cleaned her house twelve or fifteen hours a day, suffering severe mental torture whenever she saw a messy drawer or a spot on her children's clothes. When she was young, her mother was abusive and beat her. There were times when she consciously wished her mother would die. Though she expressed no remorse over these wishes and claimed she had completely forgiven her mother, her combined guilt and anger led her to decide to be the perfect daughter. She often disagreed with her mother but held her tongue. Eventually she found herself virtually blistering with anger, unable to admit it, and convinced that she was simply a bad person. She perceived each splinter of anger as an imperfection, and so she symbolically kept her anger in place by keeping her home neat.

Chronic anxiety is always significant because your fear is telling you that you're in a situation that is not good for you, be it a job or a marriage. Chronic anxiety drains energy, causes psychosomatic problems, and is life-threatening. It diverts your attention, makes you fall short of your native talent's promise, and places your focus on your failure or potential injury. You become afraid of being afraid, and this keeps you from enjoying life and simply being. Chronic anxiety should not be blamed on the environment or others even if they are the cause. The ultimate responsibility falls on you, because you've failed to value yourself and take the actions necessary to eliminate your pain.

Ultimately your anxiety is your responsibility, your signal to do something about the danger you face. When you neglect to take actions to resolve a threat, the anxiety accumulates. It is this accumulation that overwhelms you. So if taking responsibility for your anxiety seems a bit harsh, it is also necessary to name your fear, face it, and resolve it.

Anxiety and Risking

Whether anxiety is a normal, useful part of your life depends on a quantitative measure. How much anxiety is too much? If it prepares you to consider the possibility of danger inherent in each risk you face and to examine the width of the chasms you plan to jump so you can take a few practice runs on solid ground, it is serving you appropriately. If it is perceived as excitement—you feel challenged to be your best to get what you want—it is helpful anxiety, and it motivates you rather than inhibits you. The reason you get overwhelmed when you risk is that you have failed to allow yourself to feel sufficiently afraid beforehand to direct your attention to the potential dangers. You need to become familiar with the demands the challenge will likely make of you so you can take a risk with the greatest possible knowledge and manage the unknown. Still, no risk is ever completely comfortable.

If, on the other hand, your anxiety continually gets in the way of your taking the risks you need to take to get ahead, it is a problem. If you're afraid to risk because you fear losing, then the problem is that you're expecting a single success or failure to make too important a statement about your character and your worth. If you think everything hangs on one particular risk, risking is perilous indeed.

Much of anxiety is the fear of committing to a challenge that measures you. Sometimes you fear success, for example, because you feel undeserving and really believe that a success would be a fluke and you would not be able to sustain it. You really do not fear success, but losing it. You fear that the spotlight would then focus on your shortcomings. Sometimes you fear success because if you succeeded it would let someone who has injured you off the hook, such as a parent who hurt you. Succeeding would not only allow the parent to participate in your success but in some way would undermine any claim that your parent permanently damaged you. This issue is more prominent in adolescents but also appears among adults who have not forgiven their parents.

Anxiety and Paranoia

Under certain conditions anxiety can lead to feelings of paranoia, the feeling that people are out to get you. You've experienced a mild and specific feeling of paranoia upon seeing a state trooper in your rearview mirror when you've been speeding. When you are isolated from human contact, your fear stems from loneliness. You imagine others are interested in you just to believe that at least *someone* notices you, even if you suspect he or she is up to no good. Controlling people tend to suffer loneliness and, because they cannot admit their dependent need for others, often ascribe negative intentions to others, becoming punitive and suspicious. Their loneliness fills up with anger.

You are most likely to feel paranoid when you have done something wrong, have hurt someone and therefore are feeling guilty and deserving of punishment. These feelings of paranoia are not to be confused with the paranoia of psychosis. The paranoia of anxiety is transient, associated with discrete events and therefore reversible once the problem has been identified and solved.

ANXIETY AND THE THREE PERSONALITY TYPES

The same dependent, controlling, and competitive losses that cause you hurt in the present can prompt anxiety about the future. The following examples show how each of the three character types uses defenses to manage hidden feelings. As you read them, be mindful of your own defensive tendencies and think about when and why you become anxious.

A Dependent Person's Anxiety

The symbol of a forgotten loss can be signaled by a trivial or nearly imperceptible stimulus. This exchange, which took place as a call to my radio program, shows the relief that can be achieved by facing the original loss. My efforts to pin down the caller's symptoms reflect the strength of her defenses.

Gloria: My name is Gloria, and I am having problems with anxiety. Every time there's a change in my life, I have anxiety attacks.

D.V.: What kind of change?

Gloria: Something as simple as a change in my schedule. I started back to school this week, and I felt anxiety about that.

D.V.: Give me an example of the particular feeling, so I have a feel for it.

Gloria: I feel paralyzed. I just don't . . . I'm afraid to even leave my house.

D.V.: OK. But tell me, what happened this week?

Gloria: Well, I get really upset.

D.V.: What was the change that was going to happen, and when did you first think about it?

Gloria: When I woke up to go to school.

D.V.: The day you woke up?

Gloria: Yeah.

D.V.: You weren't frightened the night before?

Gloria: No.

D.V.: You knew you were going to change from what to what?

Gloria: From just being a housewife to going to school.

D.V.: Was this the first time you've made that change?

Gloria: No, this is my last semester.

D.V.: So, you've been doing it all along?

Gloria: Yes, and I'm doing well in school.

D.V.: OK. So, it was a change in your daily routine?

Gloria: Right.

D.V.: And when was the first time you felt the fear? Do you remember? Put yourself back there.

Gloria: Going out the front door.

D.V.: Going out the front door. What were you thinking of just before? Take me through it.

Gloria: I don't really remember what I was thinking.

D.V.: Remember.

Gloria: Making sure that I have everything. I wanted to know where my . . . what class am I going to? What room am I . . . what room is it in?

D.V.: Finding your place.

Gloria: Right.

D.V.: And the moment you left your place, what happened? When did you first feel that? What step were you taking when you first felt the fear?

Gloria: Leaving the front door.

D.V.: Do you remember the feeling when it came over you?

Gloria: Yeah, I just . . . I felt scared. I wanted to go back.

D.V.: Well, tell me the first moment. Do you remember the exact moment? Go to the moment.

Gloria: I had just closed my front door.

D.V.: Did you hear it close?

Gloria: Yeah . . .

D.V.: And when you heard it close?

Gloria: I got scared.

D.V.: On hearing it?

Gloria: Yeah, yeah!

D.V.: The click in the door.

Gloria: Right!

D.V.: You're outside now.

Gloria: Yeah.

D.V.: Did you ever hear a click of a door in your life before, when you were locked outside and not protected?

Gloria: Yeah.

D.V.: When?

Gloria: (*no audible answer, long pause*)

D.V.: Are you feeling anxious right now?

Gloria: Yeah.

D.V.: OK. When was that click that you heard before?

Gloria: Umm. When I was a teenager.

D.V.: What happened?

Gloria: I was kicked out.

D.V.: Why? What did you do?

Gloria: For having a boyfriend.

D.V.: And the feeling you had was what?

Gloria: Rejection.

D.V.: From?

Gloria: From being kicked out. I was rejected.

D.V.: Yes, but who rejected you?

Gloria: My father.

D.V.: What did he say to you?

Gloria: (*labored breathing*) He called me a whore.

D.V.: And you said to him?

Gloria: I didn't say anything. I just left.

D.V.: Did you ever tell him?

Gloria: No. He knows now.

D.V.: What did you say to him? He knows what? How you felt?

Gloria: Well, he knows that what he did was wrong, and he has apologized to me since then.

D.V.: Where did you go after he closed the door behind you?

Gloria: I went and lived with my boyfriend.

D.V.: What was the feeling of being with your boyfriend?

Gloria: I was just really upset.

D.V.: Upset, meaning what? Frightened? Hurt?

Gloria: Yeah. Scared.

D.V.: Scared of what?

Gloria: I didn't know what was going to happen next.

D.V.: You didn't know what was going to happen next!

Gloria: Yeah.

D.V.: You were completely rejected and alone in the world.

Gloria: Right.

D.V.: And you felt you weren't loved.

Gloria: Right.

D.V.: But you took that all inside. How much of these feelings does your dad know about?

Gloria: Well, um, he's an alcoholic, and he's been going to therapy.

D.V.: You're making a case for why you can't get him upset.

Gloria: Right. I'm afraid to tell him because I'm afraid to hurt him.

D.V.: That's what's wrong! Anytime you're on your own, it brings up the fear of being pushed out, because you still feel all the anger at your father. He's always full of

remorse, isn't he? He's always apologizing for what he
does.

Gloria: Right.

D.V.: But that doesn't make you hurt less. You still have to
tell him how badly you hurt, how rejected you felt,
and that when you hear a door click it makes you
anxious to be out on your own, alone. Has it happened on the doorstep before?

Gloria: Yeah . . . it's . . .

D.V.: Is that where it happens?

Gloria: Yeah.

D.V.: So, when it does, you are reminded of being pushed
out into the world and being left alone with the angry
feelings you never resolved. It's time to go back and
tell your father that you still have pain over this and
that you're not so interested in him apologizing as
you have a need to let him hear how much pain you
were in. You need to share this to let the pain out, and
then the anxiety will decrease, because part of the
fear is losing control of your own anger at your father
and risking further rejection. You are always making
excuses why you can't get angry at him. Poor Dad,
he's just a drunk who's trying so hard in therapy and
Alcoholics Anonymous and everything, but he's still a
person who injured you, and you still have to tell him
how you felt. Letting him apologize without you getting out the pain is not really forgiving.

Gloria: You're right.

D.V.: Your anxiety is telling you that the time has now come
for you to make that repair.

There were many leads to follow in this case. The change
that Gloria really feared was a recollection of rejection.
However, she could not admit it because it was hidden.
The sound of the click in the door was the part of the past
that intruded, a mechanical, nonverbal sound not likely to
be concealed by a defense. And yet it symbolized all of her
concerns. Because she feared being rejected again for being angry and so needed to reestablish the relationship
between herself and her father, Gloria continued to conceal

her feelings just to have him back in her life, the ultimate dependent conflict: wanting to be loved, fearing rejection.

Linking anxiety to its source is crucial to resolving it.

This case also illustrates how unexpressed anxiety, like unexpressed hurt, is stored as emotional debt. Anxiety from one unfaced fear combines with others and is pooled together as a generalized apprehensive attitude. In addition, stored hurt feelings are difficult to separate from accumulated anxious feelings, so both can be released when the fear is triggered. And so Gloria experienced some bitterness and resentment as well as anxiety in confronting her past.

Gloria's case also illustrates how the mourning process becomes frozen until the full force of a loss is admitted and felt. Until it is, the person suffers from apparently directionless apprehension, a feeling of generalized misgiving, a sense that something bad is about to happen.

When the pain of an important loss is totally suppressed, a susceptibility is created for the emotion to be suddenly triggered free and to burst forward as an anxiety attack. A panic disorder is a pattern of avoiding hurt that creates an unstable pool of dreaded losses that continually threaten to break loose. But when they reach "critical emotional mass," or are precipitated by a symbolic key, they overflow, creating great instability and self-doubt. People who suffer from this problem often feel confused. The way they dealt with problems seemed to work perfectly for years, and now it doesn't, because now their defensive mechanisms' capacity to store emotion has been overwhelmed.

A Controlling Person's Anxiety

A past anxiety does not have to be especially old to intrude into the present; even a few months can be sufficient. Barbara's call to my radio show illustrates a controlling person's anxiety. As you read, notice how transparent and unreal the anxiety seems as a symptom. Of course to the person feeling the anxiety the terror feels confusing and very real indeed.

> *Barbara:* I've been having trouble with anxiety attacks. I go into the supermarket, and my heart starts pounding. I break into a sweat and think that I am going to die. I've seen a psychiatrist, and he prescribed tranquilizers, but they don't help.
>
> *D.V.:* How long have these been bothering you?
>
> *Barbara:* Two weeks—no, two months.
>
> *D.V.:* Where was the first one?
>
> *Barbara:* In the market.
>
> *D.V.:* Always in the market?
>
> *Barbara:* Hmm . . . Yes, I think so.
>
> *D.V.:* What happened two months ago?
>
> *Barbara:* Nothing? (*stated almost as a question*)
>
> *D.V.:* (*incredulously*) Nothing?
>
> *Barbara:* Nothing I can think of.
>
> *D.V.:* Two months ago?
>
> *Barbara:* Well, my father died.
>
> *D.V.:* That's something.
>
> *Barbara:* I guess . . .
>
> *D.V.:* How did you take it?
>
> *Barbara:* Fine. No problem.
>
> *D.V.:* Did you cry?
>
> *Barbara:* Well, he'd been dying from cancer for over a year, and I was taking care of him. My mother was overwhelmed with the situation, and I had to take care of her as well.
>
> *D.V.:* And . . . did you cry?
>
> *Barbara:* I . . . I was too busy. I was cooking for him and doing the shopping and housekeeping and working at the same time. And when he died, I had to make all the funeral arrangements . . . I guess I didn't have time to cry.
>
> *D.V.:* At all?
>
> *Barbara:* I don't think so.
>
> *D.V.:* Where in the market did you have the anxiety attacks?
>
> *Barbara:* I don't recall.
>
> *D.V.:* Think for a minute.

Barbara: The meat counter. That's funny, because I'm a vegetarian.

D.V.: Was your father a vegetarian?

Barbara: No, he loved meat.

D.V.: And you used to shop for him?

Barbara: (*sadly*) Yes.

D.V.: So, when you got to the meat counter, you must have realized that there was no reason for you to stop there anymore.

Barbara: No, there wasn't. (*sighs*) I didn't think of that.

D.V.: As you passed the meat counter, you must have had some realization that he wasn't here anymore. And since you hadn't yet mourned him, the recollection of his loss must have felt new, like something was about to be taken away from you.

Barbara: Oh! (*shocked*)

D.V.: Do you miss him?

Barbara: (*a moment of pregnant silence, then audible sobs*) Yes . . . yes, I do.

D.V.: Next time you go by the meat counter and start to feel anxious, remind yourself that you are just missing your father. You may start to cry, but it will solve the problem. When you suppress a loss that has taken place, it tries to break through until it is known. Now you know, so experience the sadness of losing your father.

Barbara called back the following month to say that the next time she felt anxious at the meat counter she'd reminded herself that she missed her father and broke down into tears. The anxiety stopped and has not returned since.

Barbara wished to control her feelings about her father by organizing and taking care of details, typical controlling adaptations to loss. However, these activities were insufficient to contain the reality of losing the father she cared for so deeply. Taking responsibility instead of expressing hurt while he was dying was her attempt to be certain that she would have nothing to feel regret about afterward.

Not allowing yourself to feel vulnerable enough to

mourn is the problem behind much controlling anxiety. Whether controlling people suffer the loss of a person or the loss of power or money, they usually make a strong attempt to be in control and carry on business as usual in spite of the loss. Feeling a loss is always fearsome for they wonder what other vulnerabilities lurk behind it waiting to be expressed.

A Competitive Person's Anxiety

Competitive people experience anxiety as the threat of failure. Frequently they don't really believe in themselves. They have merely convinced themselves they are worthwhile only because they've put themselves into situations where they can easily win without testing their real abilities. They find little time for enjoying success except at the moment of victory and don't allow enough slack for dealing with modest reversals, believing they will always be able to move forward by sheer enterprise and energy. This may be the way they motivate themselves to act, but it is also the source of considerable anxiety. Incidentally, others may provoke this same anxiety by pressing them to prove themselves in a never-ending quest for more and better. After a while this use of anxiety as a prod eats at the marrow of their belief in themselves.

Notice how Ted's concerns relate to being able to perform and reach for more. He needs the trappings of success to feel good. When his ability to keep up appearances is compromised, he feels afraid.

> *Ted:* I don't understand it. I should feel solid after getting a promotion, but I don't. I got the promotion I've been working for for years, and now that I have it I'm anxious all the time.
>
> *D.V.:* What do you do?
>
> *Ted:* I'm a sales manager for a top company. I know I can do the job, that I'm qualified and that I deserve the position, but I'm having anxiety attacks again.

D.V.: Again?

Ted: Yes. Right after I was told I got the promotion.

D.V.: Again? An earlier anxiety. When did you first feel anxiety?

Ted: Four years ago.

D.V.: What were you doing then?

Ted: I was in sales for the same company but on the road.

D.V.: When did the first attack occur?

Ted: I can't remember.

D.V.: See if you can; try.

Ted: Well, I was in traffic.

D.V.: Where were you going?

Ted: I don't know; downtown somewhere.

D.V.: Why?

Ted: To buy a pair of pants.

D.V.: What kind of pants?

Ted: Dress pants! For a fancy party.

D.V.: Were you in tight financial straits at the time?

Ted: (*laughs*) How did you guess? I'm always in financial difficulty.

D.V.: Why did you need the pants?

Ted: Well, that was the question I was asking: Did I need them? Could I afford them?

D.V.: What did you decide?

Ted: (*laughs*) That I didn't need them and that I couldn't afford them, but I was going to buy them anyhow. (*another laugh*)

D.V.: How did you plan on paying for them?

Ted: (*with great convincing ease*) Oh, I would just work harder, sell more product, and make more on commission. Actually, I was always catching up.

D.V.: Wait a minute. In your new job as sales manager, are you on commission or on salary?

Ted: Salary (*seems sad*).

D.V.: What was that feeling?

Ted: A little discomfort.

D.V.: So you're trapped in a fixed salary. There is no longer a way to make up for your impulsive spending.

Ted: You're right. Because the first thing I did when I got the promotion was to start looking at a new car, and I realized that I couldn't afford it, and I felt anxiety in the showroom. I thought it was from sticker shock, but it was from being limited financially. I do feel trapped.

D.V.: I guess you're going to have to learn how to live within a budget.

Ted: You mean live without incentives?

D.V.: That's what the spending means to you? Incentive?

Ted: I rewarded myself for doing work that I disliked. Feels like I'm stuck facing it alone now. I'm the boss. No one to please.

D.V.: So that's what the spending means.

Ted: My gold card was my reward.

Competitive people fear the loss of anything that signifies success. They do not want to be shown up as inadequate or second best. Much of the anxiety they suffer is in preparation for difficult tasks and falls into the category of stage fright more than anxiety attacks. Examined closely, their fear can often be linked to concerns and self-doubts that have long been troublesome. When you suffer paralyzing anxiety prior to an important risk, it may mean that you're trying to accomplish too much too soon and with too little preparation. However, competitive people often feel as if they are impostors and do not deserve to succeed, so they often wonder if the present risk will be their complete undoing.

The loss of control concerns not only controlling types but also competitive and dependent people. Dependent people fear the loss of control over what they love just as much as controlling people do, while, like Ted, competitive people fear losing control of their reputation and financial rewards.

WORKING THROUGH ANXIETY

The kinds of things that make you anxious also reveal your personality type. At different times in your life different issues concern you, and often you feel a mixture of concerns. However, the dynamics of anxiety will always be the same: you are anticipating a loss of love, power, or esteem that you feel helpless to prevent.

To work through anxiety, allow yourself to feel the fear, then determine what it is you fear losing, do what you can to prevent it, and move on. Almost all significant growth is accomplished with some anxiety. The life and the risk are yours. Not finding happiness is a high price to pay for the dubious comfort of avoiding being afraid.

Anxiety is your signal. No one else hears it, so no one else can be expected to care. You are the only one who can take care of *you.*

It is your responsibility to respond.

9

The Skills for Coping with Anxiety:
A Handbook

ANXIETY AS A SPECIAL SENSE

Being emotionally free is being able to use all of your feelings as special senses without defending against them. If you could admit when you're afraid and find the source of your feeling, you would be far more comfortable and self-assured than if you pretended to be brave.

Your fear is like an antenna. If you're open, you can sense danger before you can discern it with your mind. This is not extrasensory perception but rather the ability of the senses to respond to very low levels of stimulus and trigger an integrated emotional response. Just having the notion that something doesn't feel right is usually the first clue that you're in trouble, alerting you to define the problem and thus relieve the stress and, hopefully, the danger.

Cultivate your feelings as a special sense. Don't be afraid to go on hunches. Make a call to a distant friend when you're thinking about him. You'll discover, as many people have, that you're in touch in ways that defy explanation. When you feel anxiety even at a low level, search your mind and be alert. When the overstimulation of modern life threatens to put your senses to sleep, wake up!

172

Feelings, especially anxiety, offer an emotional window to the soul. Know what you fear. Let it help you conquer yourself.

FACING FEARS

Fear can paralyze us or empower us to seek emotional freedom. Let's address some of the most universal fears.

The Fear of Death

Until we've accomplished something we feel truly represents our essence and worth, we all have some fear of death. The feeling reflects a fear that life is being wasted. It begins to fade when life approaches its promise. When you say you fear death you are really saying that you fear you have not lived your true life.

This fear cloaks the world in silent suffering. Let *your* fear of death motivate you to risk examining your true worth and to have a dream for your own life. Let it help you value the moment, act on it, and live in it. Let the fear of eternity inspire you to contribute to building a better world. Let your work become your monument.

The Fear of Illness

Everyone fears debilitation, physical impairment, and helplessness. It is the fear of being dependent on others for our needs without any choice in the matter, the fear of becoming like a child again with no say in our own destiny.

The idea of suffering is universally feared and motivates the healing arts to relieve pain as much as it does the lively arts to make joyous the time of recuperation from fatigue, illness, or boredom.

Let the fear of illness cause you to take care of yourself.

The Fear of Being Hurt

So much of the world is full of pain and much of it is caused by our own indifference or our failure to allow others equal access to life's promise. If we give to others, we fear we will be diminished, when in fact the opposite has always proved to be true. We can never be without pain, but we can live without fear of being hurt when all of us feel we have a life worth holding on to because we all have the same chance to be better.

Ironically, avoiding pain does not produce pleasure. In fact, shutting off pain usually increases anxiety. Consider your fear of pain as a guide to emotional freedom. Accept that you cannot eliminate hurt, but learn to know what hurts you most, where the hurt may come from, how, and when.

Don't allow the fear of pain to prolong the painfulness of whatever injury you suffer. Let your fear of injury enhance your resolve to solve your problems as quickly as possible.

The Fear of Abandonment

The fear of abandonment or rejection is much like the fear of death. At the bottom of this fear is the dread of loneliness, of being unlovable. Dependent people especially suffer from these fears.

Let your fear of abandonment inspire you to find a self you love, relate to, and enjoy being with.

Become a person you do not mind being alone with.

The Fear of Failure

Everyone fears failure.

The fear of failure can inspire the search for perfection or invincibility, and indeed it is a fear that motivates many a success, especially those measured by wealth or accomplishments. However, success measured in material terms is mocked by the fact that the success can be compared with one that is greater.

When success is not measured in personal terms, it is always fragile.

Become the standard for measuring your own success. Don't be afraid to move at a pace that is different from that of others. You are your own story, unfolding as you live your life. No one else knows the plot.

Let your failures point out your most important experiences and teach you the most valuable lessons. Be humble. Don't move off the field of battle without assessing the damage and calculating the cost to yourself. If your cause is right, it will gird you toward victory. If your cause is misguided, it will give you the resolve to rethink your plans.

Let your fear of failure prepare you to win, to stay on the field in the midst of the struggle.

The Fear of Missing Out

One of the most powerful universal fears is the fear of being left out, of not having everything life offers. Advertising manipulates this fear when it proclaims which style is fashionable, what restaurant is the right one to be seen in, and what vacation spot is in.

Everyone wants "the good life." But most people will settle for fulfilling a personal dream, being able to pay their bills, being loved and loving back. The truth is that without this nothing else matters. You can ask anyone who has ever been there.

It is not what you have that makes you rich, but what you don't need. A rich man needs nothing.

Let the fear of missing out cause you to cherish friends and to be loyal and compassionate.

Know that you need to belong to yourself before you can belong to anyone else. Forgive your own shortcomings and forgive others so that you can live free of resentment.

Your best life is having the freedom to be yourself. Insist on it. The rest will fall into perspective, and what doesn't come your way won't matter nearly as much.

The Fear of Self-Acceptance

None of us is as good as we want to be or as bad as we fear. Self-acceptance is fearsome because we don't want to believe we are what we are.

Failing to accept yourself leads to pretentiousness at one extreme and continual self-belittling at the other. You must accept yourself just as you are. After all, you're all you've got. No matter what people have praised or criticized about you—your teachers, your parents, your boss, your mate— your life is always evolving and can change in any minute to a higher road, toward a new destination you have never even heard of.

Be open to your heart. Understand that you have a future only when you're true to yourself. You cannot imitate another person's style and be happy. You have a life only when you live your own.

No one who has found himself is poor.

The Fear of the Unknown

The unknown serves as a blank screen onto which we project our ignorance and imagine the worst that can happen to us. We know we are continually falling short of our best intentions in the struggle to create our lives, and we invest the unknown with the same self-doubt. This fear of looking into the unknown limits our creativity and growth.

We fear the unknown will rouse unresolved past problems from forgetful slumber to haunt us in the days of our uncertainty.

We fear the unknown will reveal past deeds and hold them up to derision and scorn.

We fear the unknown because we are afraid we will not escape punishment.

We fear the unknown because we forget that we are good. However, the unknown is empty.

Remember your humanity and have no apprehension

that you will be maligned or mocked for simply being yourself, for telling the truth you perceive.

The Fear of Exposing Weaknesses

We are all afraid of exposing our weaknesses. We're all flawed—selfish, inconsiderate, hurtful, childish, stubborn, rebellious, compliant, and irrational. Instead of dreading exposure, why not simply admit to shortcomings when they're a problem? The fear of exposure can be paralyzing, keeping you from acting and doing your best. All you can do is do the best you can in this moment and when you think you have no more to give, to give just a little more. Giving this extra effort is how you grow.

No one can take advantage of your secrets when you know and accept yourself.

DON'T BE AFRAID OF BEING AFRAID

More than any other feeling, anxiety builds on itself. Remember, anxiety is the least real feeling because it is the expectation of injury that has not yet occurred. Anxiety easily degenerates into worrying for the sake of worrying when you begin imagining even worse situations than the one you're worried about. By constantly worrying about what will happen, you eventually lose your ability to act decisively in the moment. You exaggerate the meaning of an event, making a single loss symbolic of all of the losses you've ever suffered. You hold people up to retrospective analysis of your life and group them with your collection of assorted villains and monsters when they are probably guilty only of a minor mistake.

Most of what happens to us does not matter in the whole scheme of things. That may be an unpleasant concept, but it is largely true. What really matters are the principles we stand for, the truth we cherish, and the love we give as a conduit for a greater love of the world.

But you may not matter in the greater scheme of things.
And yet *we* matter a great deal.

Remember this. It will help you keep your perspective on
what happens to you. The person most afraid of fear is the
person who fears that his life has little going for it. Anything that reflects his self-doubt paralyzes him with fear.

You do not have time to be afraid of being afraid.

You have work to do.

If you don't know yet what that work is, begin looking to
define it.

Anxiety Won't Kill You

It just feels as if it will.

The purpose of anxiety is to alert you to danger.

Don't rush. Take your time to discern whether the danger
is real or imagined.

Decide whether you must act or retreat, speak or observe.

Consider making the simple comment "This makes me
feel uncomfortable."

Putting others on notice that you have a concern brings
their witness to bear on the situation, involves them in
facing a real danger with you, or at least makes them aware
of your discomfort so you're not alone. Most people are
kind, as well as familiar with anxiety, and therefore will be
pleased to assist.

Take a little time to act as strongly as you can.

Be patient.

Expect it to pass.

When it does, let it go.

Investigate the Source of the Fear

Take an inventory. Ask yourself:

"What just frightened me? Something I saw, heard,
smelled, felt, remembered, or dreamed?"

"Is this real, or am I imagining this?"

"Am I in danger? From what?"
"What am I afraid of losing?"
"How can I be hurt?"
"Why is this important to me?"
"What does this feeling remind me of?"
"What am I really afraid of?"
Decide what danger you are in and then act:

- If it is a real danger, protect yourself.
- If it is a realization of a previously unseen problem, learn from it.
- If it is a confirmation of a dreaded belief, try to understand it.
- If a loss has taken place, try to limit the damage.
- If the damage is complete, accept it and save what can be saved.

There is no truth you can discover about yourself that can make you less worthy, even if your worst fear about yourself were proved. In fact you'd be better off, because by knowing the truth you'd learn what problem you had to work on.

Don't make anxiety the problem. Make yourself the problem. There's work to do on yourself—goals to redefine, situations to correct, people you need to notify about your feelings, people you need to forgive, others you need to give up on. Go to work on it.

Anxiety is like a roadside rest area on a busy highway. When you pull off the road, all you do is worry about the road. You don't get any closer to your goal and you don't get any rest. Worse, your vehicle is rusting, and it's running out of fuel. No matter what, you still have to complete your journey.

Confront the Fear

Name your fear. A fear without a name is always made worse by being part of the fear of the unknown. Say to yourself, "I am afraid of . . ." and complete the sentence with the first words that come into your mind. Those words might be "dying, going crazy, losing my mind, losing control, not being able to breathe, going out of the house," but they do not name your real fear. Probe until your answer names the specific loss you've just anticipated.

When you're able to name what you're afraid of, you will find some deep hurt you've ignored. Deal with this hurt using the steps we've outlined. Once the old injury is resolved, anxiety will diminish and fade.

AN ANXIETY JOURNAL

If anxiety is a recurrent problem, you'll find it useful to keep a journal of episodes to help you understand them and put them into perspective. Keeping an anxiety journal is a great way to get a clearer picture of what you consider truly important. If you're in a high-pressure job, isolating your anxious moments and taking time to define the underlying issues will go a long way toward building your confidence. Try keeping a journal for at least a week or two. If you have recurrent anxiety, you might want to keep track for a month or longer.

Put each episode on a separate page of a notebook, as soon after it happens as you can. For each, indicate:

- the time the anxiety started
- how it manifested: as fear, hives, intestinal cramping, involuntary talkativeness, giggling, getting unexplainably high, taking a few drinks, using a chemical substance, or eating compulsively
- what you were doing or thinking at the time it started and just before: Did someone speak? Did you hear or see something?
- the interval between that stimulus and the symptom of anxiety

- what you felt and did in that interval
- what you were afraid of
- what made it worse: Did you contribute to it in any way?
- what made it better: What did you do that helped?
- how long it lasted
- why it ended

After you've made several entries, compare them. Ask yourself:

- Do they have a common thread? Do they all take place at the same time of the day? What is happening then?
- What brings them on? Is it change? What loss could be implied by the change? The loss of love, power, or esteem?
- What runs through your mind before each episode?
- In each case, what gives the stimulus the power to trigger your anxiety? (This is an all-important question.)

If a review of your journal suggests you always have *irrational* fears, you probably haven't probed deeply enough below the surface. It is not terribly useful to admit that you had fear over leaving the house a dozen times. You already know that. Spend the time between episodes trying to label the underlying meanings:

- What reality do you fear facing?
- What failure are you avoiding?
- Why?
- What judgment about yourself do you wish to escape? That you are bad, unlovable, weak, or unworthy? How did this come about?
- Besides fear, is there another emotion you are afraid of expressing? Feeling anger toward a loved one, living or dead, is a good prospect because it is an

emotion you need to express but dread the consequences of. Admitting and expressing hurt is
another.

Using the Journal to Analyze Anxiety Attacks

If you're suffering from anxiety attacks, try to search your
memory and write out your exact recollection of the very
first attack you ever experienced. Each subsequent anxiety
episode has been triggered in some way by similar events,
but the trigger becomes more generalized and harder to
recognize with time. If Barbara, who lost her father and
then experienced anxiety whenever she was by the meat
counter, were not treated, her anxiety might progress over
the years into a phobia. Her anxiety could then be triggered
not only by stopping at the meat counter but by just going
to the supermarket (where she might find herself at the
meat counter), going shopping (where she might find herself in a supermarket), driving (where she might pass by a
supermarket), and finally just leaving the house (for she
might find herself in a car on the road that might pass by a
supermarket). By then, of course, the real source of Barbara's anxiety would seem hopelessly obscure. The older the
anxiety, the more diluted it seems. Eventually, a person
with untreated anxiety just feels afraid of everything.

For this reason it is important to exhaust your memory
collecting the facts, the where and when of the first episode. The why will come later. Take time to examine that
first event in detail. When there are gaps in memory and
understanding, focus on those lapses and try to remember
what went on. If you can't remember for sure, write down
your best guess. The first one that comes to mind without
editing is a good place to start. Analyze your later episodes
of anxiety in the same way. The event that triggers anxiety
has a strong relation to the feelings that are hidden and can
provide a valuable clue by helping to name the fear and
understand it.

MANAGING YOUR ANXIETY

Analyzing your anxiety and coming to understand your fears are challenging but worthy tasks. They won't be completed overnight, but the more you learn about your feelings, day by day, the closer you'll come to emotional freedom. While you're working on this lifelong effort, there are practical ways of managing your anxiety and minimizing its deleterious effects on your everyday life.

Get Through It by Doing as Much as You Can

The more you go about your regular activities, the less likely anxiety is to bother you. Remind yourself that you are remembering an old fear. You overcome fear not by pushing it out of the way but by moving right through it, being aware as you do that you are afraid but are doing what you have to do. It's an old feeling. It can't hurt you.

When you stop your normal activities, you are in effect creating evidence you can point to and say "This stopped me." Go forward. You can always go back to your fear if you have to, but for the moment, keep going forward. Then you can say "I *was* afraid, but it's over now." So keep moving and tell yourself:

"If I don't allow my anxiety to stop me, I will stop my anxiety."

"If I give in and let anxiety get the upper hand, it will take over more and more of my life."

Don't give in and hide. Playing it safe means playing it scared. If your anxiety is so bad you find yourself unable to function, it is best to become involved in an uncomplicated but familiar routine. The more your body is involved, the better, because the more of you that is involved in a normal activity the more normal you will feel.

Some Suggested Activities
• Clean the garage or straighten up some shelves.
• Paint the patio furniture.

- Weed the garden.
- Go to the gym.
- Take a hike.
- Take a bath, do your nails, or give yourself a facial.
- Indulge yourself in one of the arts.

Make your own list of projects to undertake at such times and pick up the necessary tools or equipment beforehand to keep in a special place. Plan projects that will take about an hour.

Resume your normal activities when you're finished. If the hour is late, spend a few moments organizing tomorrow's schedule. Tomorrow, get up an hour early and get into the day.

Don't give in. It's a choice.

Expect It to Get Better

Things will improve in time.

How much time?

How tightly do you want to hold on to your fear? You can hold on to anxiety and run with it or conquer it and move forward.

Most fears are momentary, but if you allow anxiety to gain a foothold, it will exercise emotional squatter's rights and influence how you feel about everything.

Admit It When You Start Feeling Better

If expecting the anxiety to pass is important, recognizing when you feel better is crucial. The moment you admit you're feeling better, you'll get a surge of confidence and feel even better still.

If you question whether the anxiety is lifting, you will find evidence that suggests it is not.

Look instead for evidence that suggests it is passing.

Admit it and believe it.

Be a Little Braver

The highest form of emotional freedom is not measuring your emotions or worrying about being right all the time but being spontaneous so that the emotions you express are current, immediate, and direct. If you can accomplish this, you will be free of all psychological symptoms. You will still have feelings, but they will rise and wane in the moment they occur, and you will move on. This is how you create your life:

State what you feel.

Don't be afraid of offending others.

Don't hold back.

Don't hold on.

Express yourself and move on.

It all boils down to this: be a little braver. Not a lot braver. You don't have to conquer the world. You just have to be a little bit braver.

Face the fear. Go ahead.

Postpone quitting in the face of anxiety. Keep doing what you were doing. It'll pass.

Remember you are fine, no matter what you're feeling.

Do yourself a favor by assuming the best.

Nothing is going to happen.

If something *is* going to happen, ignoring it for a minute or two isn't going to make a difference. If you truly believe that the next few minutes can make a difference to your ultimate fate (and you're not jumping out of the path of a speeding truck), you're probably fooling yourself.

So if nothing is going to happen in the next minute, maybe nothing is going to happen in the next hour or day or week, maybe even the next month or year.

Take the time to be a little braver. All you have to do is believe that nothing is going to happen this moment. Be braver in this moment.

What does this mean?

Saying no to opening the refrigerator, taking that drink, lighting up.

Take a few slow deep breaths and follow the air in and out.

Count to ten.

Stretch. Wash your face and return to wo

Write out the words BE A LITTLE BRAVER on and post it wherever you tend to have mor ness.

When you act a little braver and don't gi come a little braver.

Now, what was it you were so frightened a ago . . . ?

10

Understanding Anger:
The Resentment over Being Hurt

While anxiety is the anticipation of being hurt, anger is the recollection of experiencing hurt.

The purpose of anger is simple and straightforward: to help express the hurt.

Anger takes many forms, ranging from being annoyed, irritated, displeased, critical, teed off, resentful, indignant, harassed, exasperated, vexed, or embittered to feeling animosity, enmity, rage, wrath, hate, fury, or vengeance to being homicidal.

This range of emotions makes it clear that the more time that has elapsed between the hurt and the anger, the greater the intensity of the anger and the less rooted in reality it feels. Indeed, at its extreme the longer you hold on to anger the crazier the anger feels.

Thus the wisdom of expressing hurt when it occurs is obvious. And, in fact, the purpose of anger is to provide you with the energy to display hurt when it happens. Understanding this makes the main characteristic of anger clear. Anger is naturally inclined to be expressed, not a reflective feeling like anxiety or a passive, self-absorbing sensation like hurt. Anger is designed for action, such as retaliation or self-defense.

The more emotional debt you carry, the more you dread getting angry for fear of losing control of stored-up emotions and the more out of touch with reality you become. When a hurt in the present preoccupies you and leads you to believe you'll lose control, it's a good indication that you're living in the past.

No one likes being angry. Anger is difficult to contain; it has a way of leaking out all over the place, making you feel disorganized and brittle. The feeling is contained in the muscle groups. You raise your voice and slam doors. You get rough, push and pull too hard, break things by mistake, and drive too fast. Angry energy turns innocent everyday activities into angry expressions. It alters the way you perceive reality.

Usually just as you're about to act, your mind takes over and you reconsider your situation. Do you really want to start something right here and now, in front of these people? Do you want to risk getting hurt in return? Do you want to voice the terrible comments you've been rehearsing and go to war? Are you taking it all too seriously? Do you instead go within and wait for the day when revenge will be yours? Do you turn the other cheek, snub the other person, considering him too far beneath you to be angered by him?

THE DYNAMICS OF ANGER

What happens when you get angry? The pattern is always the same. You suffer an injury, delay a moment or two in its expression, and feel resentful over being hurt. You measure the moment, try to determine what went on, and decide what to do. Then you make your hurt known, often by expressing it in an angry way.

To achieve a satisfactory resolution and let go, the volume of anger you express must feel appropriate to the injury you've suffered. If your anger is insufficiently expressed, the remnant resentment queues up waiting for expression at the next injury, when it joins forces with the rest of your stored-up anger. On the other hand, if the anger you show is excessive or vindictive, you end up hurting the person who has hurt you. You are most likely to be venting old stored-up feelings when you snap at people, bark, lecture, criticize, undermine, deprecate, or point out in excruciating detail how your hurt proves that the other person is bad.

Some people are themselves so easily and deeply wounded that you feel inhibited about hurting them with your anger and tend to hold back to protect them. Don't! Deal with these people by expressing your present hurt simply and fully. Chances are that they will indeed feel guilty about what they did, but you have avoided a build-up of anger that would hurt them—and you—more deeply.

HOW THE THREE PERSONALITY TYPES EXPRESS ANGER

Each of the three character types suffers an anger that has a unique flavor, and each is inhibited in expressing it according to its particular defensive systems.

Temper Tantrums—the Dependent Pattern

Dependent people tend to swallow their anger or deny it for fear of offending or risking rejection by the person on whom they depend. Their resentment builds up inside. Finally, when the stored-up hurt is no longer containable, they dissolve into a fit of anger and act much like children, expressing their anger and hurt at the same time. This display often prompts the people they need most to reject them or disregard their complaint as overstated, adding further fuel to the fire.

Private Ruminations—the Controlling Pattern

Anger is at once the easiest and most difficult emotion for controlling people to express. On the one hand it gives them a sense of strength, but on the other it makes them feel anxious about losing control of all the other anger they stored up; so they have to hold themselves in check. Because they tend to *think* about feelings rather than feel and express them, they often obsess about their anger, exaggerating it so that when they are triggered into feeling angry they fear being overwhelmed. It is this fear of losing control that masters them more than their fear of how the other person would retaliate. They prefer to go back to the revenge planning board and get lost in angry fantasies, all the while leaking anger to the world around them with their critical unsupportive attitude.

Public Displays—the Competitive Pattern

Competitive people tend to be explosive in their expression of anger. Because they've pretended for so long not to have been hurt, when a feeling of anger is permitted into expression it quickly kindles an outburst, often full of spite and surprising cruelty. The competitive person is displacing self-hatred onto others. The angry performance is usually quick and very often over as soon as it has begun. Include here drinks thrown into someone's face at a party, stepping on a rival's gown, making a cutting remark, asking embarrassing questions in front of the entire staff, pointing out obvious shortcomings in an attempt to humiliate.

Of course, as a mixture of all three types, the way you express anger involves a combination of responses. When you're disappointed by someone whose love you depend on, you can act like a dependent person, especially in the privacy of your relationship (which is why relationships sometimes seem to bring out the childish side of your personality). In situations where you are struggling for control you may express your anger in a punitive way, and when you suffer a failure or feel exposed in public you may try to retaliate in a public way.

SOURCES OF ANGER: HOW TO REACT

Betrayal

The violation of trust is an insult to your self-esteem. The act of betrayal is a statement that someone does not regard you as deserving respect, loyalty, or consideration.

There is no point in trying to get even or make things right with a person who betrays you. Such people have a low sense of morality, social justice, or fairness, as well as little sense of their own self-worth. Appeals to their sense of decency go unheeded, and trying to communicate feelings to them is largely a waste of time because they do not understand these issues. Fighting with them just lowers you in their estimation and validates their actions. There is little victory in the conquest of fools.

The way to deal with people who betray you is to separate from them as cleanly as possible with as little emotion as they felt in hurting you. An attempt to get even feels like maintaining contact with them, and they can interpret any feelings toward them, even rage, as meaning you still care.

Betrayal most commonly occurs in love relationships, when one party has been unfaithful. The first time it happens, it is important to address the betrayal and display your hurt feeling. That way you may come to new ground, where you are certain that the problem has been corrected and a greater level of honesty has been pledged. A person who betrays you twice, however, is likely to betray you forever. One who cannot feel pain in seeing your hurt the first time and learn from it will be hardened by subsequent lapses not to feel at all.

Lies

Being lied to means that someone does not feel you deserve to hear the truth. It hurts deeply.

Love can function only in a truthful relationship, because love is the truth, the one incorruptible standard of your life.

Someone who lies to you is not loving you.

Someone who lies to you is telling you that you are
without worth.

Someone who lies to you is insulting your intelligence.

Someone who lies to you is merely hoping to postpone
the time when you'll know the difference.

How do you know when someone is lying to you? You
have the thought, This doesn't make sense. You wonder
why you're being given this information in this way. You
have a vague sense of hurt, the pain of deception. The
other person is blinking, avoiding eye contact or staring
right in your eye for an uncharacteristically long time,
seems fidgety or constricted, sweats, stresses, and exhibits
a need for you to buy this version of the truth. You know it's
a lie but can't say why.

When you suspect someone is lying to you, just say "Is
this the truth?" "This doesn't sound right." "This doesn't
make sense." "Why are you telling me this?" "What difference does this make?" "Are you sure you're not making
this up?"

If you're sure the other person is lying but won't admit it,
listen to the answer dispassionately and finally say "OK,
let's assume what you say is so. Now, what do you want?"
You want to know the motive. It will make it easier to deal
with the situation.

If the person admits to having lied, ask these questions:
"What were you afraid of telling me and why?" "What did
you want?" "Why didn't you trust yourself?" "Why are you
telling me the truth now, and how can I be sure you are?"

When you find yourself lying to someone, correct yourself as soon as possible, even in midsentence if necessary,
saying: "I just misspoke. What I meant to say was . . ." "I
exaggerated a bit. The truth is really that . . ." "Is this really
true? Wait. I may be wrong here." "And then again it could
be . . ."

Allow yourself the flexibility to be open. Do not cover up
your lie. You do not need to explain each and every one of
your past deceptions to others, but do work on discovering
some sense of what you lie about. The lies you tell are

merely a way of avoiding a painful truth. Try to understand what you are hiding.

Malicious Intention

The most difficult part of being hurt on purpose is not the hurt itself but the betrayal of your trust. Finding out that the other person was *not* better than you expected makes you question your judgment and wonder about your ability to protect yourself. Were you too trusting, too blind, or—let's face it—too needy?

The fact is that there are people who don't care about other people's feelings and who will do whatever it takes to get what they want. You need to identify these people as quickly as possible. Someone who has hurt you on purpose is doing you a favor. Now there is no mistaking the intentions of such people—they have made their true selves known to you.

When you have a suspicion about another person, don't bury it. Allow it to come to the surface and ask yourself:

"Is this person out for himself?"

"Is this person desperate?"

"Is this person mean-spirited?"

"Who else has this person hurt? Why?"

These are difficult questions to ask only if you're afraid of the answers. When people you love hurt you with malicious intent, your love and your need to be accepted often buy your silence and diminish your willingness to dispute them. You hope you aren't hearing what you think they're saying.

Your hope is your enemy.

You need to accept the truth when someone hurts you maliciously. If you continually tolerate injury by this person, you're trapped by your need to win his approval, which you should have already won by who you are, not what you do.

Speak up as soon as you realize you've been hurt. State your case succinctly and directly. All you want to accomplish is to make the other person aware that you are on to him. Don't tolerate any more mistreatment. If you need what the other person has been giving you, let your pain remind you that it's time to start providing for yourself.

The first time someone hurts you maliciously it is his fault.

The second time it is yours.

Indifferent Treatment

You feel inner turmoil when you are ignored, your pain is discounted, your suffering is belittled, and your interests are disregarded.

You tremble with a mixture of self-hatred and anger when your best efforts are minimized by others, and you wonder why you're wasting your time and energy.

You want to matter.

You want your contribution to make a difference.

You want to have meaning and purpose in life.

You want your love to be able to heal others.

You want your gifts to be appreciated.

You do not want to be forgotten.

It is because of your innate goodness that you get hurt and angry at the indifference of others toward you. It is because you want to matter and be part of the bigger picture of humankind that you are hurt by anything that suggests that you have nothing to say, nothing of worth to contribute.

But the larger truth is that when you're treated with indifference your inner doubts are awakened and your old self-castigation is revived. You know that you may not be all you want to be. You know you've fallen short of your goals, perhaps by taking the easy route. You review the evidence on which you think other people are basing their indifferent reaction toward you and wonder if they may be right.

So the degree to which the indifference of others can hurt you is a measure of your lack of self-acceptance.

Remember your worth. You are not perfect. You are growing, getting better. Accept your faults and weaknesses.

Don't expect others to recognize your gifts, encourage you to risk, or be supportive of you. Most people are consumed with their own fears and uncertainties. And the fact that they are is a gift in disguise. It keeps them from looking too closely at your mistakes and failures and gives you time to perfect yourself and learn from those mistakes before you try again and others do take notice of you.

You're most susceptible to the indifference of others when you most doubt yourself, and there may be good reason for that self-doubt. Perhaps your work is not of the quality you desire or you're not functioning at your best. Let your dissatisfaction with yourself lead you to work on your shortcomings. Then the indifference of others will not matter so much, for the truth is it is your indifference to yourself and your failure to do what you need to do to grow that causes you the most pain.

Just beginning to be better will make all the difference in the world.

Devaluation

What is more painful than being told that your feelings don't matter, that you're exaggerating, blowing events out of proportion, making it all up, or being too sensitive?

A person who does not care about your feelings does not care about you. People who devalue others are insensitive, jealous, or envious, insecure and afraid they won't make it. They're critics who cannot create or angry people bearing grudges to vent the self-criticism they cannot admit. It's quite possible that they don't value their own feelings and don't love themselves.

You can never please someone who is not pleased with himself. You can care about others only the way you care about yourself.

What can be more disheartening than to be told your best efforts are not special? When you feel you're being devalued, your first step is to make your feelings known. If you discover that the other person really does not care about you, you have to question why that person has such a place of prominence in your life. The truth is that the anger you feel when you're devalued comes largely from your own low opinion of your work and your failure to believe in yourself enough to make it better.

You have to make yourself the standard for judging your performance and work to please yourself. So do what gives you pleasure. Follow your love. It will always lead you to the right place.

Exploitation

The problem with the anger you feel upon being used is that so much of it is directed at yourself for allowing it to happen.

When do you get used?

You get used when you give more than you should to get more than you think you really deserve or could receive if you just let matters be. Your neediness opens you to be used.

You get used when you try to buy someone's affections, loyalty, or friendship.

You get used when you sacrifice yourself for the sake of others.

The fact that people use others is not proof that they are bad but rather that others were available. Most people aren't evil; they're just lazy, full of self-doubt, anxious about failing, and uncertain about their worth. They don't believe in themselves. They have seen inferior people find their way to the top, persistence rewarded over talent, and love go to the unworthy suitor. When they see a chance to move forward and find your hand outstretched, they take it, pull themselves up, go forward, and may not even say thank you. Nothing personal. Actually, you do it too.

In fact, when most people use others, they don't even think they're doing so. More likely they believe they're making the best of an opportunity.

When you give to other people, do so openly, because it pleases you, and without expecting to get anything in return. Your disappointed expectations cause you to feel used far more than the insincerity of the person you think is using you. The people who are the angriest and most disappointed at being used are those who give with the expectation of being rewarded.

To avoid the anger of feeling used, let go of other people and allow them to be free to seek their own level of performance. Then the people who love you will love you. Those who do not will leave you alone. The people who work for you will be working for themselves and will appreciate the freedom to be their own boss.

WHEN YOU FEEL INHIBITED IN EXPRESSING YOUR ANGER

When you don't express anger, you sullenly drift into your usual day but are a little more likely to find fault with others, a little less likely to see the humor in a joke. You are not as free to provide a creative response to a problem. Your memory is a little slower. You gravitate away from emotionally interactive challenges toward the mechanical. Thus you are more likely to work on getting the computer screen to focus than to write the report.

Your held-in anger is sometimes blurted out inappropriately—at the wrong time, at the wrong place, toward the wrong person. As it remains unresolved, you become single-minded. Your hatred is sometimes the only purpose you feel, and for this reason alone, staying angry seems to justify itself.

Holding in anger also has a way of shaping your attitude. Remember the old question "Is the water glass half full or half empty?" Saying it is half full suggests you are an optimist, while saying it is half empty implies you are a pessimist. The greater truth, of course, is that the glass merely contains water. It is not merely your perception of the water but your choice of the scale to measure it that skews the evidence. If you're in emotional debt, the water glass is never half full or half empty. It is always empty. Your attitude becomes the reality.

Sources of Ambivalence in the Expression of Anger

It's a rare person who does not experience some ambivalence in expressing anger. How does such a natural feeling become inhibited from expression? Here are some of the main reasons.

- It's not nice. You've been taught that it's not nice to express anger toward your parents and other people you're supposed to respect. The damage to a child who was prohibited from expressing anger over a modest hurt is greater than the damage to a child who suffered great hurt but was allowed freedom of expression.
- Someone could get hurt. Your anger has built up to the point where your angry fantasies make you concerned about your goodness. You worry about being evil and exposing yourself and so hold back.
- You fear being misunderstood. Reciting the details of old injuries is like trying to describe a film you saw when you were a child. It's too distant to be confident about the details. Therefore, discuss the *impact* the source of hurt and anger had on you, not merely the details you remember.
- You fear rejection. Anger frightens you, for it eclipses your self-love. You're afraid that expressing anger will make you feel you *deserve* rejection for being an angry person.
- You fear losing control. Your reason for trying to stay in control is to appear strong and good, but revealing anger presents evidence that you have a negative side.

• You fear admitting vulnerability. To admit feeling angry is to lose the protection of your feigned indifference, and admitting vulnerability can feel like too great a risk to take.

EMOTIONAL DEBT: THE STORY OF ANGER

To understand the dynamics of anger you need to review the concept of emotional debt. A person in emotional debt is living ineffectively and with diminished pleasure in life. Emotional debt is the story of anger—its origin, development, and dynamic legacy. Managing your feelings effectively means staying out of emotional debt. Taking a detailed look at emotional debt will make this clear.

Reactive Emotional Debt: Hurt Becomes Anger

Consisting of the feelings created in response to a particular hurtful event, this is the emotional debt of the moment. It is in the period of reactive emotional debt that you find your bearings, come to realize that you have in fact been hurt and that the particular loss or injury is important to you. You usually express yourself and get over the problem.

This is the "Hey, wait a minute" emotional debt in which you overcome your feeling of being stunned and gather your strength to express your hurt and anger. This period of reacting can take a while if the loss is life-shattering. Still, this is the shallow part of emotional debt, for the emotions being dealt with are in immediate memory and usually related to a specific well-defined loss or injury. This period lasts for a few minutes to a few weeks.

The resolution of reactive emotional debt is in the initial reaction, in telling the person you are injured, negotiating the injury, notifying the person who hurt you of your displeasure, and in so doing, revealing your vulnerability but also affirming your intention to resolve the conflict, find peace, and move on.

Recent Emotional Debt: Hurtful Events Merge

Recent emotional debt defines a collection of current losses or injuries that have not been expressed adequately and so are presently accumulating.

Sometimes you're so stunned by a painful event that you suffer a second, third, and even more losses before you're able to deal with the first. Sometimes your ambivalence and confusion prevent you from taking timely definitive action.

As the unexpressed anger from these recent feelings combines, it builds and from time to time overwhelms the defenses that fail to contain it. Thus the scene is set for easily triggered emotional outbursts.

Often the feelings contained in recent emotional debt have been generated by the same ongoing problematic life situation. The most typical example is a love relationship during a period of unresolved recent conflicts. The partners become guarded, so additional hurts are also at least partially held in. This stretches their defenses to the limit and creates an unstable situation in which any or all of these recent feelings may seek expression at the same time, when some new hurt brings them to the surface. This is why certain couples seem to fight all the time.

When these recent feelings do burst forth, additional injury may occur. But this can also be an opportunity to clear the air. If the partners are truthful in expressing themselves, positive feelings often suddenly reappear, right in the middle of the fighting, seeming to validate the love that has been there all the time but forgotten in the hidden resentment. This can also, however, be a time of desperate action. The feelings of recent emotional debt are usually accessible, even preoccupying, and the pressure can motivate you to implement important decisions when you're not at your most clearheaded.

Recent emotional debt can tip the balance of expression either way. The combined energy of the feelings contained tends to push them all toward expression, creating an opportunity for you to develop emotional openness. Or the negative implications of these unexpressed feelings may cause you to doubt yourself and thus repress your feelings even more deeply.

The situation is further complicated as feelings contained in recent emotional debt awaken older feelings from remote emotional debt. For example, a dependent person who experiences several rejections in a short time denies those rejections, which causes the injured feelings to accumulate as recent emotional debt. The hurt is then converted into anger, which lowers the dependent person's self-esteem. In time the person recollects as a sense of negative familiarity similar feelings stored in remote emotional debt, which leads to the feeling that the present situation is the way it has always been and will always be. "What's the use?" the person asks, giving up and inviting further complications into his life.

Remote Emotional Debt: Resonant Association

The feelings contained in remote emotional debt have long been bound by the defenses and so are "remembered" through resonant association rather than direct recall. This occurs when an event in the present parallels something in the past that you cannot fully recollect, especially something dreaded, and brings it into awareness as a vague feeling of disquiet.

At first this recollection is incomplete, often consisting of the memory of the feeling without any other concrete facts. As the memory of the feeling grows, specific details come forward, especially visual images. However, this progression into integrated awareness can be shut off at any point as your defenses regroup and you try to maintain some sense of emotional equilibrium by holding the fearful past in check. Sometimes the point at which this recollection process stops can remain the only accessible memory for years. At other times a breakthrough takes place and the past is recalled in detail.

This pattern is typical of traumatic childhood experiences that have been defensively intercepted. The child experiences a painful event, typically an abuse, and wishes to forget it. The child blocks out the memory, but the painful old feelings resonate associatively throughout life, continually suggesting dreaded implications in innocent situations. A vague feeling of having been involved in something bad can actually make the child believe he is trying to hide some terrible secret about himself, something bad he has participated in but cannot define. His self-worth is placed in doubt. This forms an inner core of insecurity that defies all attempts at reassurance, because down deep the child believes he is bad.

This residual belief that he is bad persists and can motivate self-destructive behavior and extreme moodiness. Flashbacks of traumatic events that have been worked through incompletely use the same mechanism of resonant association. The original events are finally brought forward by actively desiring to know or when reality reinforces surges of awakening that can no longer be denied.

When Skip, a forty-year-old businessman, was sexually propositioned by two men while innocently walking down the street, he had a feeling of panic and ran away. He was struck by the urgency of the feelings that suddenly took him over and directed his flight. Over the next few days he began to remember having been raped by an older cousin while another restrained him. After the violation he defended himself and informed the cousin that he would retaliate and inform his parents.

He was never bothered again, but he kept the matter secret. For almost thirty years he blocked the memory, and when it returned by associative resonance Skip was overcome by a welling up of remote anger and fear that had been suddenly summoned into consciousness. If prior to the proposition he'd been asked about the incident, he would have been unable to remember it at all. However, being placed in a *similar-feeling situation* energized his dormant memory and brought it forward.

This example represents the characteristic way current injuries or threats of injury activate hidden old memories through emotional resonance. Again, the feeling is often reawakened without specifically recalling the event originally associated with it. When this happens, the person either suppresses the reawakened feeling again or is driven to make sense of it and resolve it. When the insult involves sexual abuse, the victim typically feels a certain amount of guilt for remaining silent, for not doing more to protect himself, or is angry at himself for being so vulnerable and helpless. So recalling details directly can be fraught with horror. When there is sexual arousal on the part of such a victim, even if it is only slight, it can confirm to the person that he is bad. Thus the incident is more often repressed to protect the victim from himself, not from the villain.

When reawakened remote emotional debt does not bring forward a specific recollection, it often presses itself into awareness as a sense of nostalgia, a vague but urgent longing for something that cannot be defined, an obscure emptiness, an unexpected empathy, or a sudden poignancy associated with commonplace things.

WORKING THROUGH ANGER

If you deal with your present emotions, you lower the stress in your daily life and thus diminish the power of present events to activate old memories and throw you into demoralizing helpless states. In fact, while learning about the sources of your past injuries may go a long way toward granting you insight, it is the practical techniques of dealing with feelings in the present that will free you from suffering. If you can make your emotional transactions in the present more spontaneous and appropriate, you will feel much better even if you're burdened by old emotional problems. In addition, as you learn to express your hurt in a timely fashion, some of the older pain will be pulled into

Character Type and Emotional Debt

	Dependent Type	Controlling Type	Competitive Type	Mature Type
Gets angry at anything that symbolizes:	Powerlessness, being controlled, helplessness, abandonment, being bullied, rejected, abused, teased, taken unfair advantage of	Being cheated, disobeyed, lied to, deceived, bested in a power struggle. Any injustice may launch retaliation.	Being embarrassed, failing, committing a social *faux pas*, rejection in favor of someone else, being made a fool of, mockery and scorn, humiliation, defeat	All of the preceding can hurt, but the mature type is most disappointed with personal shortcomings, failure to do or be his best, being dishonest, giving up too soon.
Fear that inhibits expression of anger/ hurt:	That expression will make matters worse and push people further away. That the person will be even worse off, more alone	That expression will bring attention to his mistakes, weaknesses, imperfections and invite further rebellion	That expression will reveal the depth of the person's hurt and show others that he really cared and was defeated in a cause he really wanted to win	That expression will hurt others unnecessarily and do further damage. Tends to do something to make it better rather than complain or feel self-pity.

	Dependent Type	Controlling Type	Competitive Type	Mature Type
Nature of the emotional debt	Angry vulnerability, resentful, whiny, sees rejection everywhere, acts hurt, guilt producing, throws tantrums	Vengeful and punitive, angry obsessional thinking, energy directed inward as controls take over, constricted, critical	Brittle anger with histrionic display, vindictive, spiteful, may ignore injury entirely and become hyperactive to prove invincibility	Tries harder to correct mistakes, uses the lesson contained in the injury to show the way. Lets others lie in the beds they made without rescuing them. Lets go as soon as possible.

the expressive emotional pathway and be resolved by proxy.

No matter when an injury occurred, all pain is resolved in the present.

To begin this process, try to maintain an attitude of hopefulness and self-belief. It's possible to get better by simply being more honest with yourself. You will be amazed by the extent to which your past problems seem to resolve as you do.

Describing a problem as very deeply hidden simply means it is old. Superficial emotional problems are merely of more recent vintage. While each new crisis has the potential to stir old problems into awareness, it also presents the opportunity to look more deeply within, understand yourself, and grow once more.

11

The Skills for Working Through Anger: A Handbook

PROBLEMS IN EXPRESSING YOUR ANGER

Since anger is old hurt, whether recently experienced or long buried, it is often difficult to express it in a way that relieves it and at the same time makes sense to the person with whom you are angry. The other person may have forgotten the incident you wish to bring up, and a denial may complicate matters by deepening your hurt. Because you may be aware of only part of your old hurt, when you bring it up you may be told that the way you remember it is not the way it happened.

You may have a tendency to become tongue-tied and frustrated when you express your feelings. You may retreat when you meet the first sign of resistance, pretending that the matter was unimportant. If you try to bring the matter up again later, you will only annoy other people who will think you are beating a dead horse—so it will be even harder to make your point.

Your anger may have swelled within you to such frightening proportions that you believe expressing any of it could do damage to everyone.

This chapter provides practical techniques for overcoming these obstacles. To start with, always bear these points in mind:

- No matter how diplomatically you express your anger, someone is likely to be at least uncomfortable and perhaps hurt because of it.
- Other people have other viewpoints. You should not expect to change them. You have to work with them as they are.
- In the *very best* of all expressive emotional transactions you are allowed to express your hurt. The other person is willing to hear your side, listens quietly without correcting, and expresses some sadness that you have suffered. If you expect more than that, you'll be disappointed.
- Your point of view, while it makes sense to you and feels right, is not the absolute truth but a composite—distorted, perhaps exaggerated—of many stored memories. So don't be surprised if the other person disregards the seriousness of your petition.
- When you create an expressive opportunity, get as much out as possible. Remember, it is a moment in time when the past and present communicate. Old wounds reopened are naturally inclined to close and heal as quickly as possible. Repeated attempts to go back and reopen an issue interfere with the healing process. Make the adjustment you wish to make. Let all your concerns come forward, leaving minor additions and corrections for later. Then let the healing proceed.

EXPRESSING CURRENT AND RECENT HURT

Ideally, whenever you're hurt, you should simply say so, using the techniques we've discussed, and be done with the incident right there on the spot. The matter is settled while the feelings are fresh.

However, most people are not so aware of their feelings: the time isn't always right to be open; bravery falters; other people walk into the room; the other person is vindictive or in a position of power, so the feeling is postponed. The result is, of course, that the hurt is allowed to evolve into anger and is stored in reactive emotional debt.

To express feelings of this reactive type, all you need to do is to get the other person's attention, recall the incident that just happened, and state your hurt.

Do not begin by stating your anger. Starting with your anger makes the other person defensive, which is the worst place to begin. Instead, begin by revealing your hurt. Indicate your disappointment, betrayal, injury, and loss of faith. Admit to being angry if you're asked, but even then come back to being hurt. If you express all of your hurt openly, you'll find some anger is naturally attached to it and will resolve as the hurt is released.

Don't use this opportunity to make the other person feel guilty. If you do, you'll find yourself embroiled in a bitter argument, suffer more injury, and leave the scene mistakenly convinced that you'll always be misunderstood in addition to being resented for being punitive and irrational.

It is typical after expressing hurt feelings to feel additional brief surges of hurt and anger of lesser intensity for a day or so, but they should subside quickly. If some additional hurts come to mind afterward and you want to state them, having already broached the subject should make this easier to accomplish. Keep these additional comments to a brief phone call or a one- or two-minute meeting. Remember, the other person will already feel chastised, and it's easy to overdo it and start venting again. So approach the person with a feeling of friendliness, say thank you beforehand, and state that you're also calling to see how he is doing and to support completeness and closure. Weave your additional comments into these remarks without making them sound like you're continuing to pile on complaints. Close by telling the other person you feel better and appreciate being listened to.

Of course if you happen to be saddled with unrelated older anger, you may find that after expressing your recent hurt, waves of old anger still come forward, spurred into awareness by resonant association with recent events. Stay focused on releasing the present hurt. Try to keep your expression under control, remembering that communicating your hurt is your goal, but acknowledge to yourself that there must be other reasons why you are so angry.

To discover them, ask yourself:

- "Who else am I angry at?"
- "What other hurt do I remember?" The very first injuries that come to mind deserve your attention, for these are the past injuries stirred to awareness again.
- "Are there other people who need to know they hurt me?" Name them!

These older feelings are your responsibility to resolve, and even though they may have been recalled by a particularly hurtful act in the present, expressing the overflow to the person who just hurt you is almost never wise. You will only hurt the other person and end up feeling guilty and further inhibit the expression of your old feelings.

EXPRESSING AN OLDER INJURY

How do you express older feelings, feelings you can barely grasp? How do you confront someone when the events that caused your hurt have likely grown remote from that person's memory?

How do you deal with your anger at someone who has mellowed with age, with whom you now have a "good" relationship, without undoing the hard work of reconciliation you achieved over the years?

How do you bring up issues from the difficult past that have never been discussed openly, especially in a family that will only accuse you of making the good times bad?

These are common problems in psychotherapy, where patients are continually uncovering old emotions, reexperiencing them with great intensity, and feeling an urgent need to disclose their secret hurt. The answer is straightforward. If this situation is not handled carefully, however, it can create more problems than it resolves.

First, it's especially important to remember that the defenses that have kept your feelings in place have also distorted them. All of us in this position collect and arrange information to support our own case. We rationalize and explain and carry on internal justification. Most of this supporting evidence is so remote and personal that it is inaccessible and cannot be corroborated, so count it as inadmissible and accept that you have a one-sided view of your situation. Bombarding the other person with facts, acting controlling or critical, is not going to get you closer to your goal. It will only cause further alienation, and you will be labeled the hurtful party. You will only be hurt again.

Remember, your goal is to release your feelings and let the other person know of your hurt and close the matter.

Second, before going ahead, consider how important it is to you to express your feelings to this person. Sometimes just becoming aware of your hurt without telling the other person will be enough to resolve the situation. If so, don't waste your efforts on trying to achieve total victory.

Third, be aware of the possible frustrations. How amenable is the other person to listening to others' opinions in general? Some people just won't listen to anyone and will automatically shut you off. This doesn't mean that you shouldn't try, but know what you're up against.

Fourth, be sure you know what you want to get across. What do you want to tell this person? You should be able to state your concern in a few words that relate directly to the hurt you suffered. Be definite and clear in your own mind.

Finally, keep a specific goal in mind. What would be the best result you could reasonably expect from an open interchange with this person? Remember, you can't get blood from a stone. Allowing yourself to come up against an impossible challenge will only fill you with defeat and a sense that expressing feelings and finding relief is futile.

Getting Old Anger Out

If you've decided that you need to tell the other person so you can find peace, go ahead, but keep your wits about you. You don't want to present yourself like a returning emotional comet, demanding the clock be turned back.

To begin with, tell the person who hurt you that you've been undergoing a period of growth during which you've been reevaluating your life, your goals, and your feelings and that you would appreciate input to help you sort out what you're recalling.

If possible, sit down face to face with the person. The sort of matters you'll be discussing are probably going to be serious, and you'll have emotions welling up in you, so it's important that you begin in the most amiable manner possible.

Be generous. Share your appreciation for the opportunity to talk.

Matter-of-factly bring the person into the subject area.

Set the scene—how inexperienced you were, how frightened, how confused, what your expectations were, what you'd been going through just prior to the event—and then indicate that you were hurt.

Tell your hurt, how it felt, why you couldn't speak up, what you wanted to do, why you could not, why you held it in, and how it has affected you.

Stay in the hurt state. Don't allow it to progress to anger.

When you're finished, ask for a reaction.

The other person may be surprised, dumbstruck, pained, embarrassed, flooded with guilt, may just not give a damn, or may be angry you brought this up again.

Remember, even if there were no painful disagreement between you, the other person would have a point of view quite different from your own. When your pain is involved, you're more likely to interpret the other person's insistence on his point of view as an attempt to avoid taking responsibility for the injury, but doing so may be natural, not an avoidance.

After you've expressed your hurt, be still. Don't expect anything. Just feel your sense of release and the relief it brings. As you do, indicate that you feel better just for getting this off your chest. Don't exaggerate the feeling of hurt to make your point.

The other person may or may not respond. Continue to listen and observe the emotional posture revealed in dealing with your disclosure. Remember, your communication is going to be perceived as a bombshell. So just observe. With your hurt out of the way you have a chance to view this person with more objectivity. Don't waste the moment by demanding that the other person agree to an unconditional surrender. Use it to learn by seeing how he or she manages this stress. You may finally understand that you are dealing with an emotionally nonfunctional person. You may suddenly find yourself face to face with the old villain. You may discover a new ally. So approach this moment from your most mature point of view to see both the possibilities and the impossibilities of getting the other person to change and understand.

Thank the person for listening.

If the peace pipe is passed, accept it and offer forgiveness.

Repeat how much better you feel.

MANAGING THE ANGER IN OTHERS

WHEN THE REAL TARGET IS SOMEONE ELSE

It is impossible to live with someone and not be targeted from time to time with old stored-up anger. This is truer nowhere than in your close relationships, for it is here that you lower your guard, where your greatest unrealistic expectations lie, and where the unsolved pain of your past symbolically tries to have its most frequent expression because it is stirred to awareness by your relationship's intimacy.

When you're in the middle of an argument in which you're receiving more criticism or accusation than you feel you deserve, try to put the absurdity of the attack in perspective before responding.

If the attack feels inappropriate or so overblown that it clearly doesn't fit the current context, you can change the direction of the argument from useless escalation to clarity by using a few simple techniques:

As your partner is expressing the feelings that don't make sense to you, hold up your hand. Don't speak until your partner stops. Then ask, "Does all of this have to do with me? Is it possible that you're really angry at someone else?"

Don't respond even if you're attacked.

Wait for the situation to subside and ask again, with understanding and sincerity, "This doesn't feel like it's about me. To whom should this anger really be addressed?" Be sure you're not using this technique to avoid taking responsibility for hurting your partner before continuing.

You can also say, "I know you feel hurt because I did what I did, but the amount of anger you're expressing sounds old and more properly directed at someone else." If you think you know who the real culprit is, you can suggest something like "I think you're angry at your mother for disappointing you, and when I disappointed you, you just remembered the old hurt and took it out on me. I understand. If you want to express your anger at your mother, I'll be happy to listen and keep you company, but I don't see any reason I should be the target for all of this. I'm on your side."

Invite your partner to take the stage and portray anger at the person from the past. You can act as coach, but be aware that egging your partner on excessively will feel manipulative. Once your partner is openly expressing past feelings, you can just let things proceed.

This technique must be used with care:

- Because it requires too much knowledge of the other person's inner life and requires a tacit permission to discuss personal details, it will not work in a casual relationship.
- *Always* be sure you're not

using it to avoid taking responsibility for your own actions.

- You can't allow yourself to get consumed by the anger of the moment. You need to retain some distance when things get heated up so you can identify the inappropriateness of the feeling. If you do get involved in the heat of the argument and then try to divert the anger away from you, it will be seen as a ruse—and at that stage it may well be.

WHEN YOU *ARE* THE CULPRIT

If you should happen to be on the receiving end of someone's expression of an injury, here are some pointers to keep in mind:

- Don't try to prove your innocence. Doing so will be read as an avoidance.
- Just hear the pain. That is the greatest gift you can give.
- Say you're sorry that the other person has suffered.
- Refrain from making statements of blame or saying that the person deserved it, is exaggerating, or is making it up.
- Again, accept the other's pain as real. There is some truth to it even if the story feels out of touch with reality.
- Thank the other person for being so brave and telling you and say that you hope your relationship can be more open and freer as a result of this communication.
- Remember you will probably hear a lot of distortion, outright confusion, and some things that are not true. Avoid the temptation to set the other person straight. Just listen. Realize that the person whose feelings are being given expression is a much younger self, trapped for years in resentment and hurt.
- If the other person has a valid point, concede it. Explain your viewpoint, but vulnerably. Admit what responsibility you feel. Provide additional facts, but not as an excuse. Say you're sorry once more. Listen and consider yourself fortunate for this opportunity to reach a greater level of intimacy.

TECHNIQUES FOR EXPRESSING ANGER IN ESPECIALLY DIFFICULT SITUATIONS

How do you deal with someone who just does not want to hear, who denies or hates you, who has hurt you on purpose and is glad of it and would do it again given the chance?

How do you deal with someone who is punitive and controlling, who will view any expression of hurt as a revelation of vulnerability and a good excuse for attacking you?

How do you deal with someone who is crazy, debilitated, or deteriorated?

How do you deal with someone who will just make matters worse if you tell the truth?

How do you deal with a boss who hurt you?

How do you tell someone who is dead how he or she injured you?

These all represent troublesome situations because expressing feelings is either physically impossible or will create more problems than it resolves. There is a law of emotional economy that must be observed. You can't waste your life energy resolving trivial hurts, and yet you still must find some way to be emotionally free.

The following techniques, designed expressly for these difficult situations, adaptable to a wide variety of circumstances, may seem primitive or even a little like voodoo. Keep in mind that the mechanisms they activate are subtle but valid. More important, they can be extremely helpful in externalizing anger and finding relief.

Making a List of People You're Angry At

Make a list of all the people at whom you're angry. This is your hit list—not a pleasant or civilized term, but it does suit your purpose. Indicate beside each person's name the nature of the injury.

For significant others—that is, people you care about deeply—you may require a separate page to list all the injuries they caused you. Only the people you love are allowed close enough to hurt you deeply and repeatedly.

If you have unsettled business with people who are now dead, their names definitely belong on the list. Don't worry about what you will do with the material; just collect your feelings.

If your list is very long, you are revealing not that so many people have hurt you but that you don't know how to defend yourself properly, speak your feelings, or forgive others in a timely manner.

Looking over the list, do you see any people you will absolutely not forgive? Why? These, then, are the people who exert control over your emotional life. The injuries caused by people you will not forgive live within you like hidden spoilers. For example, if you won't forgive your parents, you may secretly fail so as to disappoint them. I can't think of a higher price to pay for not forgiving another person.

Just for the experience of doing so, and with no intention of following through, next to each name, put down the punishment you would like the person to receive for injuring you and how you would like that to take place. You can be as severe or as lenient as you want, but spell out the punishment. Don't hesitate. Just put down whatever comes into your mind. Writing it down will make you feel better. If you feel you need to explain why the punishment is so severe, you can indicate that, but this is for your eyes only. The truth is that even thinking about beginning to let it out feels better. If you think just writing down the punishment may hurt the other person, you believe in magic and have been living in your head too much, one of the reasons you are so angry now.

If there is something you want to be sure to tell the person, write that down next to the person's name as well.

Keep all of these names and their secret fates in a private place where only you can get at it. From time to time, remind yourself of who is on your list. If you feel forgiveness, you can remove that name from the list.

Writing a Letter

Whether you intend to send the letter or not, the following technique will help you resolve your feelings.

To begin with, you must gather your feelings, recall details, and organize them.

At the top of a page, write down the name of the person you're angry with. Below the name, indicate the things you most want the person to know: how you were hurt, how you felt about it, why that hurt so much, what additional damage you suffered as a result of the person's thoughtlessness, and anything else you feel is important to convey.

Write down everything you feel just as it comes to mind. Don't attempt to put anything in order for now. Just get it all out as it comes. Be as precise as you can. Put down specific facts, hurts, times, places, circumstances, and reactions. When you've written down all the particulars you can think of, gather your written material and put it in a separate envelope for each person.

Keep that envelope in a safe place, preferably where you can see it, such as on a bookcase, just barely visible between two books. Keep it there for a few weeks. Whenever any additional hurtful or angry thoughts come to mind, write them down on cards or scraps of paper and just add them to the envelope.

After a while you'll find that you're running out of new comments to add. When an angry thought that you've already expressed crosses your mind, remind yourself that you've already put it in the envelope. When you think that thought, visualize the envelope in the place you put it and remind yourself that your angry thought is contained with the rest. The point of all this is to tell yourself that the angry thought is out of you. Then you can dismiss it because you know you have already expressed it.

Wait at least a month before ending this accumulation period. At that time, take down the envelope and organize the material in order of importance to you. Begin a letter as follows:

"I have some important feelings that I must share with you. I realize that much of what I have to say may seem only vaguely familiar to you because it is not recent information. Some of this you may have heard before, but not as completely as I now need to tell you. I hope that by your understanding my feelings and point of view we can come to a new understanding."

Then begin with "I have to tell you how you have hurt me." Follow with your list of hurts. Allow a brief paragraph for each hurt, putting down the information important to you.

Conclude by thanking the other person for the attention and say you feel better for sharing all this.

When the letter is complete, read it aloud to yourself. Correct any mistakes. Add and delete as you go.

Take your time to write this letter, but don't make a career of it. Just get it out.

Put the completed letter back in the envelope and wait at least a week. Then reread the letter and correct it so that it perfectly reflects your feelings.

Now that you have your letter or letters, several options are open to you. You can keep the letter on the bookshelf, refer to it, add to it, keep it in a file, and not mail it. Again, from time to time, focus on the fact that these feelings are now outside you. Remember and feel the relief that writing the letter has produced. If just thinking about the letter brings you relief, it's already serving its purpose.

You may use the letter as the basis for organizing your feelings about the other person.

You may use the exercise as a way to train yourself to be more expressive and spontaneous when you're hurt in the future.

Making Contact

If you continually think about the letter, chances are you should consider mailing it or using it as the basis for a conversation with the other person.

There are several ways of going about this.

You can call the person and say you are sending a letter and would like a response to it. If you do this, you are putting your timetable in the other person's hands. If, for example, you're writing to a parent about a childhood hurt, it is likely that the response may be much delayed or not forthcoming at all. In the meantime you will only suffer, anticipating rejection.

If the matter is of great importance to you, it's best to ask to meet with the other person and deliver the letter in person. You'll need to be alone for this conversation. Hand over the letter and ask the person to read it in your presence. Or you may read the letter aloud and hand it over when you're done. You can have the person read it silently while you read it aloud from your copy. This makes the voice of the letter stronger. Delivering the letter is especially useful when the other person inhibits you from being verbally expressive. Ask to read the letter without any interruptions. Be sure the letter takes no more than five minutes to read—ten at the very longest.

When you're finished, invite the other person to respond. You need to hear the other person's pain as well if this closure is to last. Besides, there will always be circumstances that you were unaware of. You want the confrontation to result in a higher level of truthfulness between you. For this to happen you have to be prepared to hear both sides of the truth, let go of the hurt you're expressing in the letter, and allow the matter to come to rest.

Letting go of hurt is the primary act of forgiveness.

People who don't want to forgive keep their hurt smoldering to keep from feeling guilty over their anger. This is also a good definition of suffering.

If the person expresses remorse, you've accomplished your goal. If you want the other person to grovel, eat humble pie, tear his heart out in mourning, and beg you for forgiveness on bended knees while offering to repay you for whatever damage you suffered, you're going to be disappointed.

If you don't feel you have received enough of an apology,

you may be seeing the emotional limits of the other person, and before you express dissatisfaction you should consider whether anything can be gained by expecting or demanding more from the interchange.

The best you may accomplish by such a confrontation is that the other person becomes willing to hear your pain and anger and, while not agreeing with every detail of your story, accepts it as your view of your experience. If you've gotten to this point, you've achieved a great deal. If you haven't, there may be nothing more to accomplish right now, and you may find yourself dealing with a new understanding that you are coping with an emotionally constricted person. It is sad to reach this point, but it is also freeing. Once you see the other person without the impairment of the defenses that bound your anger, you may even feel pity and sometimes a bit foolish that you expected so much from someone so limited.

Venting Pent-Up Emotions

If sending the letter or meeting with the other person face to face is out of the question, when the letter is completed, write it out perfectly as if you were planning to send it, for in a symbolic sense that's what you're going to do. You need to ceremonialize the externalization of your old hurt and anger. To do this you need to express your feelings in a symbolic way that is both memorable and expressive so that you can remember it later on as the time when you let go. The following pages contain several techniques for doing so.

RIDDANCE EXERCISES

I

Go to an empty part of the beach alone just before sundown. The sea, a lake, or a river will do.

You should be alone.

Take off your shoes.

Sit in the sand at the water's edge with the letter in the envelope lying before you on the sand.

Contemplate what you are about to do.

Breathe easily.

Sense your place on the planet. Feel the expanse of water and sky. Focus on where you are right now.

Remember your purpose: to release the feelings in the letter.

When the sun is just a ball touching the horizon, stand up and read your letter in a loud clear voice, expressing all of the emotion it deserves. Don't hesitate to scream or cry or shout whatever comes to your mind during the reading or after you have completed it.

Sit down when the thrust of emotion has past.

Put the letter and the envelope in a little hollow in the sand.

Remind yourself once more of what the letter contains. Remember how you just felt.

Now let calmness take you.

Take a match and light the letter. As you torch it, say "I release these emotions."

As the letter burns, see your pain and suffering being consumed by the flames. See the dark part of yourself cleansed.

When the letter has been burned, gather the ashes in both hands and walk into the water.

Holding the ashes over your head, say aloud, "I am free."

Release the ashes in the very next breeze and let the wind carry the past away.

Wash your hands in the water and wet your face as well.

Step out of the water, stretch out your arms, and say "It is done."

Improvise a dance of forgiveness. You may also laugh and cry.

Later, when similar feelings return, and they do for everyone, don't be dismayed. Don't push them away. Just shut your eyes and remember the scene of riddance and the sense of release you had. Allow yourself to feel whatever

emotions that have momentarily returned and simply release them as you do.

From then on each sunset can symbolize the promise
you made to yourself.

II

Climb a mountain and perform such a riddance ceremony
at the peak. Burn the letter and bury the ashes under a
stone marker.

It is good if the spot can be seen from a great distance so
you can look to it and remind yourself that you released
your feelings in that place.

III

Go to a special place accompanied by a loved one for
support and to bear witness to your act of riddance. You
should be careful in choosing the site of the ceremony. I
encouraged a patient who had a lifetime of manipulation to
write a letter freeing herself from her controlling mother.
Since sending it was out of the question, she decided to
take her letter to a place on a hill overlooking the ocean
and read it with her husband observing her. She had never
been able to express any feelings to her mother, so this
event was filled with expectancy and promise. She went to
the chosen spot and began to read. As she came to the most
emotional part of the letter, which she'd been looking
forward to releasing, her husband called to her in a hushed
voice, "Be quiet. There's a bull behind you." They had
neglected to examine the field and found themselves in a
precarious situation. The bull stood around for the better
part of an hour, during which the woman had a total reca-
pitulation of her frustrated attempts to be open when expressing her feelings to her mother. The feelings built to an
unbearable point, and finally, when the bull meandered
away, she exploded with the rage of a lifetime. That expression changed her life. Still, it's best to pick a safe place for
your ceremony. Choose your site carefully, considering
privacy and freedom from interruption for your recitation.

IV

Take some of the ashes from one of these ceremonies of riddance or burn a copy of your letter and mail the ashes in an envelope without a return address to the person to whom your emotions are directed. That the ashes represent what they do makes the action symbolic for you.

This sending of the ashes is a powerful gesture. Be mindful of what you're doing at each step of the riddance ceremony—burning the letter, placing the ashes in the envelope, addressing the envelope and its contents, mailing the letter.

Remember the mailbox you used. It is your expressive point. Each time you pass it, reexperience the release.

At the Graveside

If your letter is addressed to someone who is dead, it is a powerful experience to bring it to the grave. Because such excursions can be unsettling, you may wish to have a friend accompany you. If the person is buried in a distant city, consider taking the letter with you the next time you visit. Think of this ceremony as a pilgrimage of riddance. This is not small talk, but a way of commemorating the expression of your hurt and anger and closing a painful chapter. Be earnest. Be brave. Take this seriously.

Stand in front of the grave. Announce, "I have come here to complete unfinished business with you."

Read the letter aloud.

At the end, declare, "I forgive you for all the hurt you caused me, and I now release it."

Burn the letter just in front of the headstone.

Crush the ashes into the sod.

Stand there for a moment, aware of the situation and what you have just done.

From now on, every time it rains you will know that the ashes of your emotions are filtering downward.

The painful feeling is out of you.

OTHER EXTERNALIZING DEVICES

Eliminating Feelings

Take a picture of the other person and tear it into shreds. If you don't have a picture, write the other person's name on a large piece of paper and tear it into tiny pieces with a vengeance. Take the scraps of paper and put them in the toilet.

And with total awareness of what you are doing, use the toilet and flush.

If this is bringing a smile to your face, you're experiencing a release merely by visualizing releasing your angry feelings.

The reason this device works so well is that you actually do something to get negative feelings outside. That is a powerful directive. The nice part about this exercise is that you can repeat it over and over again until the anger subsides.

The next time you see the person face to face, remember your secret. It will give you strength and a feeling of being in control.

The Telephone Call

You can have any of the confrontational conversations that have been outlined here on the telephone. For many people communicating directly is too threatening, especially when they are dependent on the other person and are not yet ready to make a declaration of autonomy.

It is sometimes helpful to call the person you're angry at and when they answer listen for a moment, say nothing, and then put your finger on the release button. With the sound of his voice still fresh in your ear, tell the person what you feel. This emulates a conversation but of course is one-sided. The voice of the other person can be a useful stimulus for the expression of old feelings.

Be sure to keep the button depressed.

A Lesson from Tibet

Tibet is a land filled with prayer wheels and prayer flags, drums filled with prayers that turn in moving streams. As these prayers are physically brought into motion, the faithful believe that their prayers are activated. Who is to say they are not?

Here are some suggestions to create your own expressive device.

I

Write the name of the person you're angry at on the sole of your shoe and be aware as you go through your day that the name is beneath your feet.

Allow yourself to feel good about it.

II

Write the person's name on your tires and be mindful that it is there as you drive through hazards, water, dirt, and so on.

Allow yourself to feel the release.

III

Wrap a paper with the person's name around a rock. Throw the rock into the water.

Be mindful of what this symbolizes as you watch it sink.

IV

Write the person's name on a piece of paper and place the paper in a foul-smelling place, like a portable toilet—or a series of portable toilets around the city—and imagine what people are doing on it.

Just don't tell the Dalai Lama.

Visualization

If you can't be fully expressive of your angry feelings toward someone because of the position of power the

person holds over you or the awkwardness of the relationship or for any other reason, the following imaging technique can be helpful.

When you are with the other person, stare at his face for
a moment and then imagine him dressed up in a bizarre
outfit such as a duck suit or covered with feathers from
head to toe. Keep the image in mind as you deal with this
person.

As you imagine this person in a ridiculous disguise, try
to keep a straight face. The release of tension is what you're
trying to achieve.

If the other person asks you if something is wrong,
respond by saying "Everything is fine" and *think to yourself*, "You just look like a duck, that's all."

Anything else you wish to imagine that works for you
will do.

Letting Go of Anger

The following technique works well when you're breaking
up with someone and still feel a powerful yearning to get
back together even though you know the relationship is not
good for you.

Make a list of all the things you dislike about the other
person and the relationship, putting one item on a line.
Include the ways that the relationship hurt you, inhibited
your growth, isolated you from others, and kept you from
being your best. The list can be as long as you want.

When you go to bed at night, read the list slowly, com-
prehending the meaning and impact of each item, remembering the way it caused you pain.

Do the same thing in the morning when you awaken.

Carry the list around with you during the day, and whenever you feel the irrational yearning for the other person,
take a moment to go over the list in the same deliberate
fashion.

Don't just read the list. Meditate on each item.

A listener who once heard me suggest this technique on

my radio program was having trouble leaving her husband, so she created her own list. She read it several times a day for five or six months and gradually stopped. She left her husband and started a new life. After a year she called to tell me that she came upon the list in a drawer, read it, and declared, "I am no longer this person."

This simple procedure will allow you to put any negative situation behind you. There is no way you can appreciate how effective it is until you try it and stay with it.

A Personal Calendar

The following exercise will help you make additional sense of your emotional life. Create a calendar in which you list the anniversaries of all of your important victories and defeats, significant births and deaths, advancements and setbacks—all the important days that made a difference in your life, both positive and negative. It's helpful if you can see the entire year at once, such as on a year planner. Emotional reactions that happen on the anniversary of an important event are called anniversary reactions and can reveal the hidden sources of your forgotten feelings. They include the remembrance of losses whose mourning is incomplete. While it is typical to become sad on the anniversary of the loss of a loved one, becoming mindful of the anniversary date of other old hurts also helps locate the lost feelings, put them in perspective, and resolve the hurt. When you insert a loss in your calendar, say to yourself, "Grandmother died in March." "I was fired in July." Don't hesitate to ask members of the family for assistance with dates.

Recalling the times of your success also helps to remind you of what you have accomplished and renews your self-esteem.

It is typical of emotional reactions that forgotten feelings tend to manifest themselves in the seasons in which they originally occurred, presenting themselves as vague feelings of yearning and disquiet. While you may easily recall that it was on a snowy day that Grandpa died, the fact that you anticipate winter with sadness as a symbolic recollection of this loss may elude your understanding until you see it on a calendar.

Drawing the association between the anniversaries of losses and the seasons in which they occurred may explain some old mysteries. It's always surprising how easily you forget and how much relief you can experience when you make these obvious connections.

REVISITING YOUR PAST WITH A MAGIC LAMP

Your understanding of the principles discussed up to this point sets the scene for a unique opportunity to put them into practice to help resolve the feelings of the past.

Consider the worst moments in your childhood, the times when you were most alone, most in need of friendly advice, most in need of understanding, most hurt.

List those times.

For each of these troublesome times, write a separate note from the self you are now to the child you once were.

Assume that by some miracle you can go back in time and leave the note for this troubled and misunderstood child. Write the note in the language that you could have understood at that difficult time.

- What do you most want that child to know?
- What does that child need to know or hear most at this difficult time?
- Why does the child want or need to know it?
- What do you most need to say to that child?

In your mind's eye, go back in time and find that child in distress. Locate the room. Note the lighting. See that child's facial expression. Place the note where the child can find it.

Hold this mental image for a moment.

Now surrender to this fantasy and become that child again.

Visualize yourself alone. You are still yourself, but as that child at a different time. Remember. Be there as that younger you, looking out the same eyes, but years ago.

- Where are you?
- What have you just been doing?
- What are you feeling?

Now see yourself discovering this note and reading it.

Read it aloud to yourself as if you were this younger child, feeling the impact that it has on you.

- What effect does reading this have?
- What damage will this prevent?
- What understanding does it give you?
- What release do you feel?
- What strength does it awaken?
- What questions does it answer?
- What questions does it raise?

Now for a powerful leap of faith:

Imagine that this is not a fantasy but a real memory, an actual recollection of you discovering the information contained in your note when you were younger. Assume that you had read it and integrated as much as you could into your life experience but had forgotten about it until now. After all, some part of you did have some of the awareness you have now but did not know what to make of it. Maybe you even felt crazy for knowing what you knew or feeling what you felt. What you did not understand was that your feelings were the truth, for they were new to you then and probably confused you by challenging what you had always been taught or believed.

But in your heart you knew the truth contained in your note. Even if you were not completely aware of it, you felt it.

So in fact this note is a reminder to your earlier self. It says:

- You have a greater awareness than you know.
- You know and understand more than you realize.
- You are stronger than you realize.
- You will survive even though now you think it is hopeless.

This note is from the survivor to the part of you that *knew* you would survive but feared you might not. This is a communication between the older and younger parts of the same higher self—the eternal, ageless you. In a real sense you can return to your past, awaken this knowledge, and allow it to be reintegrated into your experience. So when you visualize discovering the note and feeling the strength that it gave you, accept that strength as having existed as part of you then, even if you think you were unaware of it. Accept that the knowledge in the note existed in you at the time of your suffering.

Now, awake to this understanding. Release this knowledge from the rigid bonds of time and allow it to be ever present as part of your memory of yourself.

Let it heal you and make you whole.

Repeat this exercise for each difficult period on your list.

No matter which of these exercises you use, allow yourself to surrender to them. The benefit you receive increases with the sincerity of your commitment.

Your emotional integrity depends on mastering the skills for working through anger. When it is all said and done, the difference between being happy and not is knowing what to do with your anger.

12

Understanding Guilt:
When Your Anger Hurts You

When anger cannot be expressed outwardly, it must be redirected within. Anger's intention is always the same: to seek a target. So if anger cannot be expressed externally, it will seek an inner target. Unfortunately, there is only one such inner target—yourself.

Anger directed at the self is called guilt.

THE RANGE OF GUILT

Guilt ranges in intensity from feeling sorry, apologetic, ashamed, regretful, or rueful to bemoaning and lamenting one's fate, to feeling resentful, bitter, remorseful, or conscience-stricken, to feeling contrite, at fault, culpable, reprehensible, punishable, or deserving of condemnation.

Guilt comes from swallowing your hurt and anger because you feel expressing your feelings would confirm that you are a bad person. Sometimes you feel guilty over being angry about someone else's injury of you. Other times you feel guilty about hurt you actually have caused to others.

231

Most of the time when you hurt others by expressing your
anger, however, you did so to break free of their influence
and control to express what you needed to express, which
you should have been doing all along. Had you insisted on
being free and truthful in the first place, rather than holding back your feelings out of fear or weakness, you would
have avoided the need to turn your anger inward, that is,
you would not feel guilt.

WHAT BUYS YOUR SILENCE

In the world of emotions whatever causes you to withhold
your feelings owns you. There is nothing so powerful as
being controlled by your own inhibitions. To some extent
you are taunted by some secret feeling you are afraid of
admitting. You may not even be aware of what the feeling
is, but it makes you doubt your self-worth and fear looking
closely. Everyone has some such doubts.

You don't need to have done anything bad to believe that
you are bad. When you are unsure of yourself, you can
easily compile a wealth of negative evidence to bear witness against your own character. You are both judge and
jury. Your conscience testifies unopposed in favor of the
victim of your crimes, and the rules of evidence are over-
ruled by your low self-esteem. As a result it takes recalling
only one negative act to conclude you are bad.

It's not the evidence you provide that proves your guilt-
worthiness, but how you feel about yourself that leads you
to create and weigh that evidence. In part you wish to be
punished to relieve your guilt, to set matters straight so you
can be free to act again without the painful burden of
being unforgiven and unforgivable.

Your tendency to exaggerate your feelings of low self-
worth whenever you do something wrong and reinforce
them with the recollection of old unconfessed transgressions is a self-deprecatory path you've been taking for
years. For this reason it is altogether too easy to torture

yourself when you do something wrong or when you hold in your anger.

GUILT AND EMOTIONAL DEBT

Inwardly directed anger makes up the majority of the feelings you don't express. Like the pattern of other stored feelings, the way you feel guilty falls into three distinct patterns depending on how old the feeling is. The immediate reaction of having a guilty conscience comes from your doing or saying something hurtful or morally wrong right now. Feeling self-deprecation over being angry is the emotional debt of recently accumulated feelings. Finally, feeling ashamed of who or what you are and where you came from is typical of the guilt of remote emotional debt.

The Guilty Conscience: The Guilt of Reactive Emotional Debt

You feel guilty when your actions lead you to conclude that you are not as good as you think you should be or when you fall short of your standards of behavior. In this category are guilts of omission and forgetfulness such as forgetting anniversaries and birthdays, breaking appointments, and all the thoughtless comments you make that hurt others. The guilt you feel about these offenses is also reinforced by recollecting fragments of similar hurtful acts and angry thoughts. The self-resentment from these acts immediately touches you with pangs of conscience. The feature that distinguishes this category of guilt is that the injury is fresh and you can easily identify the source of your wrongdoing and correct it.

The rule of thumb to set all of these problems right is to tell the truth and correct the mistake as soon as possible. If that seems too simple for you, it's probably because you're afraid of admitting the truth.

Common Sources of a Guilty Conscience

Included here are some basic categories of wrongdoing and hurting others. They are most forgivable when they result from pressures of the moment, such as being overwhelmed. But they can also result from more long-standing problems such as not trusting your own worth and, therefore, not believing that you would get what you want if you just acted straightforwardly. So these hurtful acts also result from not really liking yourself, from insecurity, or simply from being childish.

The fact that the following actions make you uneasy is a sign that you have transgressed your ethical or moral standards. Remember, feeling remorse is also a sign that you are good. A psychopath who committed these offenses would never think twice about them. The ease with which you admit these wrongdoings is a measure of your goodness and goes a long way toward relieving your guilt.

Dishonesty and Lying   You lie not so much to deceive others as to hide your weakness from yourself. All dishonesty is an attempt to portray reality in a way that makes you look best. A dishonest person thinks he deserves more than he has and so feels entitled to take what is not his. All dishonesty and lying comes from low self-esteem and lack of self-acceptance. Tell the truth. Make it a habit to correct lapses.

Stealing   An honest person simply does not steal. Once you steal and rationalize what you're doing, you're in trouble. Saying everyone does it or that you deserved more only weakens you. Stealing from your employer because you feel underpaid only lowers your self-esteem. You should ask for a fair deal, not cheat to catch up. And you need to feel good about yourself in the first place to ask for what you deserve. Stealing only encourages more stealing.

Believe in yourself. Give to yourself by standing up for your worth when it matters and work toward your own goals.

Taking Advantage   Taking unfair advantage of others' transparent weakness, by intimidating them or providing them with the minimal reward to keep them involved, is a violation of innocence and trust. Included are all seductions, insincerities, and exploitations of others' ignorance—anytime you give people what they say they want to take more from them.

When you take advantage of others, you rob yourself of the self-esteem you would have developed if you had done your best for yourself.

Selfishness   Being petty, cheap, or giving the absolute minimum to make an impression only reflects the belief that you are needy and don't have enough for yourself.

Be selfish enough to take time to understand yourself and grow. Only this fills you.

Cheating   When you believe you would lose in honest competition, you may succumb to using your superior position, influence, or contacts to achieve an unfair advantage over others. A narrow line to draw: when is being preferential to a good customer an incentive, not a bribe?

When you cheat, you forget how good you really are. You do not grow. Worse, you lower your self-esteem by believing you have to cheat to win, a loser's mentality.

Infidelity   Being unfaithful is not being willing to work out the problems between you and your loved one in an open manner. Besides reflecting a lack of commitment, being unfaithful is almost always the sign of both a lack of communication and a fear of what needs to be communicated. Whatever argument you had before you were unfaithful loses its legitimacy to you. Your guilt keeps you from finding the best solution because you don't feel you deserve to be happy.

Hurting Others   Overreacting and hurting those you love has the power to lower self-esteem more drastically than almost any other item in this collection of guilt-producing activities. This is mostly the result of not expressing your feelings spontaneously and exploding to hurt others later.

Being Defensive   Not being one's best can be a source of guilty conscience for people who are driven to excellence. The amount of discomfort you feel in realizing you have been defensive or were not being your best reflects your motivation to grow. Learn to accept your humanness, imperfections, and inconsistencies gracefully.

Self-Deprecation   When you hurt others accidentally, you feel guilty but find it possible to apologize and be forgiven.

When you hurt others on purpose, you feel so ashamed of yourself that you often hold back and suffer and remember other offenses you committed.

Then again, having a guilty conscience doesn't always mean you've done something wrong but that you've done something you think is wrong.

On vacation in Hawaii my friend Sharon turned to me and asked, "Why do I feel guilty for not bringing the kids?"

"Did you want to bring the kids?" I asked.

"Not really," Sharon said with a laugh.

"Do you think you should have wanted to bring the kids?" I pressed.

"Yes. I do think that."

"So what does that say about you if you don't want to bring your kids on vacation?"

"That I'm bad?" Sharon was looking a little apprehensive.

"Maybe that you're normal. Having three young kids climbing all over you all the time, making demands and clamoring for your attention, isn't easy and isn't fun."

Sharon nodded.

"And you are the world's most patient mother. I've seen you deal with them. Don't you ever get angry at them?"

"Yes, but not much."

"Not as much as you sometimes feel?"

"OK, I admit that."

"So where does that anger go?"

Sharon shrugged.

"Maybe it sometimes becomes a wish that you were alone and away from them. So you view your wish to have relief from them as an angry thought. Now, when the wish has come true, you start to think you're a bad mother."

"So, it's OK not to want them here? To tell the truth I am pleased that no one is pulling at me. Hey, you know, I feel better."

A little understanding of the fear and hurt underlying your internalized anger goes a long way toward relieving your guilt.

Bitterness: The Guilt of Recent Emotional Debt

Most guilt results from the accumulation of unexpressed anger from a succession of recent injuries. The anger is redirected inward. In a sense you become angry at yourself for being so angry. Since withheld anger is managed mostly by the mind, it breeds terrible angry fantasies whose gruesome negativity and bizarre quality make you doubt yourself. You are ashamed of your pessimism, cynicism, and desire for revenge. After a while this inner-directed anger subtly undermines your self-esteem in ways that are difficult for you to understand or share.

When you feel angry at yourself, you believe you should suffer. You take yourself to task and go on hunting expeditions into your past, looking for everything you've done wrong. In time you prove a case against yourself that no one else could make or believe. The evidence is one-sided and entirely prejudiced against you. Such is the heavy-handed way of guilt.

If guilt is allowed to fester in this way, a pattern of internalizing all negative feelings becomes more established, and you're required to use increasing amounts of energy to hold your anger in place. You become more defensive. You lie to yourself, justify your actions, and make preposterous excuses to convince yourself either that what you did was not so bad, that you had good reason to do it, or that how you acted is the way the real world is. But if how you feel or what you did wasn't so bad, how come you still can't get it out of your mind? You don't make good sense.

In hiding your guilt, defensive alibis know no limits. For example, when Betty's fiancé, Mickey, infected her with genital herpes, he not only denied it but accused her of infecting him and insisted that she knew all along that she was infected. He came to believe this, and rather than admit the truth he self-righteously called off the wedding.

In adolescence, when the defenses are easily overwhelmed, young people often have difficulty handling internalized anger because their self-esteem is so fragile. It is also typical of adolescents that when they have guilt that they cannot manage they act out in ways that lead others to apprehend and punish them. This explains why some adolescent guilt-producing activity is so flagrant.

Tommy, a fourteen-year-old boy who lived with his alcoholic mother on an army base while his dad was stationed overseas, could not deal with his resentment. He was demoralized by the violent outbursts in which she belittled him and compared him hatefully to his absent father. One day, unable to tolerate his anguish, Tommy stole an army truck, crashed through the security gate of the base, and headed out of town on the main highway. Running out of gas, he stopped near a parked patrol car where a state trooper was giving a motorist a ticket. He slipped into the front seat of the trooper's car and drove back into town at speeds approaching one hundred miles an hour, but somehow eluded capture. He parked the car in front of the police station and honked the horn. No one noticed. Finally, Tommy threw a rock through the window of the police station, shouting, "Isn't anyone here going to arrest me?"

While this story may sound exaggerated, it was fairly typical of the hundreds of incarcerated adolescents I interviewed who were considered to have emotional factors that influenced their crimes. I did not find one such child who did not have an emotional problem. All of the criminal acts were related to the guilt of low self-esteem, usually from repressed anger over being abused. Sometimes when these adolescents could contain no more anger, they committed crimes.

Confessing your transgressions is a powerful release because it cuts through your defensive activities. You come clean. You state the simple truth, that you were selfish, dishonest, or resentful. You list the examples of your wrongdoing, and so you are set free. Confessing your guilt is the beginning of redirecting your hurt outside again.

Relieving the sting of such guilt also requires admitting that you've been hurt and expressing the hurt to the person who hurt you, just as in the dynamics of expressing hurt and anger. The problem is that a guilt-ridden person may interpret showing anger as confirming he is bad. How to solve this problem will be discussed in Chapter 13.

Shame: The Guilt of Remote Emotional Debt

Shame is the long-term belief that who you are or what you have done is bad. People who feel shame usually have had childhood experiences that proved to them that they were not good. These experiences are of several kinds.

Children whose parents were too emotionally impoverished to invest time or affection in them, or only pretended to love them but were really manipulative, develop low self-esteem and are highly susceptible to internalizing their family's shortcomings and incorporating them into their character as a feeling of being ashamed. This is typical of children of alcoholic parents. Mostly such children feel worthless for being angry at their parents for not loving them. They seldom discuss this openly. Sometimes these children become supercompliant high achievers but secretly still hate themselves for their anger. Unable to express their anger directly, they punish themselves. A good example is anorexia-bulimia. The gorging and purging of bulimia are symbolic of the attempt to get rid of these bad feelings. Anorexia expresses anger by bringing everyone's attention to the child's terrifyingly thin appearance and making the point "See how unnurturing my parents' love is." This public display embarrasses mother—an intentional hurt—but because the act is also so self-punitive it limits the guilt the daughter feels. This way of relieving guilt over one's anger is typical of all self-punitive behavior.

Suffering physical, emotional, or verbal abuse in childhood underscores the child's belief that he is bad, stupid, or worthless. While it is a rare person who cannot recall a parent's loss of temper and name calling, the people who suffer from this sort of abuse can rarely remember anything else. The parent on whom they depended for their first sense of self-worth gave them the message "You are bad and deserve to have bad things happen to you."

Still, this abusive situation by itself is not enough to produce shame. After all, you can eventually come to view your parents' activity as crazy, decide that they are sick and unhappy, and conclude that you don't have to be that way. However, this declaration of self never comes easily because you always carry some expectation that your parents will love and give to you if you are just a little better. And so you may try to be perfect just in case your parents change. Giving up this expectation is the prerequisite for placing distance between you and their abuse. It is always painful to let go of hope, but the sooner you do, the less damage is done, and the process of healing can begin.

The fact that makes abuse most damaging is the child's eventual acceptance of it. Even healthy children are aware of doing things wrong. Imagine how children who are unloved must feel when their parents continually call them bad names and cite endless examples to back up their point. The children come to feel that they must be undeserving of love. They suspect the worst about themselves. The concept that their parents are unloving is too frightening to occur to them, and when it finally does they often deny it and redouble their efforts to please their parents.

After a while internalized hurt begins to produce resentment and rage, and this leads unloved children to conclude that their parents were right in their assessment. They become determined not to show anger and try to please others. These attempts usually fail. Their anger deepens and turns into the guilt of shame. They feel they are bad for feeling this way about their parents. These attitudes can become established at an early age.

The adolescent rebellion of these children can be overt manifestations of antisocial behavior with criminal activity based on rage, or they may develop the same addictive problems as their parents. On the other hand, the fear of expressing any anger may totally inhibit the rebellion, and these children may become passive and dedicated person pleasers. In later years the inhibited anger often expresses itself in abusive outbursts toward their own children. This rekindles their old sense of shame as they fear they are no better than their parents.

Children who are sexually abused are invariably compromised. They feel they are part of a terrible secret. They feel they have done something wrong. They feel horrified at the perpetrator and often at themselves for being stimulated, curious, or passive. They feel that they are co-conspirators even if they were forced, even if they were paralyzed with fear. When children keep their silence, these feelings of shame are intensified. If they tell their parents and nothing is done, or they are not believed, their low self-opinion is reinforced. What is worse is that the nonabusive parent now seems part of the enemy camp, and the children's hurt and subsequent anger increase to fuel their sense of guilt. This evolves into the pattern of shame as the children feel confirmed in their belief that they are bad.

In dealing with shame, no matter what happened, how you were compromised to believe you were a willing participant, how much you took part in, tolerated, or even enjoyed the abuse, or how much anger you had following it, you must come to the belief that as a child you were innocent.

You were innocent even if you were arousable.

You were innocent even if you were silent.

You were innocent even if you acted seductively.

You were innocent even if you feel you asked for it.

You were innocent even if you were angry about it.

You were innocent even if you did terrible things because of it.

You were innocent because you were a child.

THE IMPACT OF SHAME

People who feel ashamed find it difficult to take risks because they feel undeserving. When they do risk, they often undermine their efforts just at the point where success is at hand, for they see failing as a punishment that will balance their anger and make them feel better.

The perversion of shame is that it leads people to accept pain and suffering, to endure loveless marriages, and to seem to invite additional abuse as well as to perpetuate social and financial hardship. Often people who were abused are unwilling to accept that they were injured or to admit that their parents hurt them on purpose. Because of this they perceive being abused in their marriage as familiar, like home. Often abused children first realize that they were abused when they have a child of their own and find themselves loving the child and feeling wonderful in being a loving parent. The question crosses their mind, "Why wasn't my parent as good to me as I am to my child?" Then they realize the impact of being abused. They may then gain the courage to grow, but as their buried rage surfaces, they may lose control and abuse their children, having no other place to release their anger. In this way abuse becomes a self-fulfilling prophecy. When it does, the guilt can be more than they can stand, and they get angry at their children because they remind them both of having been abused and of being abusive—a childish, destructive self-contradiction.

Like most feelings in remote emotional debt, shame is activated by resonant association. Committing a shameful act reawakens old feelings of shame and intensifies all feelings of loss and depression.

GUILT AND THE THREE PERSONALITY TYPES

The three character types deal with guilt in their own typical manner. The following chart may seem extreme,

	Dependent	Controlling	Competitive
Dynamics of the buildup of anger in emotional debt	Holding in resentment over repeated rejections during which anger was repressed to keep the person appearing lovable. Little angry outbursts betray him. Tearful bitterness.	Long-standing failure to admit vulnerability leads to internalizing all hurt and anger. Preoccupation over others' malicious intent makes him cynical and negative. When someone is good to him, he can't accept. Others pull away.	Withheld anger rises to the point of deep bitterness in which the person's self-punitive failures and selfishness combine to lower his self-esteem. He can't perform with the same magic anymore. He doesn't believe in himself.
How guilt is precipitated	When his anger leaked out, he broke ranks, acted rashly, and went over to the enemy side, betraying others, losing their support. Feels cut off, self-destructive, panics.	A vindictive punishment backfires, leading him either to be abandoned or actually to do damage to another person that he cannot explain away and that is worse than what was done to him.	His anger or playacting cause him to lose something he really cares about and on which his good feelings depend. *(continued)*

	Dependent	Controlling	Competitive
Nature of the guilt	Guilt and desperation interchangeable. Reluctant to take responsibility for his angry acts but insists on being victim. This keeps him from accepting that he has hurt other people. Stays in abusive relationships to punish himself.	Disturbing revenge fantasies, casting hexes, damning the other, wallowing in a sense of evil. Dark and rigid. Not approachable, protecting his vulnerability with a gloomy shield.	Walking out on the job, running away, acting out the low life. Self-punitive or punishment-seeking behavior.
How guilt is relieved	Accepting his role in injuring others and apologizing to them almost requires the other person guaranteeing to forgive him in advance.	Often leads to depression with some letup after the person feels he has punished himself sufficiently.	Crashing of self-image leads to sorrowful admissions of how much he cared and how badly he needs what he cavalierly abandoned. Prodigal son returns.

but keep in mind that the depth of feeling being shown here is severe and defines guilt at the level at which it interferes with the ability to function productively.

13

Forgiving: A Handbook for Letting Go of Hurt

Forgiveness is a vital part of emotional freedom.

Without forgiveness we're bound to the past. Sometimes we hurt others by misunderstanding them, by not giving them the benefit of the doubt, by misrepresenting ourselves, by acting out of anger, pettiness, or selfishness, or simply by not being our best. So from time to time we all need to be forgiven. And because sometimes we are hurt, betrayed, ignored, taken advantage of, deceived, and treated shabbily, we also need to forgive others.

The more you've been hurt, the more you need to forgive the person who hurt you.

You don't want to forgive?

Perhaps you feel you were hurt so badly and so thoughtlessly, so maliciously and cruelly, that you can't find it in your heart to forgive. If forgiving sounds like selling out and letting others off the hook, then what follows is of special importance to you.

When you don't forgive others, it is because you don't want to free them from obligation or guilt. But when you don't forgive the person who hurt you, you end up living in resentment. As you've seen, contained anger is a dangerous business since it lowers your self-esteem and productivity.

Not forgiving hardly feels like a victory. It isn't. Because when you don't forgive, you become a prisoner of your own anger, carrying an unnecessary burden of pain around with you.

BEARING GRUDGES

When you bear a grudge, you're intentionally preventing your anger from resolving. Nurturing anger and letting it build to fortify your resolve for vengeance is the stuff of Shakespearean tragedies. Basically, what you're doing is preparing to murder someone. Fantasizing about that may give you some satisfaction, but it doesn't resolve the problem. If anything, it makes you question whether or not you're any better than the person who hurt you. When you don't forgive, you end up destroying yourself.

When you don't forgive you're forced to keep alive the hurt that the other person caused you to sustain your anger. You recount your pain and how you were damaged. You play the innocent victim and make the person who hurt you into a monster. You take less and less responsibility for your injury and do not gain from your mistakes.

After a while other people don't want to be in your presence. A person who has suffered a similar injury might tolerate your angry outbursts and even encourage them, releasing anger by proxy. In fact this is typical of the dynamics of conversations in support groups, one of whose benefits is providing an opportunity to share pain and anger. After all, no one else really wants to listen, most people want to let go and get on with life. The problem with support groups is that some people become so dependent on them that they keep their anger alive just to belong and stay in them, either as members or as leaders who may be still venting their anger vicariously.

Try to keep in mind that anger does subside. The world does turn. You do heal. To sustain anger artificially is always self-destructive.

WHY PEOPLE DON'T FORGIVE—THE THREE PERSONALITY TYPES

There are three basic reasons people don't forgive.

The *dependent person* uses the role of victim to gain moral superiority or to manipulate from the passive position, making the offender seem even worse. The dependent type gets even by flaunting this helpless attitude and despairing appearance in an attempt to arouse sympathy but is more likely to elicit even more scorn that feels remarkably like parental chastisement.

The dependent person needs to forgive to grow. If you can blame someone for crippling you, you never have to look within, find your inner strength, take responsibility, risk, or do your best.

The *controlling person* fears revealing vulnerability. Forgiving means admitting injury. This person punishes by using the courts, tightening rules and purse strings.

Controlling people need to forgive more than anyone else because they can always rationalize and excuse their own shortcomings. This only makes them seem rigid and old, because they appear so resistant to learning and growing. They need to give up the privileges they think being right confers on them and release others. Otherwise, others will simply release themselves and abandon the controlling person. No one likes to be unforgiven.

Out of false pride the *competitive person* pretends not to stoop to the other person's level, while maintaining vicious contempt. Competitive people punish by snubbing, creating bad publicity through gossip or rumor, and creating scenes. They need to forgive so they can drop the facade of indifference. Otherwise they become bitter, convinced that the whole world is undeserving and that their efforts are meaningless. This can lead to a self-generating cycle of self-destructive behavior.

WHY FORGIVE?

When you do not forgive you come to believe that retaliation against the person who hurt you is justified. Unfortunately, when you fail to make your original hurt known even a minor punishment feels unjustified to the person you are trying to punish. Anger expressed by punishing will not bring release because it will just hurt and anger the other person. Your old hurt will be difficult to substantiate and your attempt to punish will seem unreasonable and therefore easy for the other person to use against you.

The reason to forgive other people is not to let them off the hook but to free *yourself* from the burden of hating. If the injury that someone caused you turns you into a hateful person, the worst damage you suffer is the damage you caused yourself. Initially the correct response would have been to defend yourself from the hurt. Perhaps you were unable to because you were so young and you were taught to respect the person who hurt you. But what is your excuse now? How do you justify holding in all of your hurt and living for revenge? You only hurt yourself in the process and get in your own way.

Everything you want in life depends on your being open, free of old anger.

You need to forgive.

To forgive another person is to release the hurt, to say that you're no longer suffering.

Forgiving should be a common part of your everyday communication with others. Whenever you express hurt or anger, you need to express a gesture of forgiveness. When you forgive someone, you indicate that the pain you felt is gone, and you release it. If you cannot tell the person face to face that you forgive him, you need to do so in your heart. You forgive a person and release him at the same time. You may choose never to speak to that person again, but you need to feel free of the pain. That's why this is so important.

BEING FORGIVEN

You need to be forgiven.

Think for a moment of a person you once deeply hurt.

It's not pleasant to recall.

Now become aware of how you feel as you remember the incident. Dark feelings that raise questions about your worth surface. You've probably answered many of these questions yourself. You may have reasoned that the other person was at fault, did not take responsibility for himself, or in some way deserved to be hurt, but these are merely the excuses with which you have coated the incident to make it seem more acceptable and to make yourself less of a villain. Under the excuses remains the fact that you did something that hurt someone.

It doesn't feel good.

Now imagine that the person you hurt has called you on the phone and says, "Remember how you hurt me? Well, I've gotten over it completely, and I no longer hurt."

What would you feel?

You would feel relieved and unburdened, happy that the other person is no longer suffering. You would also be glad for yourself because now whatever injury you caused is healed. The evidence that could testify that you are a bad person is diminished.

Powerful stuff!

As a matter of fact, forgiveness comprises some of the most powerful emotional content in your life. Forgiveness, absolution, cleansing, a fresh start, being reborn, renunciation—these tear at your very heartstrings as you yearn to be released from your negative actions, made whole and good again. You want to redeem yourself.

LETTING GO

You need to let go of your old pain and move on.

The fuller life you want depends on letting go of your hurts and resolving the hurt you've done to others.

The exercises in Chapters 7 and 11 define the way to let go of your old hurt, and you should commit to the process they describe. You need to let go.

When you do decide to use one of these devices for letting go of your hurt and forgiving, be sure to include the following points, no matter how you release your hurt, even if in a letter that you burn at a grave site.

"I no longer hurt from what happened between us."

"Because I care so much about us and myself, I promise never to let the hurt build up between us again."

"I will make my hurt feelings known as soon as I feel them from now on."

"I feel better now."

"I forgive you."

Again, you don't have to tell the person that you forgive him, but you do need to come to peace in your heart. The damage people do to others eventually comes back to haunt them. You don't need to take on the role of grand inquisitor—the other person's guilty conscience will do that. You need to live happily, but being joyous in your survival requires forgiving those who hurt you and dedicating yourself to the goodness of life.

MAKING AMENDS

This will not be easy.

Compile a list of people you have hurt.

Probably many of the people on that list are people you are living or working with right now, not from the distant past.

Next to each name, write down the injury you caused. The shorter your description of the hurt, the more likely you are on the road to forgiving yourself, because you can state it clearly. The longer your description, the more likely you're being defensive and making explanations.

Next to each name, start a sentence with "I'm sorry for . . ." and speak the hurt you wrote out loud. This is the message you need to give the other person, in a note, in person, or in a telephone call. If the person is no longer alive, consider a letter such as the one described in Chapter 11. Ask for forgiveness and grant it to yourself only as you finish the letter.

When the event you're asking forgiveness for is in the immediate past, just mentioning to the other person that you were wrong and that you're sorry should be sufficient to open a conversation in which other details are discussed, but don't get too involved in the initial communication. Just set up a time when you can express the remainder of your apology in person. When you do communicate face to face, remember that your natural tendency is still going to be to defend yourself, especially when the other person feels comfortable enough to respond by letting out hurt. Remember that allowing the other person to express hurt is the act of forgiveness you seek.

Don't try to justify your actions.

Just listen.

Don't make excuses for your actions.

Just keep listening.

Thank the other person for expressing pain and be sincere when you say you hope it helps.

Don't act hurt even if you have somehow triggered an outrageous display of hurt from the other person. Many of the things the other person says may be exaggerations, distortions, or outright lies—after all, the other person has been living with this hurt as long as you have been living with yours. Even so, let the other person have this moment. It will go best for you. This is especially true if the other person is your child and is wildly exaggerating a complaint. Bite your tongue. Just listen.

You can correct an important fact or divulge information that expands the truth, such as that you didn't know certain facts at the time. But keep this sort of comment to an absolute minimum or you will hurt the other person again by denying responsibility.

Does this mean you should be a doormat? Sure, if that's what it takes to allow the other person to speak his hurt and end his suffering. Permitting the other person to express hurt is what love is all about. Besides, you can always coat yourself in the protection of knowing that you're doing a good thing and not let it bother you. This is called being therapeutic. It will give you strength to get through this. Love isn't always comfortable, because it demands that all the truth be spoken.

Asking forgiveness for a remote injury that you caused requires making a more complicated and detailed communication. Whether you speak face to face or in a letter, the ideal message should contain a selection of the following points:

- "I'm sorry I hurt your feelings when I acted the way I did."
- "I was selfish and didn't care about anyone else at that time but myself."
- "I acted out of greed and fear."
- "I was not my best."
- "I've often thought about how I hurt you, and it has caused me pain."
- "I want you to know that I haven't forgotten, that I've suffered in recalling my unfortunate actions."
- "I wish I could take back what I said or did, but I can't. What has happened lives in me as discomfort."
- "I know I can't make your pain go away, but I hope you understand that I'm deeply sorry."
- "Please accept my apologies."
- "Please forgive me."
- "I wish you the best."

Don't let your pride or false self-righteousness get in the way of following through on this. If you express your hurt over your actions, you'll start to feel better even if the other person can never forgive you.

If you have been abused you need to forgive your abuser. Even if your family will not believe you, even if you cannot make peace with the perpetrators of the crimes against you, forgive them anyway and release them. Then go on and live your life. Everything good in life depends on it.

You deserve the best. You deserve to be forgiven and to forgive.

The negativity of the past, when forgiven, becomes the lesson learned and the motivation to move ahead.

14

Understanding Depression:
The Cost of Withholding Anger

Sadness is not depression, although every depressed person feels sad. Sadness is the feeling of being depleted and experiencing loss. Depression is a much deeper, much older feeling, but because it is actually a pattern of avoiding feelings, it is a complicated emotional state involving all of the emotions discussed so far.

Depressed people feel hurt because they've been hurt and because holding in feelings is hurtful.

Depressed people are angry because old hurt becomes anger.

Depressed people are anxious because they fear they will lose control of their repressed anger and hurt someone.

Because they have redirected their anger inward, depressed people feel guilty and worthless. While we all suffer blows to our self-esteem from time to time, depressed people have allowed their guilt to erode the very foundations of their self-worth to the point where they cannot see their goodness at all and have difficulty finding any meaning in life.

THE RANGE OF DEPRESSIVE FEELINGS

Depression ranges from being sullen to moody, gloomy, defeated, woeful, melancholic, suffering, afflicted, miserable, tormented, tortured, hopeless, or despondent, to feeling despairing and condemned and suicidal.

THE DYNAMICS OF DEPRESSION

The dynamics of depression are straightforward:

1. A person is hurt but internalizes the hurt instead of expressing it.
2. The hurt turns into anger.
3. Anger unexpressed is directed inward as guilt.
4. The energy used in rerouting the anger inward and confining it in emotional debt uses up emotional reserves. This depletion of energy is called *depression.*

The more firmly established this pattern of concealing emotions becomes, the deeper and longer-lasting the depression.

SETTING THE STAGE FOR DEPRESSION

Usually acute depressions are the product of emotional overload from one or a series of distinct losses. It's important to realize that it is a rare person who goes through life without accumulating feelings in emotional debt that can lead to depression.

When you consider that stress is the pressure of an unexpressed feeling, you realize how many feelings are being shunted into emotional debt every day of your life. You suffer unresolved concerns over your self-esteem, your relationships, your children, your work, and your parents.

You deal with the competition of coworkers and the arro-
gance of bosses. You struggle with your personal finances
and failures. On top of this you deal with self-doubt as you
question whether you're doing your best or what you're
supposed to be doing. The world around you bombards
you with additional concerns: wars, famines, epidemics,
financial crises, political scandals, taxes, inflation, crime,
pollution, and environmental degradation.

You're not expected to solve all of these problems, but
you are exposed to them, and they worry you. There is a
limit to the amount of indifference you can muster to adapt
to a world going mad. After all, indifference is the state of
pretending not to care, and it creates an emotional debt all
its own. It's easy to get lost by saying your problems are
insignificant compared to these events and so ignore them.

What do you do to cope? You try exercise and sports. You
divert yourself with the arts; you make love; you travel. You
bury yourself in your work. You hide your feelings by
eating too much, drinking too much, sleeping too much,
working too much. Each day you defend against an army of
almost imperceptible hurts and hide from them instead of
being open. After all, none of them is really that important
to you, and you are too busy or powerless to change the
world. Besides, there is always something more important
to do. You are in a rush. This is the nature of our time.

While expressing your feelings openly in the present
does relieve some stress, many feelings still manage to
build up over the years. It is this accumulation of nonde-
script minor old hurts from many sources, the disappointment of your private life and the world around you that,
combined with the loss of energy and self-esteem of aging,
makes you sensitive to suffering depression. The accumulation of feelings in emotional debt *is* psychological aging
and why you tend to get rigid and irritable when you get
older.

In a so-called mid-life crisis you're overcome by the
realization that your life is running out, so you feel pushed
to get what you can before it's too late. The dynamic for
precipitating this situation typically involves falling in love

either up close and requited or at a distance and one-sided with someone outside your marriage. The vulnerability that love confers makes you more open to the feelings you've repressed over the years, and you decide you haven't been true to yourself. Often rather than admit the "affair" you claim to need more space and time to find yourself. A more truthful confession would be that the rat race no longer works for you and you no longer have the energy to pretend.

A similar accumulation of unresolved feelings sets the scene for the development of involutional depression, the menopausal depression in which a woman feels she no longer has a purpose when her childbearing years are behind her. (Obviously, there are hormonal changes that aggravate the situation as well.) Contributing to her emotional debt may be suppressed resentment of many instances of self-sacrifice or a particular hurt; such as an unhappy marriage, a thankless child, a career path not taken. Unfortunately, such women often turn all their anger on themselves, suffering guilt over their resentment. They often develop psychosomatic illnesses that symbolically contain their unexpressed feelings in a safe expression of their self-victimization.

As we grow older, illness and the aging process lower the energy to cope with life, so we become more fragile and emotionally sensitive. Isolation caused by the negligence of family and friends either imagined or real and feelings of being abandoned and discarded can break your heart. With few reserves left and no place to go or energy to do what used to give you pleasure or divert your attention, depression is often the result.

Given all that, it is amazing that more people do not suffer from depression.

ACUTE DEPRESSION

You can become suddenly—or acutely—depressed after suffering a brief series of losses that overwhelm your capacity to feel openly. Your defenses were designed to cover your emotions until you're ready to process them, allowing them out a little at a time as you're ready to deal with them. Unfortunately, when the sheer volume of the losses exceeds your ability to manage your pain, most of your painful feelings are shunted into emotional debt.

Now you're confronted with an emotional overload that creates unfamiliar feelings of vulnerability. You try unsuccessfully to cover, but instead you become irritable and snap at people. You're preoccupied, negative, brooding, and find little joy in the world around you. People have difficulty making contact with you. At first you smile an automatic smile, and then you stop smiling altogether. Little things that never bothered you before now unnerve you. This makes you feel brittle, and your perceived fragility lowers your self-esteem and courage. You're looking to solve a problem, but some of the pieces of the puzzle have been obscured by your defenses. It's as if part of your mind isn't working, and your usual methods of coping don't feel right anymore. Your sense of conviction and the motivation that believing in yourself once generated are absent.

On the positive side, all of these symptoms of acute depression may frighten you enough to make you take stock of yourself. Your new vulnerability opens you up to examine your feelings and consider whether you really want what you claim. You see the futility in impossible quests, trying to win just to please someone else. You admit failure. You realize you have nothing to lose and so resolve to do what you want, what pleases you.

As the events that contributed to your hurts are resolved, acute depression usually resolves. Mostly it is mild to moderate and is a simple matter of getting on with the business of identifying your losses and mourning them.

CHRONIC DEPRESSION

The most seriously depressed people not only accumulate the daily insults that everyone suffers but also have a long history of holding in important feelings of loss whenever they occur. Their low self-esteem has prevented them from coming forward with their hurt and anger when it was fresh, so they've been swallowing these feelings for years. They come to fear facing any of their feelings at all.

While some present loss or injury often precipitates a depression, solving the present difficulty does not solve the real problem for these people. When people have been depressed for years and have not sought help, the sources of their hurt and anger often lie so deeply buried that they often seem inaccessible. Such people are mistakenly labeled as having endogenous depression, meaning that the depression comes entirely from within, from no discernible source. In truth most of these so-called inner depressions are a collection of reactive depressions whose cause has been forgotten. The original depression and cause of low self-esteem have gone untreated for so long that they have been compounded by subsequent insults.

Unfortunately, this search for the sources of the original depression is often sadly neglected in therapy today, and symptoms are treated instead. (See the section about chemical imbalance on the next page.)

THE SYMPTOMS OF SEVERE DEPRESSION

The anger repressed by depressed people causes nightmares, which eventually interrupt their sleep pattern. They get up early, lose sleep, and feel even more fatigued. They also avoid sleep to escape the nightmares. Some depressed people sleep all the time but never feel rested or refreshed. Since their energy is already being consumed by redirecting anger inward, the loss of sleep further taxes their strength.

As their energy is drained, less is available to invest in the outside world, so their attention becomes focused increasingly inward. The world then gives them little in response. They cannot be bothered playing with their children, so they feel like bad parents. They can't pay attention to the movie they have been taken to, so they feel even more depressed by comparison to others. They cannot enjoy a good day; they feel that there is something wrong with them, and turn inward even more, wishing it would rain to fit their mood or that there would be an earthquake to swallow them up.

Their appetite decreases, or they may eat all the time to fill their emptiness. They tend to become constipated. Their speech and walk become slower, and their thought process becomes leaden.

Suicidal thinking surfaces as a form of mental self-punishment. Such thoughts sometimes become preoccupying as a way to escape the pain. At such times, when financial reverses hit hard, the loss of a spouse in the twilight years leaves them feeling abandoned, or the pain and hopelessness of chronic illness disheartens them, severely depressed people can become motivated to act on the thought, but often they lack the energy to carry it off.

Suicidal thinking is part of the guilt process, and often just expressing the feelings behind it relieves the pressure spawning it.

A WORD ABOUT CHEMICAL IMBALANCE

It has been demonstrated that when a person is depressed an imbalance occurs at the level of the neurotransmitters in the brain. Many factors affect these neurophysiological dysfunctions. Whatever the mechanism for the problem, the situation is made significantly worse when emotions are not expressed. The propensity not to admit one's feelings is most likely the result of defenses and character development, but it is also possible that over a long period of time such withholding of emotions also alters the way the biochemical mechanisms function, putting them out of balance. It has also been shown that such a chemical imbalance tends to reverse when a depressed person copes with the problem with therapy alone. You can also experience relief from psychopharmacological intervention in which the biochemical mechanisms are brought back into order. However, this doesn't alter the life situation that originally caused the problem. Administering antidepressants may reset the biochemical order, but the propensity of your character and defenses to re-create the loss that caused the imbalance in the first place remains unchanged. You still need to learn about yourself and what your feelings mean.

To believe that your problem is exclusively biochemical in origin would rob you of your humanity and your desire to take responsibility for your life.

Life is never that simple.

There is a price to be paid for the use of antidepressants:

- A rapid rise out of depression may be nothing but a chemical avoidance of your real problems, a pharmacological "flight into health."
- An antidepressant may give a suicidal patient the energy to follow through on self-destructive thoughts.
- The worst legacy of antidepressants is the belief that you could not do it alone and that you can't cope without drugs.

- If you continued in your old defensive ways after successful psychopharmacological intervention, it would be only a matter of time before similar biochemical problems recurred.

It's important to bear in mind that while antidepressants can change your life dramatically, they are only tools that increase the brain's energy level, making more energy available for examining and solving your problems. That is, they can produce lasting cures only because the biochemical damage caused by emotional debt has been momentarily set right, allowing you to take responsibility again. Once that redirection is accomplished, you need to seize the opportunity to grow. Combining the work of self-understanding with the use of drugs is of critical importance to the healing process. In fact, the new insights you develop when your defenses are lowered, often not even shared with the doctor who prescribed the antidepressant, may be the self-therapy that gives the antidepressant its curative effect by leading you on a more honest path.

PROPENSITY FOR DEPRESSION BY CHARACTER TYPE

Each character type has a special predisposition toward depression. Some *dependent people*, because they are so sensitized to loss, perceive losses everywhere. Even when this tendency is not pronounced, it dampens the joy of the moment. Failure to resolve feelings about perceived losses that are merely trivial or imagined places a burden on the storage capacity of emotional debt. Through the years dependent people store so much resentment over minor and exaggerated hurts to which they are especially sensitive that all of these hurts coalesce, blur, and lose their identity. To the dependent person this hurt is real and immobilizing and smolders within.

Some *controlling people*, because of their defensive structure and their tendency to hold feelings in place, function mechanically throughout life and seem to be emotionally cool toward love and tenderness. This is their equivalent of depression. People who don't take responsibility for their feelings can't resolve them. Any person who lives defensively will become depressed after a time.

Competitive people are continually storing all that hurt they pretended not to care about. As the years pass, their massive emotional debt makes them more irritable and prone to acting out their anger in sudden irrational outbursts, hurting others and embarrassing themselves. All of this hurtful activity eventually overwhelms the competitive person's ability to pretend that none of it matters. When age or illness intervenes, the usual sources of self-esteem such as being admired for physical beauty and the ability to perform are often early casualties. This lowers self-esteem even further and sets the stage for depression.

TREATING DEPRESSION

The cure for depression is not to release the anger but the hurt from which the anger evolved.

This point is critical.

Therapists who help depressed patients come to realize that they are angry and encourage them to let it out often discover that their patients' overtaxed and rigid defense systems will not allow the anger to escape. So when anger is mobilized, it is sometimes immediately turned inward again and directed against the depressed person, increasing guilt and deepening depression. In fact mobilizing such anger may only confirm to depressed people that they are bad—a dangerous tactic.

The psychotherapeutic treatment of depression should be aimed at identifying the most recent hurt that precipitated the anger that in turn overloaded the person's emotional balance. The patient should be encouraged to face the new injury, see how it affected him, and express the hurt he feels. He should be encouraged to come to terms with similar old hurts and express his hurt about these as well.

The patient should be helped to survey his older hurts and come to understand why they were held in, how they built up and added insult to injury, as well as what he was afraid of expressing and why. Similarities between these old hurts and the new should be pointed out.

The patient is guided and supported in the expression of his hurt. Some anger is bound to come to the surface, and the patient should be made to understand it as the result of being hurt.

Once this process is begun and the depressed person has started to open up, some anger can be expressed at safe targets, such as a widow getting angry at the insurance company for delays in sending the check and the like. Even so, expressing volumes of anger even at these safe targets should not be encouraged. The defensive system of the depressed person is fragile and overloaded to begin with, and the expression of anger requires self-esteem for it to be a worthwhile enterprise. Even a healthy person finds expressing a lot of anger disruptive and uncomfortable. A depressed person can find it shattering.

A Remarkable Treatment for Depression

A mental hospital occupational therapist, believing that punishment had a role in reversing the guilt of depression, came up with a therapeutic activity for depressed patients. Each patient would be assigned to a desk containing eight bottles of tiny beads, a different color in each bottle. The occupational therapist would then empty the beads into a larger bowl, mixing them up with her hand, and give the bowl to the patient with the instructions to sort them all out again and fill the bottles. When the day's work was done, she would tell the patient he had done a good job, and right then, in front of the patient, would empty the bottles into the larger bowl again, mix them up, and set them back on the desk for the next day's work. This went on for two weeks, five days a week.

At the end of this time all of the patients showed improvement. Some were well enough to go home.

The dynamics of this are clear and relate to the heart of the problem of working through depression. The patient was doing repetitive meaningless work that could be viewed as punitive, like writing "I will not talk in class" five hundred times, but without even that amount of meaning. The patients sorted out the details of the daily work, felt resentful at the occupational therapist when she made them stay at their purposeless task, and complained to other patients about how stupid it all was. This gave patients something safe to vent their hurt and anger at collectively, relieving the guilt that they had difficulty putting into words.

I remember my residency days at Boston State Hospital, where depressed women would come onto the ward and turn into housecleaning demons, scrubbing the floors and ceilings. The nurses never objected and even directed some of their activity to where it could do the most good. It is clear that the act of contrition makes a person feel good by physically undoing guilt.

All this suggests that volunteer work, giving socially, even when you don't feel you have the energy, and common activities such as cleaning up the garage and putting things in order all have the potential to offer some symbolic help in relieving depression. The next chapter offers more specific suggestions for working through depression.

15

Working Through Depression:
A Handbook

LEARNING FROM A DEPRESSION

While it is hardly recommended that you become depressed to learn life's lessons, suffering a depression does offer special opportunities to learn. Some points to guide you:

*You wouldn't be depressed unless what
you lost was important to you.*

- What did you lose, and how was it important?
- What could you have done to change matters? (Don't blame yourself; merely see how you did not take responsibility for your actions or feelings.)
- How did you allow your feelings to build up?
- Why didn't you do what you feel you should have done?
- What got in the way?
- Why did you let it get in the way?
- How many of the things that got in the way can you still change?

If you feel the world is too overwhelming or that you have sold out to a standard of living that does not make you happy, you need to look more closely at that. Sometimes you achieve success doing something you don't love, and you hope to have more time to fulfill yourself someday. Your depression is a fair warning that today is that day and maybe you cannot afford to ignore the yearnings of your own heart any longer.

Is there any bright side to what you've lost?

Don't be afraid of admitting it, because it's what you have to fall back on. If you lost your business, at least you're free of the tension of going to work and waiting for disaster. If you've lost a loved one after a long illness, at least that person won't be suffering and you won't be living in morbid expectancy.

Find something to be grateful for!

When you get depressed, you often give up trying to please people, doing everyone else's work, and trying to keep everything under control. It's possible to realize that some of your activity was really unnecessary and that perhaps you were doing it all to prove something to other people. Maybe you can give up some of it without any serious negative consequences.

Attachment to a lost cause brings everyone down.

What do you need to give up? There's no shame in calling it quits when it's over. You cannot begin to learn the lesson of an experience until you admit the mistakes you made.

The new requires the death of the old.

See your depression as a time of mental housecleaning. Streamline your life. What really makes a difference to you? Redefine what you love.

Know how you got into this mess.

- Understand your weaknesses.
- Remember your strengths.
- Take responsibility for your suffering.

It's difficult to believe in yourself when you're depressed, because you feel so tarnished by your hidden anger. Accept that what you're going through is the logical result of not dealing with your emotions in time. Accept everything about the situation as the way things are. Do this simply, without putting yourself down. All the truth that you can admit and absorb becomes the foundation for the future.

Just because everything is dark right now
doesn't mean it's not going to get better.

If you learn and grow, this period of depression will enable you to enjoy the good times and value them more. Much of the time when you feel well you don't work hard or with purpose. Remembering your depression can serve as your inspiration.

A depression gives you greater understanding of your emotional reserves and limitations. You understand better what is important to you and so become wiser and more respectful of your need to be open.

This is what growing is all about.

SPEAKING DIRECTLY ABOUT YOUR FEELINGS

Speaking as truthfully as you can is healing yourself. Anything that deviates from honesty has the propensity to lead toward depression. Using defenses is just another way of being less open, lying again. Expressing an honest view of your hurt is resolving it.

There is a healing way to speak of feelings. You need to speak of your emotions in clear language.

Instead of saying "I'm depressed," be specific and say

"I'm feeling depleted because I just lost my job," or "I'm sad because my girlfriend left me." It's much more painful to speak this way, but the directness initiates the healing process.

Each time you mention the source of your hurt you resolve it a little more.

The healing begins when you tell the truth about the hurt.

Instead of saying "I have a panic disorder," say "I'm afraid of being fired," or "I'm worried about not having enough money." Even if these seem obvious, being specific about what you fear is critical to initiate the process of organizing your thoughts and doing something to protect yourself. If you don't identify what you fear, you end up fearing everything. If your fear seems ridiculous to you, do not speak it. Do not say, "I am afraid of being alone." Think a little more deeply. Instead say, "I feel that my resentment has pushed others away." Locate a fear that doesn't seem so irrational and state that. In other words, don't say, "I'm afraid of germs," say, "I'm afraid I haven't done anything with my life and will die leaving nothing important."

In the same manner, speak your anger by identifying what has hurt you and express the hurt, not the anger. And then do something about the problem to make it better (see Chapter 13).

DEALING WITH DEPRESSED PEOPLE

When you think about it, it's pretty obvious that the people who are most likely to hurt you are themselves overflowing with old anger and suffering because they are in emotional debt. Often you become so caught up with how they hurt you or how embarrassing their behavior is that you miss the opportunity both to be helpful and to limit the damage you suffer at their hands.

The following comments should help when someone is

hurting you unnecessarily. They will give you therapeutic distance and with it the upper hand over the situation— only take care that you don't use it to manipulate the other person. These comments also protect you from needless suffering. If you're sincere and pleasant, you'll be helpful, and the other person may even thank you.

The next time someone acts irritable or hurtful, try one of the following statements. To assess their potential impact, always consider how you would feel if you were in the other person's situation and someone said this to you.

"You seem disappointed."

This opens the door to expressing the hurt.
State it sincerely.
Wait for a response.
Listen quietly.
If you're targeted for unreasonable anger, at this point, you can add:

"I wonder if you might be a little disappointed with yourself."

This is a slightly riskier comment, so to diminish the possibility that it will be seen as cross-examining the other person, be casual and avoid eye contact. Don't be confrontational. You're just making an observation.
Just listen.

"Having a difficult day?"

This is a statement of bland but sincere sympathy. By providing an explanation that you sound willing to accept for behavior the other person may not even be aware of, you open the other person up to start expressing feelings.

Don't get involved in a discussion. You don't want to debate the other person, just to help him lower his defenses to express the hurt he is carrying around so you can work with him better or relate to him more openly. If you live with someone who is having troubles, this is the way to get him to initiate discharging his feelings.

You may not feel like being the emotional facilitator in the other person's life and may wish to avoid taking such an active role. So consider this: when you are in a close relationship and are not willing to lend a sympathetic ear to hear the other person's troubles, you always end up in a more emotionally closed environment. Unexpressed, these very same feelings become stored and will make your life even more unpleasant.

Think of listening as your best investment and your most loving act. You don't need to comment or advise. You don't need to be a therapist. You don't even need to be smart. Be present and show that you care. Don't coddle. Don't baby. Just invite the person to express feelings and try to understand.

"I see you're not feeling good about yourself."

This also implies, "Do you want to tell me about it?" If the other person responds, you've helped. If the other person doesn't respond, at least he knows you offered. You can let him know that the offer still stands by maintaining an attitude of openness and indicating that you're always willing to listen.

This comment implies some risk because it can be taken as an accusation by a defensive person. To minimize this possibility you should use this comment as your understanding that explains the other person's negative behavior. Remember that you're not attacking the person for being thoughtless or hurtful; instead you've reminded yourself that he is basically a good person and that you believe the only reason he would do something so hurtful is that he doesn't feel good about himself. So you're just giving him the benefit of the doubt. "Oh, you're having a bad day" is what you say.

If you meet resistance or are attacked, just say that you were only wondering aloud and go on and do something else. Let the comment do its therapeutic work.

PART III

WHERE YOU ARE GOING

16

Finding Your Gift: The Action Board

No one is freer than you are when you have discovered your gift and are sharing it with others. For then you have found yourself and are making a difference in the world. You create your own happiness by doing what you love. You stay young because you expect to get better with everything that you do. You're easy to love because you don't need another person's love to make you happy. You're already happy.

Finding yourself does not magically make life perfect or render you impervious to the problems of the world. The capriciousness of fate and the heartlessness of the world are still to be reckoned with. However, you're no longer crushed by indifference, humiliated by your mistakes, or paralyzed by loss. You act as your own person with your own identity.

It doesn't matter how big or important your gift is. All that matters is that it's yours and you're free to give it. Giving your gift does not deplete you but rather validates and fills you, because giving reaffirms the meaning of life.

When you find yourself, you're the custodian of your

corner of the world. You're responsible for yourself. Your job is to see that you take advantage of the opportunities you seek. You create your own luck by being prepared to take risks in your own best interests whenever and wherever they appear. To do this you need to know what you want. Knowing yourself is the best preparation.

It's hard to go comparison shopping when it comes to finding your best life. You can't try out someone else's life to get a better understanding of your own. When you try to emulate a lifestyle that you don't come by naturally, you always lose some of yourself and become a prisoner of your needs. And if you try to resign yourself to the wrong path, doubts will surface when your life seems unfulfilling. It's disheartening to go through life always wondering if you've made the right choices or missed your true calling.

The life that's best for you must exert a special seductive pull on your senses and have the capacity to arrest your attention, wiping the numbers from the clock face so that your work alone determines the passage of time. Being happy in your work is being successful.

The person you finally become is always a part of what you do. If your work is the right work, it's the friend who never lets you down, the master who drives you to work harder, and the therapist who best knows you and understands the growth you've made. It's your love object, your amusement, and, finally, your memorial. While you want to be thought well of by your friends and family and to be missed when you're gone, it's what you do that makes a difference—that is your lasting tribute.

The case can always be made that you are the love you give to others. Of course this is true, but how much happier you would be if the love you had to give was the love you expressed in your work. If you were doing what you most loved as your work, each day would be fulfilling. The work might continue to be difficult, but at least it would bring you closer to self-realization. You would not trouble yourself wondering if you were wasting your life.

The world is a big place, and it is sometimes impossible

for you to get a sense of yourself against that broader and often confused canvas. You need to be in control of a little world of your own. You need to have a sense of mastery over your own life and to be able to affect your destiny in a natural ongoing way, not out of desperation or sudden urgency but through the enthusiasm and love for the work you generate. The feedback you get from the work you do energizes you, gives you courage to go on, and instills a feeling of being in touch with yourself. It is when you like what you do and are doing your best that the way you see the rest of the world is least likely to be prejudiced.

All of this boils down to valuing yourself enough to think, If I like it, it's good. What others think of your choices should have nothing to do with your happiness. You have to live in your body, in your mind, feeling your feelings, living your life. You might as well please yourself. The reactions of others are just commentary.

So trust yourself when you feel the urge to pick up the thread of a dream abandoned long ago. When you think of an old dream, you might wonder if you were fooling yourself for believing it was possible. Maybe you were never certain you had the ability to succeed.

At such troublesome times you need most to believe in yourself. You need to find courage by believing in the necessity of the thing you are doing or are about to do so you can go forward rather than falter. Instead, out of fear of discovering your true worth you often back away from giving your best and fail.

Understand that your fear of success is mostly the fear that whatever success you achieve will be a fluke and so can be taken from you. Also, when you complained in the past that no one noticed your work, you had a sense of security, a freedom to make mistakes that you may not have fully appreciated. As a success, everything you do is noticed and matters. Ultimately, the excellence that others expect of you must give way to your own standards for measuring yourself. When you're successful, you have to work even harder to please yourself. And only people who are secure enough to tolerate their own loneliness endure as successes.

Finding the right life should be your subject of study every day. Deciding what you're going to do next should always be in your mind. When not knowing what's next frightens you, you run the risk of attaching yourself to a predictable, structured life that only gives you a feeling of security. Structure is fine as long as its purpose is not solely to protect you from the world but to give you the courage to take the risks you need to take.

It's up to you to create a life that works for you, that feels right, that makes you happy.

No one can do this for you. No education can prepare you for it. No amount of parental support ensures that you'll find the right life, and no amount of parental abuse or neglect can keep you from discovering it if you're determined. The right life doesn't just happen to you. No teacher taps you on the shoulder and tells you what is to become of you. In fact too many people go through life without knowing what became of them. You need to find the right life for yourself.

Here are a few clues:

The right life is the life in which you're doing what you love most of the time.

Just because you have to sweep the floor, balance the checkbook, or do errands for other people doesn't mean you're living the wrong life. But if all you do is balance the checkbook, sweep the floor, or run other people's errands, you should wonder about what you're doing.

The right life feels comfortable most of the time.

While you may ask questions about your destiny and the meaning of life and should ask yourself if you're living the right life, when you're heading in the right direction these questions don't fill you with fear. They're merely recurring self-inventories to measure your progress.

When you're living the right life, you're
always prepared to risk.

You're secure in knowing that you don't have to throw everything away to make a big change. The right life provides you with slack and comfort. Even if it's not perfect, it's not all wrong. You have room in the right life to make additions or deletions, to make mistakes without being ridiculed, to fail without being a loser, to succeed without having to claim victory, and to work hard without insisting that the entire world cater to you or forcing other people to walk on tiptoes around you. You feel comfortable saying what you feel and expressing what you think.

The right life feels optimistic.

You are forging ahead with plans, keeping your eye on your goal. Because you are independent, your life has a will of its own.

The right life is the place where you are
your best.

The right life feels free.

THE CREATIVE SELF: YOUR TRUE GIFT

A world of free and happy people is not an empty dream but a natural legacy. The world needs every talent it generates to make things right. Each of us is one facet of a great energy. In the best of all possible worlds this combined energy should be directed toward a positive goal, toward the survival of the species at its best. The development of each individual's talent needs to be seen not only in terms of personal fulfillment and happiness but also as a vital evolutionary step to meet the needs of the planet.

When you find yourself, the world is enriched by your discovery. You are an inseparable part of the evolution that brought you to this place and a link to the better world to come. Your development and your striving for your best is not an isolated personal event but an integral evolutionary necessity, embodying the goals of a collective consciousness. There is every reason in the world for living your life as your best self. If everyone did so, that great kingdom would be ushered into existence overnight. The problems of the world would still be there, but finally they would be addressed with confidence, sincerity, and optimism.

As mentioned very early in this book, we are all essentially creative artists—our talent, our gift defines our true selves. Everything we do is some sort of creation, and by tapping our creativity we have shaped the world to make it what it is today.

We hybridize plants, develop countries, build spaceships, and dream an interplanetary dream. We aspire to the reaches of the galaxy, yet sometimes we lose touch with the very nature of our humanness that initiates our activity, that lies at the heart of our expansionist quest for mastery of the universe. Our minds probe the building blocks of matter, and we seek by our expansion to reach God in the most distant corners of existence. Who but an artist could dream such dreams?

What we see in our mind becomes the reality we create. The power of visualization is nothing more than our dream of our creation.

When we act like artists, we are most like our childlike selves, innocent of the limitations of reality, free in the pursuit of our dream. What is that dream? What is the ultimate thing we seek?

We seek the thing we love. The thing we love is, in a word, our senses. We love the body that is home to those senses, and we love the soul that pulsates as life through that body. What compels us to create is the desire to make known what we hear, feel, see, think, or taste. We want to provide our comment on the world by creating a part of that world anew.

That is our destiny. It doesn't matter how much or how large a portion of the world we create, only that we create our own part. Our lives scale down neatly to fit our talent, and our sense of happiness and completion come not from the size of what we do but from how closely what we do resembles ourselves, how much what we do is our own.

If you cannot manifest the longing of your spirit and the bidding of your imagination, you are an incomplete person. You may be well thought of, a captain of industry or an excellent group leader, but if the evolving destiny of the race does not make further strides through you, you are in some way handicapped.

We don't, of course, need to earn our livelihood as artists to have the psychology of an artist, to have a creative attitude toward problem solving, and to view the world as a possibility waiting to be created. The basic attitude of the artist is hopefulness, the hope of creating something out of nothing, making order, finding balance, superimposing a sense of design on chaos, and bringing the world into harmony with itself. A cynic could argue that the world was fine until humans put their hands on it. An idealist would respond by creating a sense of beauty somewhere and letting that creation speak for itself.

The Three Creative Roles

In adult life we express our creative selves in one or more of three main ways. We are either the creator, the performer, or the audience. No matter which of these roles we choose, each plays a vital part in ensuring the further development of the race and promoting the continued flourishing of the artistic consciousness.

The Creator
Most people view the role of creator as remote from themselves. This is partly due to the fact that our society showers the great artists with adoration and awe. Also, to think that George Frideric Handel composed *The Messiah* in three weeks and that the fourteen-year-old Mozart composed twelve symphonies in one year stuns us. How do we

begin to compete with creativity like this? As adults, with our experience and understanding, we feel intimidated and sorely lacking in creative talent by comparison. This attitude stems in part from our lack of meaningful education. A meaningful education is one that relates to your work when your work is related to sharing your gift. How much of what we learned in school serves us and makes a difference in our lives today? The unfortunate truth is that many intelligent people become unhappy professionals who achieve great success only to find that real happiness has eluded them. When intelligence and scholarship are more important in a profession than native ability, satisfaction is difficult to hold on to. You miss feeling your work is special.

In our compromises to survive we have lost the simple ability of children to take pleasure in creation. In fulfilling the role of creator we need to recapture our capacity for spontaneity and expression, our willingness to try without fearing failure, to do what we love merely because we love it, and to trust in ourselves. Only then will we be able to give fully and freely of our gift. Only then will all of us have our moments as true creators.

The Performer

Few of us can live our whole lives as creators, but the artistic trait can still be expressed in the role of the performer. Performers are all those people who take part in the performance and make it possible, not merely the person who goes onstage and wins the heart of the audience: the support crew, publicity and advertising people, the marketing department that makes the idea available to the public, the lawyers who write the contracts for the performance, and those who design the acoustics of the hall, install the lighting, organize the stage mechanism, and build the structure that houses it.

In fact when people in our civilization have a lasting and meaningful sense of accomplishment in their work, it is usually derived from their association with an artistic presentation—the higher cause. The creative imperative that is our collective birthright as a race of artists invests in us a powerful need to take some part in the manifestation of some noble energy. We love to participate in a cause greater than ourselves, identify with the whole, and glean some sense of worth from being part of it. We love performing to the instructions of some great design of cosmic proportions and to find in our participation some sense of our own immortality.

As performers we should all have some feeling of pride in creating a better world. It is difficult to append a religious or spiritual meaning to the building of a skyscraper in these harried days, but we each still have a need to see the impact of our work on the society we live in. We each need to be performers mindful of the artistic expression we make in everything we do. Otherwise we are just making a living and feel remote from the meaning of our lives.

The Audience

The role of audience is familiar to everyone, but perhaps not in the context of being a vital link in the creative chain of civilization. The audience is also the appreciator, the benefactor and patron, the encourager, the preserver and collector, the critic and the enthusiast, the fan and the lifelong supporter. The creator may conceptualize the idea, the performer may bring it to life, but it is the audience demonstrating a need for or an appreciation of a work or a performer that keeps it all alive. The good in this world is there because the audience supports it.

As audience we need to be encouraged to show appreciation for what we like and to offer criticism of what disturbs us. We need to take an active role in government by voicing our opinions in letters and speaking out for what we believe in. These are simple virtues, but if we all exercised them, we could change the world.

It should be clear that there is a powerful link in all the art forms, in creation, performance, and audience. That common denominator is the feelings that are contained in the art. As artists we communicate our feelings in our work. By participating in what has lasted through the test of years we can get a picture of ourselves, come to appreciate our own immortality, and be encouraged to take risks to express ourselves.

Our openness with our feelings limits our understanding of art, and yet it is also through art that our ability to feel is enhanced. Art teaches us new ways of perceiving and makes us aware of the hidden emotional realities of the world. In experiencing these feelings through the artist we become more aware of the world within ourselves.

Art is the parent that civilization provides to comfort us and reassure us that we are not alone and that we have worth as people merely for being present at some place in the creative chain.

Art makes us human.

Remember your true self—the creative you—as you take the following steps toward finding your gift.

THE ACTION BOARD

The following device will help you in several ways. First, it will help you discover your gift. Perhaps you feel you've already found your gift. Go through the process anyway. Again, finding the right life should be your subject of study every day, and using the Action Board might let you see your gift in a new light, unveil a gift you weren't aware of, or simply confirm that you are leading the right life for you. Once you have found your gift, you can make further use of the device; it will show you how to develop your gift and organize your life efficiently so you achieve your goals and make your contribution.

The Action Board is a simple visual device that will help give you direction and tell you what you need to do right now, today. It will allow you to see your life in an organized fashion. It will also tell you when you have nothing to do so you can enjoy relaxing without feeling guilty.

When you've completed your Action Board, you'll have a collection of cards on a bulletin board organized to show you what you must do next.

For the first part of this exercise you'll need a bulletin board, a wide-tipped felt pen, and lots of 3″ × 5″ cards.

1. Finding Your Gift

You already have some idea of what your gift is, but because it is so natural to you, so much a part of the way you are, it can be difficult to see at first. For this reason when people finally find themselves and realize their purpose and goals, they have both a sense of relief and a profound sense of familiarity.

In a sense when you find your gift you realize that you knew it all along. It fits. It feels right. Your first response when you discover yourself is "Of course!" You never forget your direction once you've found yourself, although you may sometimes get sidetracked by others when your self-confidence fails.

Gathering Information

You should be in a quiet room where you can work uninterrupted. No distractions, television, or music.

Write the words I LOVE in large letters on a piece of paper and post it on the wall.

Now, as quickly as thoughts completing this sentence come to mind, write each down on a card. Place the cards face down in a pile.

Typical responses might include your hobbies, certain activities you do at work or at home, and entertaining and travel. Be specific. Entertaining whom, when, how? Travel where, to see what?

Take as much time as you need to do this. You won't think of everything. Typically, answers flow rapidly for the first fifteen minutes and begin to diminish. Stay with this for at least an hour. Many of the best answers come in the second hour. If they're slow at the beginning, continue to stay with the exercise for the full hour. It's important. Write down all of your completions even if you think they're trivial. Don't edit. Don't pass judgment. Just write down your responses. Feel free to add cards to your collection at any time after the exercise.

Sort the Cards

You'll need a large table for this part. Sort the cards into individual groups.

A group should contain cards that seem similar to you. You are the judge. Any way you want to group the cards is fine. Feel free to change this grouping at any time. Just break the pack down into separate categories. If you get additional ideas as you do, put them on individual cards and include them where they seem to fit best.

When you're finished, you should have several categories of cards—from as few as three to as many as twenty-five.

Define the Groups

Examine the cards in each group.

Answer the following questions to help you define the individual groups. Write down your responses on a separate card.

- What do these cards have in common?
- What goals would it take to accomplish what's contained in this pile of cards?

List those goals on a card.

Think of a word or phrase that summarizes this group of goals.

Take your summary card and try to define a single goal that would contain all of the goals of the entire group. If you come up with more than one goal, perhaps you have more than one group. If so, break the group down into its smaller parts and treat them as separate groups.

Define each group by a word or phrase that describes the common goal of the group.

Write down that common goal on a card (A). The other related goals of each group should be summarized on a separate card (B).

Do this for each of the groups you have before you.

Examine the Groups

Pin all the goal cards on the bulletin board with their summary cards just below them.

What do these goal cards have in common?

If you see any similarities among the goal cards, place them beside each other. For example, goals that have risks in common should be together.

Now put the goals that are most important to you on the right side of the bulletin board. Place the goals that matter the least on the left. Place the rest in the middle. Take your time doing this.

When you've finished this, organize the cards in each of the three sections with the goal cards that are most important to you at the top of each section. Feel free to make changes.

Keep these cards up on the board for a week. Each day, spend ten minutes looking at the board, adding, deleting, rearranging, and correcting it so the goals reflect your desires more accurately.

ACTION BOARD EXAMPLE—CHRISTOPHER

An excellent organizer, Christopher manages the sales force of a company that deals in upper-end kitchen gadgetry. His catalogs have won awards and he has been well rewarded financially. He feels trapped in the company. No matter how much money he has, it doesn't mean much to him. Lately Christopher's sense of personal satisfaction seems to evaporate when he looks at his career. He wants a change but doesn't know what direction to take.

Notice how Christopher adapts the Action Board method to his own style. Don't be frustrated by the structure provided—it is only a model. Use it to create an adaptation that fits your needs.

Christopher's I LOVE cards

Group #1

Living in the country
Vermont
Foliage
Woods
Country inns
Springtime in the woods
Country shops

Fireplaces in winter
Goal: To be close to nature
Goal: The hearty old-fashioned
life
Summary Goal: To live in
Vermont or New Hampshire

Group #2

Giving parties
Taking care of people
Making people feel welcome
Meeting people

Playing tour guide
Goal: To deal with people
directly
Summary Goal: To be a host

Group #3

Being my own boss
Working at home
Being independent
Sleeping late
Taking time to think
Running my own business

Having time to myself
Goal: To have more quality
time for myself
Goal: To be independent
Summary Goal: To run my
own business

Group #4

Reading
Going to poetry readings
Browsing in bookstores
Reading poetry

Writing poetry
Goal: To be a poet
Summary Goal: To be involved
with the literary life

Group #5

Tennis
Skiing
Running
Hiking
Camping

Goal: To be outside more
Goal: To find more time for
sports
Summary Goal: To be closer to
sports facilities

Group #6

To be happy in my work
To feel I haven't wasted my life
To be satisfied
Summary Goal: To have a
meaningful life

Other Group Summary Goals:
To get more education
To own a country home
To teach something

These nine summary cards remained on Christopher's Action Board for some weeks when Christopher got the idea that he should run his own bed and breakfast. It seemed like a wonderful idea, but felt financially impossible and posed major problems. He would have to convince his wife and children. Dozens of questions occurred to him.

Christopher wrote a new summary goal—"To own my own bed and breakfast"—posted it on the board, and wrote out the next steps, lesser individual goals that he needed to explore so as to accomplish his greater goal.

When Christopher wrote out his new summary goal he was able to be more specific and focus his direction: "To own or operate a bed and breakfast in Vermont, perhaps near an artists' colony or a college, perhaps near a ski resort; maybe even have a little bookstore as part of the operation, with poetry readings."

Christopher's Summary Goals

Then, after more time had passed, he saw that the goal was still not clear enough, so he broke it into several new summary goals:

1. Christopher's: A Mountain Inn

Giving his project a real name helped him focus even further.

Here are the goals Christopher placed below #1 on his Action Board. Below some of these goals he listed the next steps he would have to accomplish to get to these goals:

Investigate cost dynamics
Figure out downside risks
(Who will finance this? What
    will this cost?)
What would it take to run a
    small inn?
(Evaluate existing inns—who
    succeeded, who failed, why,

am I getting in over my
head?)
Investigate courses on hotel
management
Pick best opportunity
(Locate ski areas, locate
colleges, make plans to visit
these areas)

Timing
(When is the best time to make
a move, and how will I
know?)
Family impact
(What about the kids' school?
What about Barbara! Am I
being too selfish?)

2. The great outdoors

3. Poetry bookstore: Inner Landscapes

Locate poetry societies
Locate bookstores
Locate artists' colonies in New
England
Take poetry course

Notice that Christopher added to his Action Board some questions that were troubling him. Placing a question on the Action Board keeps you aware of it. This will help you state problems clearly. Again, the whole point of the Action Board is to give you a visual perspective of your direction and present plans. State your problems. Ask questions and post them. Write down your goals. Summarize. Condense. Add commentary cards that say, "Do I really want this?" to dubious goals, "This doesn't make sense" to unclear ideas, "Not yet" to incomplete thoughts. Use the Board to structure your thinking. See it as a visual editor of your mental process.

Note that Christopher did not follow the exact plan suggested in this chapter to the letter. Your life and goals are unique and your Action Board will require customization. Feel free to play with the model and make it work for you. Don't get bogged down in details. If you are uncertain about a card or a goal put it up on your Action Board and look at it for a week or two. It will eventually fall into place as important or irrelevant.

The Action Board is a process. Learn to trust it.

No matter how you approach the Action Board you will be adding and deleting cards, goals, and summaries for years. The purpose here is to get you started.

2. Examining the Board

After a week, prepare to spend an hour with the board. Sit quietly and answer these questions:

- Who is the person reflected in these goals?
- What matters to this person?
- How determined is this person?

Are there household tasks, errands, reminders on the board? If so, remove them from the board. Such daily reminders do not belong here, and the presence of busy work on your board at this point only reflects your lack of direction and need to focus your life.

Assume that on the board are the goals that will make you happy:

- What does this person want out of life?
- What has this person accomplished?
- What would make this person proud?
- What does this person most need to do?

Are you living a life that will lead you toward the goals on this board?

What would you have to change to live the life in which you could commit to or reach these goals?

If the answers to these questions prompt you to think of new goals, write them out and place them on the board as well.

For the next week, look at the cards each day and add and correct as before.

Redefining Your Goals

Go back to the Action Board and rewrite as many goals (A) as possible, making them as distinct and specific as you can. Each goal is now a project. Write the name of the project across the top of a separate card in large block letters. Be specific. If you have being a caterer as a goal, define the type of food you want to specialize in. The more clearly you see your goal, the more likely you will reach it. Also, the easier it is for you to tell how realistic it is, so you can revise it.

Directly below the project name, if appropriate, write down in smaller letters the name(s) and telephone number(s) of the key people you believe will be the most important people to be involved with this project.

Do this for every project and replace all the A cards with these redefined versions of the goal cards.

List the Steps Toward Your Goals

Now consider the related goals (B) for each of the main goals:

1. Examine the related goals summarized on each B card and use them as a guide to create a series of logical steps, filling in the blank spaces that would take you toward the main goal.
2. Place these steps in order and write them down on a card (C).
3. Write out the first and perhaps the second of these steps on a separate card (D). This defines the next step you need to take to get closer to completing your projects.
4. Pin that card (D) beneath its corresponding project on the board. You can use adhesive notes instead of cards and place that first step or two directly below the name and telephone number of your key contacts on each goal card. Save and date these to follow your progress.
5. Pin the card containing the list of steps (C) behind its corresponding goal card. This is your reference card. When you wish to reconsider where you are and how much progress you're making, refer to this list of steps.

Go through this process for all of your main goals.

Simply take all of your goals for projects that you consider important, want to start, or are currently working on and organize them into project or goal cards. Then create C and D cards for each as just described and start your Action Board from this point.

3. The Action Board Process

When your Action Board is complete, it will contain many cards, each representing a single project, with the first one or two steps toward reaching it attached right below.

The most important goals will be to the right side, the least important to the left. As each project matures and comes closer to its goal, move it from the left side of the board to the right.

When the goal is achieved, remove the card from the board.

The following is a good model for your Action Board.

I Anything Goes	New ideas. Projects you are considering. Dreams. Questions. Comments.
II To Do or Not to Do	Projects being investigated. Your commitment is to look more carefully.
III Getting Started	Projects just committed to. The organizing stage for projects.
IV To Do Now	Actively working on these projects. Your daily work is here.
V Finishing Up	Projects being completed. Final touches, implementation.

To be perfectly honest, your Action Board may not look at all like this. It may contain a wide variety of seemingly unrelated goals and preferences. Some projects you will love but not have the slightest idea how to start on them.

Others you may love less and have a dozen well-defined steps. Don't be concerned about that now. Everything belongs on the board, even if it doesn't yet fit together. (If your life could fit into an organized structure like this, you would have no need for the Action Board in the first place.) The idea is to begin to emulate a structure like the model. Adapt your goals into an Action Board that reflects your needs.

Edit the Board

When your cards have been arranged in order, you'll have a good view of where you're going. You'll see a visual display of your current direction. It will always appear incomplete. Your job is to fill in the blanks.

It takes at least a year for an Action Board to mature, to represent what you really want, and to direct you to finding what will make you happy and productive. It takes a year to separate wishful thinking from reality. Be patient.

Look at your Action Board every day for fifteen minutes during the first week.

Question each goal and how badly you want it.

Continually edit and rearrange the cards on the board.

Always wait a few days before removing a goal. When you see projects that no longer fit, move them to the bottom of the first column. Such a project is a candidate for removal from the board.

If you want a goal badly but think it is impossible, leave it on the board at the top of column I. You never know what could happen if you are stimulated to think about it for a year or two. The Action Board works as a silent prompt to fulfill your dream.

One woman had placed her Action Board on the refrigerator door with magnets so she could see it and think about her life while she was in the kitchen. Her problem was that she could not define a goal because she was afraid of the disruptive effects it would have on her household. For months no solution came to her. Off and on she rearranged her board, but she was very casual about it. One day while having a heated discussion on the kitchen telephone she integrated all of the cards on her refrigerator door into a project that she suddenly realized she had always wanted to do. Within a month she was in business for herself; she had a major financial success in the first year. Her Action Board had stimulated her creative process without her awareness. By continually placing the pieces of the puzzle in front of her, the Action Board set the stage for a creative breakthrough.

Don't underestimate the primary value of the Action Board as a visual prompt to your mind to work on the problems of your life. Whether you're thinking about your life direction or not, the Action Board redirects your thinking and in some way encourages you to fantasize solutions to the problems it poses. Your board is in continual process, just as your life is. A working Action Board should provide a visual flag of your intention and remind you of your direction and your needs.

It works!

Feel free to add new goals anytime. Adding a goal only means that you're considering it. Just put your trial ideas on the left, the most important goals toward the right.

As you make progress, the slips listing the next step or two will change continually. It's useful to help keep track of your direction and to evaluate problems by keeping a 3″ × 5″ card file to hold your next step (D) slips or cards, past and present. You can lay them all out and see where you went wrong or what you might have missed, a valuable way of checking your progress. It's a good idea to work at the Action Board for five minutes a day and to remove these next steps as you complete them. Replace them as soon as possible.

It's useful to keep a separate bulletin board available for routine errands and appointments. Avoid using precious Action Board space for mundane tasks that more properly belong in an appointment book. Your Action Board is your life goal organizer, not a diary, not a shopping list or date reminder. It requires continual attention and adjustment. It is a living representation of your life. If there are empty spaces in your life, there should be empty spaces on your Action Board. Your creativity should be directed at filling these empty spaces. Don't feel you need to have a completely filled-in board. The real value of the board is that it defines your empty spaces. In those spaces you will find your future.

Try to maintain a natural relationship with your Action Board. Don't make it your life. It is there to help you find and fill your life with what you love. Once a week, reorganize the next-step slips; once a month, spend an hour editing the board—bringing it up to date, rewriting cards, and changing telephone numbers of key personnel.

When you're reviewing your Action Board, ask yourself these questions:

- "What's missing from this board?"
- "What do I need to do most?"
- "What other options am I missing?"
- "What do I want to happen? Why?"
- "Is this going the way I want?"
- "Is this the right way to do this?"
- "How would I feel if I accomplished this?"
- "Who else should be involved with this?"
- "Who will benefit most from this?"
- "What card(s) should be removed?"

Your Action Board should be a part of your life. You should use it to bring your hidden desires to the surface. One of the great benefits of the Action Board is that it allows you to see all of the facets of yourself. Often when you have a talent it seems so familiar that you hardly notice it. The Action Board will remind you that it is there and help you to find the courage to risk developing it and point to the means for making it happen.

The Action Board also gives you a sense of balance and timing. When you speak to the person whose name you've listed below your projects, you will appear conversant with the problem, focused, and up to date. You will know when to apply pressure, because you will know when something has to be done. You will also know when applying pressure is fruitless and likely to be seen as nagging. In a word, the Action Board will make you more professional.

You need to have as many options open for living your life as possible. If your happiness and success depend on only one aspect of your talent or training, you're more vulnerable than if you have several projects going. Your Action Board makes you aware of all your passions and interests and gives you a direction and a method for implementing your dreams. It will help you discover new relationships among your various interests and create a life that is uniquely your own.

You deserve to find yourself!

17

Epilogue

Just being yourself without the need to prove anything is the highest sense of consciousness you can ever attain. High consciousness is not reaching some exaggerated state of awareness and sensitivity but merely being aware of yourself as you are being yourself. If you do this fully, you feel so natural about it that you're not even aware that you're being aware.

It seems so simple, but reaching this plane is fraught with such difficulty.

The directives are clear.

Know yourself and be aware of the forces that shaped you.

Know your weakness as part of your strength. When in doubt, lead from your strength but never at the expense of forgetting your weakness.

Speak your feelings simply and openly when they occur and share them with the person who needs most to hear them.

Let go of your hurt and forgive.

It is a simple truth: you live your best life by giving your gift. Your gift is always part of your passion for life and is given in love.

You need to judge your actions by asking what the world would be like if everyone were like you and did what you did. You have no right to ask more of the world or of others. You instruct best by being a model, not a critic.

Your assignment on this planet is to enhance the part of the world you were put in charge of. You keep that world free by living and speaking the truth.

Whatever else you believe, this is the attitude that will lead you to find happiness and fulfillment.

Your search is ever to find the unity between the self that lives in the moment and the universal self. Your goal is to seek out this higher self in everything you do. Be reverent of the artistic creations of others that have been passed down to you, for they have accomplished this goal and endured the test of time. They show you the ways to grow.

The combined gifts of all the artists who have ever lived constitute irrefutable evidence. Your life purpose is to understand what this evidence proves.

It's easy to lose your way from this higher path. You're tempted by choices that promise easy rewards. You're ground down by an indifferent, uncaring world. Addictions and possessions capture you and fuel your indifference. You're misled to prove your worth to yourself or your parents instead of simply being yourself. Still, you are responsible for what happens to you, for the life you accept, for the way you respect and develop your talent.

Listen to your inner voice for direction.

Trust your feelings for a sense of confirmation of the rightness or wrongness of your actions.

When you cling to the emotions of the past, you add a veil that obscures your ability to sense these inner directives.

In time the inner voice becomes dimmed by the murmuring of unresolved feelings in emotional debt.

If this persists, you lose the ability to hear your inner calling, and soon you lose your belief that the voice exists at all. Your sense of direction blurs, and you become lost.

Then you're adrift, on your own. Your life's meaning is not reinforced, because you do not live as a supportive part of a larger, more universal whole.

When you are emotionally free, you need only pose the question and listen for the response that echoes within to understand what you should do next.

Your dream may be to find yourself and develop your talent, but in some way your dream must also reflect the best interests of the planet that gave you life. Every gift must be given in harmony with the dream of one world. To have meaning and be supported by nature, every individual dream must add to the universal dream. Then, when you've realized your dream, you have everything.

You have nothing to prove. You have only to be your best to do your part. Don't compare yourself to others or desire what they have accumulated. Don't imitate the steps of great men and women, but seek their ideals. Don't try to accomplish what they did, but find your own path.

Your life has its own scale. Your immortality is found in being true to the dimensions of your own soul. Only then is the confidence you develop real and your work capable of touching others, because then what you create is an extension of your real self, not an imitation.

There are no final methods to accomplish this aim, only splinters of light from others' quests as they seek answers for themselves. This book has been an attempt to give you the courage to look within and become the master of the inner world from which all love and creativity flow.

There is a method here, but it is humble, neither new nor unfamiliar.

Enjoy the good.

Trust yourself.

Express your feelings.

Believe in your worth even when you sometimes forget.

Find something to be grateful for.
Come from love.
And give.
I hope that this work has helped you come closer to your special self and given you the courage to take the next step.
More than ever, the world needs what you have to give.

Index

301

and personality types,
  160–70
managing, 183–86
and risking, 159–60
as a sense, 172–73
working through, 170–71
Appetite, 260
Approval, 33
Art, 13–14, 142
Artist, 283, 298
  as childlike, 279
  as creator, 280
  as performer, 281–82
Attitudes, 32
"Audience" role, 282–83
Awareness, 201, 297

Babies, 34–35
  thought processes of, 40
Betrayal, 191
Birth, 35–36
Bitterness, 237–39
Blaming (stage of
  mourning), 130–31
"Blind spots," 80–83
  of competitive personality,
    83
  of controlling personality,
    82–83
  of dependent personality,
    81–82
Bragging (defense), 109
Bravery, 185–86
Bulimia, 240
Buzzwords, 84–89
  for competitive
    personality, 88–89
  for controlling personality,
    86–87
  for dependent personality,
    84–86

Ceremonies (ridding anger),
  221–23
Character traits, 12
Character types, 16–22. *See
  also* Personality types
  competitive person, 27–28
  composite type, 28–29
  controlling person, 26–27
  defenses of, 101–3
  dependent person, 22–27
  and forgiveness, 247–48
  stages of, 67–72
Cheating, 235
Chemical imbalance, 260–61
Child abuse, 240–42
Childhood, 2, 3, 30–72
  anger in, 228–30
  character traits in, 31–32
  competitive period of,
    56–66
  controlling period of,
    45–56
  dependent period of,
    33–45
  effects on adulthood,
    67–72
  traumatic experiences of,
    201–2
  feelings returning, 30–31
Children, 47, 48, 259. *See
  also* Childhood
Comfort, 35–37
Comparing (defense), 109
Competitive period, 32,
  56–66
  early stages of, 56–57
Competitive personality,
  101, 102, 118–19
  and anger, 190, 204–5
  and anxiety, 168–70
  defenses of, 58–59, 108–11